CHRISTINE

LIVING WITH SCHIZOPHRENIA

Christine & Jill Delahunty

For Christine, her nieces, and friends.

CHRISTINE: LIVING WITH SCHIZOPHRENIA

Copyright © 2019 by Christine & Jill Delahunty.

Produced with assistance from yourmemoir.co.uk

Book and cover design by Your Memoir

ISBN: 9781679789823

Imprint: Independently published

First Edition: December 2019

CONTENTS

About the Authors

Jill and Christine Delahunty are sisters. Christine, born in 1948, is the youngest by 16 months. While always close, their lives took very different pathways due to the serious, life-long mental health difficulties which Christine experienced from the age of 15.

An avid reader and writer, she spent much of her life in long-term psychiatric hospitals including two spells in Broadmoor. When she died in 2013, she left Jill boxes of her writings, which form the main substance of this book.

Jill lived in Brixton for 35 years bringing up her two daughters, largely as a single parent. She worked in education, health and social care. Jill has always enjoyed travel, finding her annual holiday abroad therapeutic. From 2002-2005 she worked for DFID (Department for International Development) on the South Atlantic island of Saint Helena, one of the remotest places on Earth.

Since retiring to the Kent coast, Jill has brought together Christine's writings, many of which were written while she was in hospital. Jill includes some of her own recall to create this memoir of Christine's life.

Acknowledgments

Many thanks to Marnie Summerfield Smith who has consistently encouraged and helped me to proceed with this book. Also Dyfed Edwards for his contribution.

A particular thanks goes to those health and social care workers whose great help finally enabled Christine to achieve more independent living.

Also my thanks to my friends and family, most especially the support and suggestions of my two daughters, Amelia and Louise.

Introduction

My sister Christine was still at school when she first suffered the mental health problems that were to dominate her life. She would have many diagnoses but the most consistent was Paranoid Schizophrenia. Her illness was often at the severest end of the spectrum and she spent many years in hospitals, including two spells in Broadmoor from 1971-1975 and again from 1978-1981. She was to experience the best, and worst, of mental health treatment and care.

Christine was born in 1948, 16 months after me. We already had an older sister, Anne, who we would later find out was adopted. Our parents, Marjorie and Vic met in a tunnel in Dover during the Second World War. Dad was in the Royal Signals, and Mum was in the Women's Air Auxiliary Force. They married in March 1944, Mum having converted to Catholicism. After the war, Dad started a part-time law degree then when he and Mum began their family, he became a clerical officer. After school, Mum had been to secretarial college where she trained as a tele-printer operator and had just got a job when the war began. While in the WAAF's she was vetted and approved for a high security post, but when the authorities found out she was getting married, they refused her entry.

Reading and writing were encouraged in our home. Both our parents read newspapers and both Christine and I could read before we went to school. From the minute Christine could read, she loved it, and preferred books to people much of the time. We had a comic delivered each week, Christine's was Robin, mine was Girl and Anne's was School Friend. Dad would encourage our learning by giving us spelling tests.

In 2013, Christine died of cancer. She was 64. She stressed that she was leaving to me her accumulated collection of writings. Christine was always a scribbler. She wrote a great deal while in hospital but also wrote retrospectively when, no longer having to fear institutional retribution she felt safer to record her sometimes horrendous experiences. Her unique, personal, and often insightful reflections and vivid accounts are captured in prose and verse as well as diaries and letters. She wrote constantly and read whenever she was well enough and when books, and the glasses she always needed were not denied to her. Given her chaotic life, and the disregard some professionals showed for her personal possessions, I am staggered that she managed to keep her writings in one place. Her success at doing so shows the determination that she had to try and make sense of her illness and to record her experiences. Christine had a lifelong passion for words and books and when I found her work, I was in no doubt that she wished me to publish. Although Christine's diaries and accounts of her experiences of the mental health system largely cover the period of her life from the 1960's to the 1990's I have changed names to preserve the privacy of the innocent, and also those who could be regarded as less so.

*

This is Christine's story. My part is largely to bridge the gaps and to indicate the impact that mental illness has on the whole family. It is reported that about one in four of the UK population are likely to experience mental health problems at some stage of their lives and yet the subject still remains practically unspeakable. Before Christine was diagnosed, our family knew virtually nothing about mental illness. There were no indicators – not that we would have known what to look for – and even if we had spotted something we wouldn't have known what to do about it. We had heard of people having depression or nervous breakdowns, but all in the vaguest of terms. A friend's mother would go off and have ECT, but we didn't know what any of it meant. Hindsight can be as frustrating as it is enlightening. Yes, Christine was shy, but I was too. Was her shyness a precursor to the isolation that is part of mental illness or was she just shy? I do wonder which parts of her were the illness and which parts were just her. I know this is a question common to the family members of those who suffer from mental ill health.

In collating and contextualising Christine's experiences I hope, as she did, that they will contribute to the awareness and understanding of all who live with mental health problems whether personally or as family, friends or workers. Perhaps a key question that arises is whether there have been any improvements in the way we treat people with mental illness.

When I look at Christine's writings, and think about what she did achieve, I find it amazing. But I can't help wondering how different my sister's life could have been if she hadn't been ill, or if her treatment had been more enlightened.

Jill Delahunty

Chapter One

I CAN READ

Christine

"Mum, I can read."

I had been battling with Janet and John for some time, but that didn't interest me, it was just a chore that seemed to please parents and teachers. But it was at the Primrose League one Saturday afternoon that it hit me, like a smiling thunderbolt – I could make sense of the chalked song on the blackboard and join in the Empire Anthems. The Primrose League was the meeting place where children were dumped while parents did the shopping on Saturday afternoons in the 50s. You either went there, or to the sixpenny flicks, depending on your parent's attitude. It was founded by Disraeli to encourage youngsters to learn about, and support, the British Empire and all that was pink on the map. The meeting always ended in a sing-song. My sister would stand beside me and kick me and hiss, "Sing!"

I'd say, "I can't read it."

"Yes, you can," and another kick.

But the day I actually made sense of it was a turning point in my three-year-old life. After that my life was sealed. Another memory of the early 50s was dashing to the public library on Saturdays to join the children queuing to get in. The library opened at 9am, but the adults weren't allowed in until 10am. We raced to be first in the queue. I remember saying to the librarian, "I wish the grown-ups didn't have to come in at 10, it spoils it." Of course by the time my parents came to pick me up I'd have spent an hour glutting myself on The Famous Five and The Secret Seven. It was 1953 when we got our first television, a 9" Bush, in time for the Coronation, but by that time my life revolved around books.

We were always a bookish family. I was eight when we moved to Devon and on our first Saturday there the whole family went together to join the town library.

"You're too young to join," the librarian said to me. "You have to be 10 to join the library."

"Why?"

"You might tear the books."

"Why would I do that?"

I was not just puzzled but broken-hearted. Mum had the solution: "I'll join Boots Lending Library and you can get books from there." But Boots Lending Library turned out to be a disappointment. It cost one shilling and three pence to borrow a book for a week, and I knew my mother couldn't afford to keep up with my appetite for reading. But, as one door closes another one opens. At the beach at Westward Ho! I discovered a wonderful place – a second-hand bookshop, where I could spend my pocket-money and enjoy delicious time choosing my books. The shop owner would let me have a few pence off the price of the books. I still have treasures from there, literally since 'Treasure Island' was a great find. Dad would guide my reading and help me choose my books.

When I was 13, we moved to Cheltenham, but here was something very strange – a school with no library. I remember the nuns, the lacrosse, the Saturday mornings in detention, the woollen swimsuits – but no library.

I spent much of my adult life, from the age of 15, in locked wards in psychiatric hospitals, including a great deal of time isolated in cells. If I didn't have a book I would pass my time remembering the ins-and-outs of the plots of books I had read. Papillon was a favourite, helping me fill the long hours. Even when I was on an open ward for some odd reason the Australian psychiatrist, in whose care we were, created a blacklist of books we were not allowed to read. There was no logic to this list and I don't think he had done much reading of English literature himself, but when the fortnightly library van came the general idea behind the blacklist seemed to be that we were all at a pretty basic level of literacy. When I joined the Open University (while I was still in hospital) all my OU books, tapes and videos had to be vetted before I could have them. And so, from the Primrose League to becoming a mature student at the University College of Aberystwyth at the age of thirty-five, I have always had one friend beside me – my love of literature. I didn't get to be a librarian, which was a dream that kept me going for years, but if I can write of those dreary years and bring pleasure and information and interest to a few, and open people's eyes to the horror of those Victorian Asylums, that is what I want.

Chapter Two

FAMILY

Jill

Dad was one of the youngest of eight children, born in Southport, Lancashire in 1919. When Dad was 11, his father died from his struggles with unemployment and alcohol. Hannah, the oldest daughter, was from then on charged with helping their mother to bring up the family. Even to this day Mum's background remains a mystery. She rarely spoke of it, having been orphaned as a baby. I think her father died during the First World War although I have found a photo of him, taken in Australia, that appears to be later. When I was expecting my first child I was asked if there were any hereditary illnesses. I said that there weren't, then realised that I didn't actually know. When I asked Dad he said that Mum's mother had died of diabetes, shortly before insulin became available.

Mum was brought up by Auntie Florrie and Uncle Frank who

were well-to-do in a Victorian way and held some resemblance to Jack Spratt and his wife. They were the nearest we had to grandparents. We used to visit them occasionally, and sometimes stay over, while we lived in Woodford Green. I remember spending Christmas day at theirs and watching Uncle Frank cooking a whole tongue in aspic, and Auntie Florrie hiding silver three-penny bits in the Christmas pudding mix. There was always a sense that Auntie Florrie had resented having to bring Mum up. She had been engaged in the early fashion industry and used to travel to Paris. I can't remember what Uncle Frank did, except smoke. We always had to watch our p's and q's with them. It wasn't until after Frank's death, in 1967, that any of us knew that this very correct couple had never been married. He had previously married a Catholic woman, by whom he had a son, and divorce was not allowed. We rarely saw, or heard from them, after we moved to Bideford, in Devon, in 1956.Christine would have been eight then, and I was nine. Anne would have been twelve.

Mum's mantra was to treat us all alike, but we were all very different. None of us knew until much later, when I was about 20, that Anne had been adopted in 1945/6, not long before I arrived on the scene. Mum had initially agreed to look after her for an afternoon to enable her bus-conductress mother to attend a hospital ante-natal appointment then her parents never collected her. Dad and Uncle Frank eventually found the struggling home and were told, "You keep her." Mum, who was now attached couldn't bear the thought of an orphanage, so they went through the arduous process of adoption. I felt disbelief when I was told at the age of 20, and a sudden sense of not knowing what to believe, even about myself, on the sudden realisation that I had actually been my parents first born. I found myself remembering a school science class on genetics, when I was about 11. My science teacher nun had been explaining emphatically how two blue-eyed parents can only have blue-eyed children. I put my hand up and assured her Mendel must have got it wrong because my parents both had blue eyes, but my older sister's eyes were brown. She clearly didn't know how to answer that. When I told my Mum about the lesson she replied that teachers don't always get things right. Perhaps that was the beginning of my scepticism of authority.

So Mum and Dad, neither of whom had had the easiest experiences of being parented, had become parents of three children under five within five years of their marriage while domiciled in an upper floor rented flat on the corner of Salway Hill and St. Albans Road, above the Royal London Insurance, in Woodford Green, which was then Churchill's constituency. There were 36 stairs to haul us all up and down. The building, with its spire and balcony are still there. They tried but couldn't get onto the council house waiting list because they didn't have enough points. As the youngest, Christine stayed the baby for a lot longer, particularly as she had fallen down the stairs and broken her leg when she was about 15-months-old, and soon after was in hospital to have her tonsils removed, an event that led to her having lots of people visiting her in hospital with presents and being given lots of ice cream. I was disappointed that I couldn't have my tonsils out too.

These two events led to Christine being regarded as rather fragile. As sisters we got on okay, apart from the usual bickering. Christine was always the bright one, shy, fond of reading, and somehow always getting 90 per cent plus for everything. I was often referred to as a good average with much more fluctuations in my grades, which often seemed to reflect how well I got on with particular teachers. My best and worst subjects seemed to change every time I changed school. Anne always hated school and by the time she was 15 she left to work in a dress shop in Mill Street, Bideford. She was paid two pounds ten shillings a week and always resented the fact that Mum insisted she pay two pounds of this for her keep.

My memories of our earliest years are probably clearer than many of the later ones. I wasn't the baby for very long. I can remember sitting on a seat at the end of our large old pram while Christine reclined. I even remember Mum chatting for ages on the street corner with a friend of hers called Sylvia, who had become very fat, and telling her she could have the pram. Sylvia had a baby shortly afterwards, apparently delivered by a stork. Mum always seemed strict and certainly ruled the roost. Dad generally went along with whatever Mum said, presumably for the sake of peace. We used to be allowed out to play, probably unthinkable these days. We used to go with friends over to The Dip where we made great dens from what we never realised was the household detritus of a bombed site. Our gang would always be on the look-out for the rival gang from the flats. Christine would sometimes come and sometimes prefer to stay at home reading. I wasn't much into reading, except our weekly comics, Robin, Girl, School Friend and books like Enid Blyton's Famous Five and Secret Seven. I especially liked George and soon found myself declared a tomboy like her. I learnt to ride Anne's full size bicycle before I could sit on the saddle until I was given a smaller second hand bike. Christine got a brand new one, with stabilizers, but these didn't seem to help her much as it took her ages to learn.

Dad was working as a Clerical Assistant in the Civil Service and used to leave home early each morning to cycle to Stratford. He would cook us all breakfast and take Mum a cup of tea and toast and marmalade in bed each morning before departing. Mum didn't go out to work except she used to clean the office below us to earn a bit of cash. Generally we always seemed a rather ordinary family. Rather boring really. Mum and Dad weren't very sociable. Mum tended to have a few friends, mainly among the neighbours with children, who tended to become family friends. Money was always a bit of a struggle so the answer to things we wanted was often, "We can't afford it."

The first school I went to, with Anne, was St. Anthony's. It was a penny bus ride away. By the time Christine was due to start, Mum had fallen out with the nuns. They had wanted her to buy us all white frocks for the May Day procession. Mum told them she couldn't afford it so Christine went to Churchfield's Primary and I was moved there too. Anne was transferred to St George's secondary school in Walthamstow. She was besotted with Bill Hayley and sported a Teezy Weezy curl on her forehead.

*

When Christine joined the infants, I was in the juniors in a class of 60 where my main memories are of reciting tables (which I can still do) and kneeling on our desks with our hands on our heads. As a well-behaved child I was seated at the back so was largely overlooked. Christine was by this time wearing her round, pink, national health glasses. The infants and juniors were in separate playgrounds so we didn't play together, but neither of us enjoyed playtimes anyway.

Chapter Three

HAPPY DAYS

Christine

Nobody in the family seems to have kept many photographs of our growing- up-years, but our memories of the early 50s in Essex would probably now count as social history. I recall playing in The Dip, which was actually a bombsite from the war. We found treasures of all sorts. These were from bombed homes, although we didn't know that. Bagwash is another memory. Mum would put the week's washing into bolster-cases and when the lady came to collect it, the three of us would grab it and hurl it down the stairs yelling "Bagwash!" The Rag-and-Bone-Man, who would let us stroke his old horse and give us shiny pennies and balloons in exchange for a few old vests and liberty bodices, is another memory. It is easy to be sentimental over memories – to bury the bad bits – but our childhood was very different from that of children today.

When I was eight we moved to Bideford, north Devon. Our first year there was spent in east Rousden where our parents had rented us a home in an old school, while our new home was being built. East Rousden was a dream place to grow up in during the 50s. A world of fields, woods, rivers, and beaches, unlike children today, we never learned to fear neighbours or strangers. Bideford was a world where I became a different child, so memory says. This was no upstairs flat and playing in alleys and at The Dip. To my surprise, I was somebody. I was ahead of the other children in my class. This was a place where doors were open, where drawing hopscotch squares on the street was okay, where there were lots of children to play with and places to explore.

Yes, it was a barefooted, clotted-cream summer the year I was eight. That year I swallowed a sunbeam that was to lighten many a dark corner of adulthood. The year we moved from a London dust-bowl suburb to a puppy-tail-wagging corner of the West Country. Everything smelt God-blessed and still does to me, through the tinted glasses of nostalgia. Memory has blotted out the flaws but I cannot imagine unhappiness at East Rousden. We were only there one summer. It was part of an old school and the bricks had mellowed to the breathy laughter of children. The grass was knee-high when we lived there and the bushes seemed to be just right for the making of dens and hideaways. The gates were to be climbed over and swung upon, and the hills were waiting for us as we scooted and skidded in our orange-box-and-pram-wheel carts.

School was at the bottom of the hill. A panama-hatted,

angelus-bell convent, quite amazingly filled with boarders from all over the world. The only swear word we knew was 'furriner', which applied to the summer tourists, and maliciously to the people from the next town, but never, never to our multi-coloured schoolmates. School for me meant the nuns taking us tad-poling with skirts tucked up and nets made of scraps of lacy-white curtains. Church was gloves and hats and scrambling for the honour of pumping the wheezing organ — two, or even three of us, would swing on the handle.

Church meant Father Scanlon, a cantankerous old Irishman who had carved his own character on the liturgy. There were no prying tourists the day he climbed the pulpit and, shedding tears without shame, told us the Bishop was putting him out-to-grass in an out-of-the-way village. Our parents openly wept. We were to be sent a dynamic young priest who would get our little community back on the rails, and instruct us in all the changes in the church to which Father Scanlon had obstinately turned his back.

It was late summer when we went pot-walloping, cycling over The Burrows and paying our shilling at the toll gate to enter. It had been a day of rain and sun and we joined in the joyous back-breaking tradition of re-building the Pebble-Ridge, which holds back the Atlantic surf at Westward Ho! As we piled the sea-polished pebbles the air twanged with West Country accents, a music apart from all others. The evening was rounded off with a barbecue on The Burrows and the tired muscles of the Pot-wallopers proclaimed the fact that we were safe from the wild waters for another winter.

May-poling, Regatta Week, Pot-walloping – these were the high spots, and every day had its high spots, and every night was star-studded and moon-shiny. We were otters in the river, Tarzans in the trees, and we had voracious appetites for Boots' Library books and fruit stolen from the convent orchard. All through the East Rousden summer we had watched as a row of pokey-ugly terrace houses were being built further down the valley. Finally the day came when we left our dream East Rousden and moved into Number 48, and the balloon was burst. All the familiar life-scapes remained, but summer was never quite the same again. It didn't last, for as we grew up the other children outstripped me in the growing up process and isolation and bewilderment began to set in.

*

Torrington Mayday

In a small town called Torrington, in north Devon, the first Thursday in May was celebrated as May Day. Even in the 50s its charm was in being old fashioned. I don't know whether they still celebrate it. I cannot imagine children of the 21st Century willingly practising the complicated maypole dances. The ribbons had to be twisted and plaited by the dancers, and if one child danced the wrong way – which they never did- the whole pattern went awry. May Day was an excuse to wear pretty dresses made by mother and the day was started by the Town Crier. As well as the dancing there was a carnival, a fair, a market and wonderful parties.

The Maypole

There is a streak of silver in each day,

Of all the colours of black and white and grey,

And as the Mayday ribbons twist and weave,

With one false dancer causing disarray,

So all the dancing colours of events

Compose our day, its bitter sweet contents.

A smile can pierce the thickest winter fogs.

A sour word brings purple loneliness.

The greyest sea has beauty of its own.

Contentment springs and fades as fast as light.

Times laughing stocks play multi-coloured tricks

The ribbons weave and inter-weave and twist.

The May-pole is the central point of life.

We form the pattern, for good or bad or strife.

Time will not pause, we march along with it

But all the colours come from deep within.

On looking back we see a rainbow gay,

For there is history in all men's lives.

The ribbon-patterns never work out right.

They're too complex, they're not just black and white.

Those days of 50s north Devon were days of innocence. They are tucked away in private memories. In the 60s, the world changed as if by an earthquake – a lifequake – as if all of us had lived in a quiet, sheltered world and suddenly the lights came on, the walls disappeared and we moved into a world of loud sound, of seeing and living in a world where there was nowhere to hide, no escape from life. The word psychedelic accurately describes the sudden life-flashes, life-crashes of the 60s. Some people coped with it by taking drugs, or by discarding the life rules which had guided our paths through earlier years. No family photographs – nobody bothered to recall those bewildering years.

Chapter Four

BIDEFORD

Jill

By 1955 there was talk of us all moving to Australia, which I think the family could have done for £5. Then Dad got promoted to the post of Youth Employment Officer for north Devon. He went ahead to start his job and find us somewhere to live. We soon followed him on the Golden Arrow with Pickford's delivering our chattels initially to East Rousden and into the wing of a former Grammar School. We watched our new house being built down the road, with fields and cows beyond and used to chat with the builders. But conversation was difficult as they struggled to understand our cockney accents and we found their broad Devon accents hard to interpret. Bideford was a different world. Rural and near the sea, which until then we had only seen on occasional coach trips to Southend, or visits to Southport when nine of us would travel from

Woodford in Uncle Matthew's Wolsey.

We soon made friends and enjoyed playing out with doors left open. As a family it was to be our best five years. Mum and Dad had ventured into home ownership. We got a car and Dad learnt to drive the winding country lanes. It was an old black Ford, with flipper indicators. Dad made a tin box for the back to serve as a boot. It usually needed a handle, or push to start. Our new school was Stella Maris Convent where there were about twenty children to a Class, and boarders from all over the world. No chance of being overlooked! We all started regularly attending Mass on Sunday all dressed up sedately in hats and gloves. Bideford was a friendly place. On reflection Anne and I were probably quicker to make friends than Christine who tended to be more of a loner. Anne liked the lads, much to my parent's horror. I was also getting into party mode in my later years there. Mill Street was ringing to the sounds of 'Living Doll' and my friends and I would spend hours listening to records in the record shop booth, and in the newly opened coffee bars, firstly the Cat's Whisker, and later the Cappuccino, where we would sit for hours over one cup of black coffee, playing the occasional record on the juke box and pin ball machines.

They were great days, walking to Westward Ho in the summer when the whole place became alive with tourists, regattas and fairs. We weren't allowed out with our friends on Sundays because that was declared a family day which in the summer was likely to include an outing to Instow with stripy windbreaks, sandwiches and a calor-gas ring for making tea. Christine mentions no photographs of us as children yet one of Dad's hobbies was photography, he even had a darkroom in the basement of our home in Bideford where we would watch the pictures emerge as he dunked the negatives in and out of various trays of chemicals. There were plenty of photos but at some stage Mum evidently jettisoned most of them. Strange. Family photos are one of the last things I would ever part with.

Chapter Five

SCHOOL

Christine

School. Bewilderment. Teachers. Pillars of Wisdom who got it all wrong.

"You've got all your sums and spellings wrong. Why?" (Dumb question).

"'What are you doing in group one?"

(You put me here.)

"Move immediately to group six."

Months later. "You've got it all right (accusingly), what are you doing in group six?"

(You put me here).

"Move immediately to group one."

In the intervening months, forgotten. Thank God for the mercy of small classes for today's small children. The playground where I stood alone. Always in the same place. Just across from the coat pile. Watching. But at first not allowed out: "It's too cold for you." Then, when the weather improved, I stood determinedly on the line between the swarming infants and the huge juniors.

On Monday nights we all went down to the links, which was the junior branch of the Red Cross. We were given a little card with 10 rules on it, to be offered up on demand. I learned one of them – the shortest one: Do not spit, it spreads disease. I offered it week after week the same as when I later learned the Commandments at school. If you learned the shortest one and stuck your hand up first you got it over with. You never got asked to say the first one, which seemed an endless chain of words. Much easier to simply leap up and say to the nun, "Thou shalt not commit adultery."

We didn't learn clever things like calculators, or computers. I don't think we learned much at school that would be useful in later years. When we moved to North Devon the first problem we hit was language. We were true Essex Gels- the Devon children spoke a different language from us. This problem was to re-occur when, five years later, we moved to Cheltenham – the school bullies made a big deal of this. In those days Cheltenham was a world away from rural Devon.

Chapter Six

CHELTENHAM

We were all upset in 1961 when Dad declared we were about to move again, this time to Cheltenham. It was another new build, semi-detached, on an estate at Benhall, over the road from the then newly arriving GCHQ. Anne got a job at County Clothes and Christine and I were soon fully fitted out with uniforms for Charlton Park Convent. I never did grow into my navy serge PE shorts which the shop assistant assured us had to touch the floor when we knelt down. I was tall but skinny so my waistband was disproportionately wide and I found it difficult to keep my shorts on. Cheltenham was another culture shock. Not friendly, more snobby and old fashioned. We probably all made fewer friends there. Christine recalls her unhappiness at the move. I don't remember it like she does, any arguments were between Mum and Anne. Nothing else seemed out of the ordinary to me.

*

"We moved to Cheltenham, to a dreary housing estate, and an over-refined convent school, when I was 13. In Bideford our family had never been isolated, the house had been vital, and a part of the community which loved and hated each other with brave strengths, shared tears, troubles, smiles and squabbles, but didn't on the whole go in for that coldest of human weapons – rejection of other humans. Now the members of the family began to bite at each other in their separate misery.

Jill was allowed to bicycle to school. I wasn't. Every morning in my food encrusted gymslip, with my satchel of uncompleted homework would watch the bus go as I walked across the bridge. I was always reading interesting books and had fairly well opted out of the school learning process. The two-mile walk dividing the misery of home from the separate misery of school was important. But it meant exclusion from assembly. Standing at the back of the hall to be seen by Madam Anita as she battle-shipped her way from the hall. And it meant regularly detention on Saturday, copying out the previous week's English essay. I always tried to persuade Dad to drive me to school on Saturday, thinking that otherwise the whole of Cheltenham would be saying to their other halves, 'Look, Christine's wearing her gymslip. That means she's in detention again.' Detention at Stella Maris had been fine. We did it in the sixth form classroom, where the desks were the kind that, so I imagined, Chaucer would have quilted in (more likely, actually,

Alexander Pope). In these oak thrones detention was a pleasure. Although Jill would growl, 'You shame me in front of my friends. Your name is on the detention board again.'

When I think about it, Charlton Park School was designed on the lines of a prison. So much of it Out Of Bounds. An escape attempt was nearly always spotted – the reason, surely, for us wearing vivid yellow blouses. They gave us a list of school rules. Twelve of them. A school with only twelve rules? One of them said: 'No talking is allowed in the corridors, cloakroom, classrooms, changing rooms, refectory, hall, or chapel'. That didn't leave much scope for developing the art of conversation. I took to spending my entire lunch-hour in the chapel. Not that I was a particularly religious child at all. But school dinners were awful. And had to be eaten. I remember confronting a boiled onion, as it sat alone on a plate, just a splodge of white sauce to cover its dignity. What to do with it?

'I can't eat it.'

'You have to. No-one leaves the refectory until every plate is clean.'

So I put it in my pocket. And was spotted. Spending lunch-time in the chapel meant avoiding lunch. It also meant avoiding the other girls, who threw my disorganised mind into a total panic. I had nothing to do with them, nor wanted to, and the feeling was mutual. My lisp, which combined with a Devon roll, made my speech a joke. My differences meant that it was better to walk alone. Early in my time in Cheltenham, Miss Carroll, teacher of history and Latin, said to me, 'Christine, you're a nice, ordinary girl. Don't let this place spoil you. Don't get like the other girls.' I didn't know what she was talking about.

I walked home from school, again to stretch out the break between school and home. A problem developed as I began to wet myself on the last stretch of the walk, as I walked through the estate. Woolly socks would be presented smelliely to Mum, 'I splashed in a puddle, Mum.' I began to stop at every public convenience on the way through town, and the problem was solved. I was 13 when we moved to Cheltenham, and I count this move as the beginning of the disintegration of our family, from that move. A barren housing estate. Ferocious nuns at school. Each of us struggling with our own demons.

Chapter Seven

THE NIGHTMARE BEGINS

Jill

While I am only 16 months older than Christine, we were two school years apart. I was halfway through my A Levels when the family moved from Cheltenham but since the schools in Luton were not following the same syllabus it was necessary for me to continue at Cheltenham as a boarder. Christine was given the choice of boarding or staying at home and attending a local school. She chose to board too. There were only about 30 boarders, whose parents mainly lived overseas, and were probably mainly somewhat wealthier than ours. Being in the upper sixth I was initially allocated a room to myself while Christine shared a dormitory with about five other girls.

We had not been there long when I was woken one night by the nun on duty, Madam Aquinas Maria, known as Prowler. She asked me, "What do you do when your sister has a nightmare?"

"She doesn't have nightmares," I said. I knew this since she and I had always shared a bedroom. I went with the Sister to Christine's bed where she was sitting up screaming in what I can only describe as a catatonic state. I had never seen anything like it. Her face was frozen and her eyes were wide open but unseeing. I sat next to her and tried to calm her down but I couldn't reach her. It seemed like a long time before she stopped screaming. She was unreachable, unhearing, unseeing, it took a long time before we could elicit enough response to settle her. I don't know how aware she was of what was happening but she didn't talk to me about it. She just clammed up if I tried. The nightmares began to occur with increasing frequency, and then sometimes during the day she would also get into a state and be found huddled up in some corner sobbing, curled into a ball, or she would run away and have to be found.

Our parents rang us each week on a Sunday evening, so I would fill them in with the latest about Christine, although the headmistress was in contact with them too. They couldn't understand it any more than we could and they were extremely worried. Christine was asked if she wanted to go home, but she was adamant that she wanted to stay. She could be very determined. I was asked to take her to the Doctors, and then to Child Guidance sessions.

Initially the diagnosis was given as night terrors. After a few weeks Christine refused to go. We were allocated a bedroom together to see if that would help and to ensure that I was there to care for her, but Christine's problems persisted. They were inexplicable to us all as we struggled to make sense of what was happening to her. A sort of homesickness reaction seemed the most obvious explanation but Christine was adamant that she wanted to continue boarding. Christine would talk little about it, even to me. We had never been a family to talk much about our feelings. I'm not sure we had the language to express them. None of us were really confidants in that way. Increasingly discussions were that Christine should return home. The school felt unable to carry on coping with these now frequent and unpredictable incidents.

Eventually the decision was made for Christine. She was to leave and when she was told by Madam Anita, the headmistress, and my parents one Sunday afternoon, she ran away. It took the combined efforts of many people searching for several hours to find her. Even Madam Anita was close to tears as she drove me round in the school minibus. Christine was finally found by my friend, Diana, who managed gradually to persuade her back to the school. From there she was finally bundled screaming into the car home. It was a horrendous day.

It was hard for any of us to cope with what was happening to Christine. It all seemed so inexplicable. We were essentially a very ordinary family. There had been no significant traumas during our childhood. Possibly not a lot of understanding from our parents but they, like most of their generation, had grown up in much less child-centric days and spent their young adulthood through what must have been the living hell of the second World War from which they seemed to learn not to share their experiences. They were generally more focused on practicalities than emotions and struggling to manage their finances to make ends meet.

It was about this time that our Anne left home. She had been very unhappy after moving away from Cheltenham, and was missing her boyfriend, Mike. She and Mum had been rowing a lot. Mum was very controlling and Anne, now 19, would no longer stand for it. One day while Mum and Dad were out, Mike drove up to collect her and she left a note saying, 'Gone to Mike's'.

*

It was to be 25 years before Anne and Mum and Dad would see each other again.

I finally managed to get them all together at my house in London following the birth of my second child, Amelia. I used to be allowed to visit Anne from school some Sunday afternoons as she was living at Mike's parents in Gloucester until they later married. I also successfully contrived to get Dad and her together on my last day of leaving school. I told him I had to collect a bag from her at the Coop shop in Cheltenham where she was working. He took us both out for lunch. Apart from that he also didn't see her again until 1989, by which time she had had three children, the youngest of whom had died of leukaemia at the age of nine.

Mike had died a couple of years later from a heart attack. I always thought his heart was broken by the loss of Darren. Christine and I had continued to see her occasionally. She never visited Christine in hospital. She now lives in Istanbul with a Turkish man friend and his family.

Chapter Eight

CHANGING SCHOOL

Christine recalls the time that her night terrors started: "What perversity, what cruelty to myself, led me to tearfully ask to go to Charlton Park as a boarder? Too many chalet-school stories? Fear of separation from Jill? Of change? Of going to a state school when for years we had been in convents and thought ourselves superior? Whatever it was, it was a bad mistake. While the world around us was breaking out into a Summer of Love, short-skirts, loud music and general mayhem, we were in a convent boarding school where time stood still. In fact it didn't just stand still – it went backwards! On Sunday afternoons we walked in double-file, in our Sunday suits of navy blue serge and ridiculous hats, in a silent crocodile around the golf-course. It was the only time we breathed the air outside the convent walls. We must have appeared as if we were on a film set from a different age.

A strange memory from those days is our weekly bath. It was considered sinful for young girls to see their own bodies, so when we bathed we had to cover ourselves with this rubber creation (it had a name, which escapes me now) like a poncho. The idea was that you washed without seeing yourself naked – and this in a world where free love, and lots of it, was the fashion. We were so brainwashed and battered and bullied into Catholicism that I think it would be classified today as emotional abuse. Even in those days it was all a bit strange. Oh, I wonder what the children of the 21st Century would make of being told to address their teachers as madam, and to curtsey to the headmistress. It is not just a couple of generations away but a world away from today's schooling.

Boarders and day girls didn't mix. Ever. They moved, within the same school, with their noses pointed in different directions. Two spheres, moving within a common larger sphere, yet scarcely acknowledging the existence of the other. A transition from one to another would not be easy for a gregarious child. For me it was the end. I gave up. At nights I screamed blue murder. In the daytimes I tried to run off, to hide in the woods, anything, and again the bright yellow blouse would be the giveaway and my poor sister was always ordered to head the manhunt. On every third Saturday, we were supposed to be able to go into town for a couple of hours, depending on individual requests and permits from Madam Anita. But third Saturday was always last Saturday, or next Saturday, never this Saturday. If it seemed a definite thing, then a group punishment, or an individual detention would intervene. I never made it into Cheltenham in all my time as a boarder. I made it to the village – once to Charlton Kings – where the chip shop opened at 12pm. Having to be back at school for lunch at 12.15, speed and efficiency was demanded in the eating thereof. And I bought a forbidden newspaper. Which meant trouble. On Sundays we wrote letters home. Which were read by the nuns. I used to write long letters, which irritated them. Why couldn't I write a page and a half like everyone else did to their parents? Why did I have to be different, difficult?

I made it into town when an appointment was fixed for me at the Child Guidance Clinic. Feeling awkward, sitting in the waiting room in my Charlton Park gear. Ink blots. 'What does this make you think of?

'Nothing.'

Then she was supposed to ask, 'Why does this make you think of (whatever I had said)?' But, apart from a butterfly, I had a pack of nothings. I had let the side down. Or beaten the system. I'm not sure which.

One Sunday afternoon: 'Christine, you're wanted in the parlour'. That was a place where important things happened. And there were Mum and Dad. And Madam Anita.

'You've been asked to leave.' But nobody had asked me. I didn't understand until we were halfway home that this wasn't just a jaunt, an unexpected holiday. My sister had been made to pack my bag. And I was OUT. Home. I don't remember feeling sorry or ashamed. It was what I wanted.

My oldest sister, Anne, had run away from home the night before I was sent home from school. Things must have been hard for my parents. But I retreated into my childishness, my dreams (and tearful and cruel they were −but mine). My father arranged with the GP that I would go into the Middlesex Hospital in September. Why the Middlesex, or why September? I have no idea. This was spring. It was also my O Level year. I didn't go to school for a good while, but in the summer term started at Queen Eleanor's. I chose to ignore the learning process at this school for the time being. I was a bit busy reading Dr Zhivago. In any case I had passed O Levels in English Lit and Scripture the previous year, as was expected from fourth years at Charlton Park. By dint of learning Conrad's Youth and Typhoon by heart I had gained the top marks in English Lit, and been rewarded with the embarrassment of collecting The Complete Works of Shakespeare on Prize Day. I had rather wanted the Scripture prize too, but Anne Mintoff pipped me to the post on that one.

Anyway, there I was at Queen Eleanor's. The O Levels for which I had supposedly been working were for another examination board, and had to be sat at a school in Leighton Buzzard. I nearly missed one through sitting in the cloakroom and another through sitting by the swimming pool. Fifteen minutes was enough for the general science paper. I hadn't a clue. And I might have done better in my art exam if I hadn't had to sit in a room where a class was being held at the same time. I wonder why I had been put in for a paper on flower painting? So, I scrabbled together another 3 O

Levels.

Queen Eleanor's was a bewilderment to me. I insisted on wearing my Charlton Park boater as I couldn't come to terms with the fact that this school had no school hat. And I refused to go into assembly and pray with heathens (Protestants). It was against my religion. At this school I was issued with something I had never had – a Bible. I still have and use my Queen Eleanor's Bible.

In September, instead of returning to school, I went into hospital. I don't think it did me any good at all. I was just put down, I think, as immature. A spoiled, contrary child. At fifteen. The night-screaming had stopped when I left Charlton Park. I had simply opted out of the process of growing up, and the demands that went with it. My cruel, terrible, attractive dreams were my escape. Night and day. No-one could intrude on them. No-one knew. In those dreams physical suffering came long and often. Mental suffering was a phrase I wouldn't have thought of. That came later. There was a Miss Hickson, a Behavioural Therapist, pink and blond- bunned. We would sit for our daily hour in her office, daring each other to break the silence. This continued during weekly visits when I returned to school, until I tired of it and began to spend these afternoons wandering Tottenham Court Road. I think it was a relief to my parents when I refused to go any more. It is only in later years that it occurred to me that they were paying for that treatment.

So I went into the Sixth Form, taking English and History. I was the only sixth former from whom no work, or even understanding, was expected, and none given. They thought I was dumb. I wasn't. But neither was I capable of studying and the teachers, I think, understood that. I was the only one never made a prefect (for whom could I be responsible? Scarcely for myself). I was rigid in my disapproval of the girls being allowed to drink coffee and smoke cigarettes during the break, and determinedly went into the playground to collect my bottle of cold milk. I was now wearing my Charlton Park velour as it was winter. I opted out of most of the interest in pop-stars, in dancing, in fashion. It was all nothing to do with me, and it was many years later, when the cruel day dreams were past, that I realised what I had missed by not being a teenager.

The order of events post-school is somewhat hazy, but I made an attempt at a Secretarial Course at Dunstable FE College. I was on medication, I think, because even by spending lunch hours struggling with the typewriter I was too uncoordinated to manage the touch-typing which the others soon picked up. Hamburgers in the canteen is my clearest memory of that place. But one term was all I managed before another hospital admission. Fairfield's. I'm not sure whether I was there between Banstead Hospital and the college, or not until afterwards. I was told later, by a male nurse 'You've been in here four times this year.' I didn't know. But I remember the shock of the whiteness of the place each time my parents took me back there. The reason for the admissions is unclear to me even now. I recall that my parents had fitted a bolt across the outside of my bedroom door. And a male Social Worker who used to come at my parents demand. When he turned up again it was all up. Back to hospital. Odd things I recall, that the male nurse always gave me polo-mints. Then kept me talking a few minutes. When other patients demanded polo mints he refused. He explained that by watching if I bit the sweet up immediately, or sucked it, he knew whether or not to give me a second tablet. He gave me printed papers, explaining that they meant that I couldn't go home. There was no point trying to go home – my parents always brought me back, even when I was discharged, didn't they?

Chapter Nine

IN AND OUT OF HOSPITAL

Jill

Christine was still in her teens when I first visited her in hospital. It was Fairfield's Hospital in Bedfordshire. At first I thought, if she needed to go into hospital then she must go, but then the stays became more frequent and then longer and longer and it began to seem that she would spend her whole life incarcerated.

I would find my young sister in these dreadful places, these stone building with never-ending corridors and mainly confused, elderly patients. I went to see Christine as often as I could but found the visits saddening and there was usually a distance to travel.

Fairfield's was one of the many old-style asylums built by the Victorians. These were mainly in out of sight, out of mind places. Usually I would find Christine doped up to the eyeballs in wards full of geriatric patients some of whom, I was later to discover, had probably been admitted for the 'insanity' of having a child out of wedlock and were by now deemed incapable of coping in the real world due to the compounded effects of institutionalisation. Eventually, when carried out properly, the NHS and Community Care Act released many of these by now elderly women during the 1990s. The long stone corridors, usually with cream or green glossed walls, were somehow clung to by residents, including Christine, as she developed what I can only call the institutional walk: head down; eyes down; shoulders sagged and always shuffling along close to the wall. Apart from the drugs the major treatment was endless ECT. Most of the time she was in locked wards.

When I finished school, I was rarely home again. I went to teacher training college in Southampton from 1965 -1968 and nearly always worked during my breaks, first on the Christmas post, then as a waitress. I spent two summers in Germany working in the bar and as a waitress in the NAAFI. During 1965-68. Whenever I visited Christine in the various hospitals, that she seemed to be in for increasingly lengthy periods, she was rarely very forthcoming and often obviously very drugged up, head hanging low and with little affect. During her better periods she would occasionally come and stay with me in Southampton and she could seem really well – but it never lasted.

*

When I qualified, I got a job with the Inner London Education Authority in Kilburn and initially shared a flat in West Hampstead with three of my college friends. After two years I left teaching to become a social worker with Camden Social Services.

For many years she was by far the youngest person in hospitals that were largely full of psycho-geriatric patients.

Sometimes I would visit and Christine would seem absolutely fine, with her usual intelligent conversation, and it would be incomprehensible why she was there. You never knew what to expect, or how long she would be in this time. At other times she would be teary, sullen and uncommunicative. At better times she would come and spend occasional weekends with me in London. Sometimes she was fine and would relax and enjoy herself. I would optimistically hope she was coming through it – until the next time these hopes were dashed. When she was out you also never knew what to expect. There would be periods when she seemed to be managing fine. At school she didn't achieve anything like the exam results that in good health I knew she was capable of. She somehow got good jobs, but they didn't last. The Radcliffe hospital, where she started on nurse training declared her immature. I guess they were right. I doubt she was suited to become a nurse.

Christine would occasionally come and stay for a few days. I was sharing a flat in Chalk Farm. I used to share some of my concerns, and what was happening, with a few close friends along the way. Patsy was one – she continued to visit and write to Christine through her Broadmoor days. Andy, with whom I shared a flat in London from 1969-71, was another, and later my husband Chris until our divorce in 1981. He did his best to be supportive and understanding. None of us could ever really understand. That's partly why I'm writing this.

Christine's first, and very nearly successful, attempt at suicide was while working for the Civil Service in London and sharing a flat in Victoria. For our family, it was another horrifying shock. How could things be that bad, particularly when we thought she was doing okay? It was to be the first of very many attempts to kill herself over the years, in very many ways. I was appalled that when admitted to hospital she was usually immediately discharged after a stomach pump. I don't know if this still happens.

One evening when I invited Christine to come with me and a couple of friends to the Fitzroy pub across the road she declined, preferring to stay at home. When I returned a couple of hours later I found she had stacked all the chairs against the door to the flat. After I persuaded her to let me in she told me she had been frightened. I knew she was being manipulative, trying to stop me going out and leaving her alone, but there was little I could do as she would quickly become distressed. She was due to attend a hospital appointment the next day and I was concerned that it was important to get her there. I was worried she would refuse to go. My parents, who I had spoken to on the phone, thought it might be better if they didn't come as I was more likely to manage to persuade her without them. Christine reluctantly agreed and we took a taxi.

The psychiatrist at that hospital spoke to us both, together and separately. He told me that I needed to stand back or she would destroy me. I was taken aback and knew he was making the point that Christine would take over my life. I felt that what she had done the night before had been done in anger, and was very manipulative to stop me going out. I heard his caution but knew I could not abandon my sister, nor could I let her control me. It raises the question of what she knew and could control and what she could not control. I still struggled to make sense of what was causing her unfathomable distress and behaviour. I reckoned it could so easily have been me that got the wrong gene.

Chapter Ten

IN AND OUT OF WORK

I was the only girl in my year who didn't go to University. Instead I went to train as a Nurse. My parents were stunned at the unsuitability of this. Years later, reading my hospital case-notes, without permission, I saw it written that I had been accepted at the Radcliffe, Oxford, simply because Miss Scott (the Head of Q. E.) had a friend who worked there. I didn't know about that. I must certainly have been the most unsuitable candidate for nursing ever to have been employed at that great teaching hospital. I was taken on first as 'Pre-PTS' – a trial period of four months- before entering the Training School. When, later, I was asked to leave, on the grounds of being too immature, I asked why I had been allowed onto the pre-training scheme. 'We thought you might improve' came the answer.

It had somehow escaped everyone's notice (and mine too) that I didn't know the Facts of Life. I didn't even know that men were built differently from women. Having dreamed my way in isolation through my teenage years, I had missed out on some important things. In fact I was 22 before I fully understood how the sex act works. I knew that I was ignorant, and fear took the place of knowledge, so I didn't, during all that time, have any relationships, or even real friendships, with men.

This was the Swinging Sixties, when, so I later learned, there was no better time to be young. I was still, to an extent, cloaked in unreality, still blinkered by barriers erected between myself and a threatening world over a number of years.

After nursing didn't work out, I went, for a few weeks, to a Prep School, in Sussex, as an Assistant Matron. Polishing the boys shoes, emptying the conkers out of their pockets, washing their clothes. I was quite unable to get on with Anna, the Matron, a year or two older than myself, or with the Headmistress wife, who ran the domestic side of things. I was sacked for being useless at the job and went home to my parents.

My father arranged a job for me in the Civil Service and a place at a Civil Service hostel. How this was arranged I have never dared ask, since I had no job interview and filled in no forms. So I took my place at a hostel in Gloucester Road and at the office in Ebury Bridge Road, processing work permits for foreigners to come to work in England.

*

I soon tired of the hostel and answered an Evening Standard

advertisement for a shared flat in Pimlico. For £3 a week I moved into a slummy flat with three shop-girls in the heart of swinging London. Only nobody had told me this was swinging London and I was supposed to be swinging with it. It was all nothing to do with me. I had beaten a mental retreat from the whole demanding process of living. I did my job, but that was all.

I had, around this time, a nasty kidney complaint and went to see the Doctor. He apparently spotted that there was something wrong besides the kidney complaint. He arranged for me to be admitted to a hospital called 'All Saints'. A place no more than half a large house, the upstairs being for Out-Patients and, I suppose, offices. For several days I didn't move from under the bedcover.

I had left a note for my flat-sharers saying that I had gone into hospital but would be back. The more intelligent of the three, one called Anne, who used to collect the rent, checked where I was with the G.P. and came to visit me, bringing the latest acquisition, a stuffed lion, called Sebastian. In the coming years I was to cling to that toy as a protection against all evils. It would have a chair at table in the hospitals I entered, until finally it was stolen at Fairfield Hospital. I suspected the nurses of removing it, and still do. I raised merry-hell when he went.

At All Saints my other comfort was to cling to the hand of a nurse called Pamela. I was 19. A conversation with the lady Doctor at this time stays in mind. It was vividly recalled years later when, as I earlier said, I was reading my hospital case-notes in St. Francis one night while the night nurse slept. This Doctor had said to me:

'You're a lesbian, aren't you'.

I asked her to explain the word, not having heard it before. I assumed it implied membership of a club, or Church.

She screamed at me:

'Don't pretend. I know you're a lesbian'.

She was getting upset. I told her that if she would tell me what it meant I would tell her whether I was or not. She got really angry and finally I agreed that I was. Returning to the Ward, I asked my nurse, Pamela, the meaning of the word. She told me that it meant a woman who liked to hold another woman's hand. So I said that I must be one then. Several years later I found out the real meaning of this word, when I found myself in a hospital where I was surrounded by them. That doctor had written in my notes that I was a subnormal lesbian, which stayed in my notes for years, and is presumably still being passed around the hands of doctors.

I was discharged from All Saints and went back to work. I had in my mind at this time two plans, two things that I must do. One was to find another placement as a nurse, this time as

SEN (State Enrolled Nurse), as SRN (State Registered Nurse) was clearly beyond me. The other was to kill myself. I was accepted for training at Tooting Bec Hospital. I wrote and told them, 'Thank you'. I had changed my mind. And I overdosed heavily, dispassionately, on the drugs I had been given but not taken. I do not remember being in the least frightened by this action. It was simply something that had to be done. I took some from each of the bottles, lined them up again in the wardrobe and went to bed.

Later I heard what had happened. Anne had wanted the rent. She came in that evening, but I was apparently asleep. She tried the next morning. Asleep. The next evening, desperate for the rent, she noticed that I still had not moved, and called the doctor. Three days later I awoke in the Intensive Care Unit at Westminster Hospital with my parents at my side. They had been there the whole time. A Priest came and said to me accusingly: ' I gave you the last sacrament the day before yesterday'. I'm still not sure whether I should have apologised for letting him down. The following day I was moved to Banstead Hospital in Surrey. I had meant to kill myself, but I had no great regrets that I hadn't. I just didn't care either way. I was back in the protective nursery atmosphere of a hospital ward. That was the only place I could cope. The only place where I functioned at all. I had my 21st birthday on that ward. Whether there was a party I don't know. I just recall making soft toys.

Chapter Eleven

FAIRFIELD HOSPITAL

Christine was always a prolific letter writer, partly motivated by the pleasure she derived from receiving them. She also wrote poems, and prose accounts of her experiences, and kept diaries.

> Fairfield Hospital, Hitchin, Herts
> 31st March, 1971

Dear Jill,

Thank you very much for the owl. I have christened it Parsley (after the lion on TV) and hung it up by my bed. I am getting very depressed because I am not allowed to go off the ward to therapy or any of the entertainments. I am just left on the ward with the worst of the idiots and slugs and as this is a long-stay ward I cannot envisage any change coming. You have seen for yourself what a depressing ward this is but you have not met any of the patients – there are only two who are capable of holding a conversation, the rest are toothless, frustrated, bickering old hags and it makes me very miserable having to sit with them all day.

I am sorry to write such a miserable letter but if I had any good news I would give it to you – I just can't think of anything cheerful to say! Mum and Dad came at the weekend and they brought me a lovely bunch of tulips and daffodils. The daffodils have died but the tulips are still standing. I think one of the patients has been drinking the water out of the vase because each time I look the water has nearly all gone! I wouldn't be surprised at anything here. There is one woman who gets out of bed at night and switches on the light to see whether she is in bed. She also looks at her tongue in the mirror to make sure she hasn't swallowed it! There is one woman who has been here 32 years, but most have only been here about 10 years. I can't see any other future for myself at the moment. I am writing this in bed. We go to bed at 8pm, just when all the best TV programmes come on.

Please write again soon to cheer me up.

Love, Chris xxxx

*

Fairfield Hospital, Hitchin, Herts

2nd May, 1971

Dear Jill and Andy,

Thank you for your lovely card and all the news. I haven't really got any news except that we have got all new nurses on the ward today as every three months they have a big change-over in the hospital. The trouble is that three of the new ones already know me – in fact most of the hospital knows me by now, I have been here so long.

One thing is worrying me at the moment – am I backward? Please write and tell me if I am. I don't know what to do about it. If that is why I am here what can I do to get out of here? I don't think I will ever get out of here and I don't know what I shall do if I do. Nobody would employ me because I am too stupid to hold down a job. The people here didn't believe that I was 22 but I asked Mum and she said I am, but I still get scared of dragon-flies and silly things in my dreams in the middle of the night. The other night I was looking for Sebastian and the nurse locked me up and gave me an injection and I could hardly sit down for two days after.

One morning Elaine and I asked if we could go for a

walk but we hitched into Hitchin. Her husband had sent her £5 and she spent most of it and then we came back by bus. When the bus reached Letchworth one of the nurses got on it but she promised not to tell on us, she said she hadn't seen us. Another day I went down to the hospital shop and met a hairy hippy called John and he was chatting me up. I didn't tell him my name but he found out and came up to the ward asking for me. Sister said she would grab him by the hair and throw him down the stairs! I haven't seen him since.

I am writing this sitting in the court-yard with a couple of dozen nuts, wandering around talking to themselves and eating the stale bread that is meant for the birds and talking to the male nuts through the fence. It is really gorgeous weather and I hope it is like this for you and Chris when you go to Aberystwyth. When are you going? Don't forget to send me a post-card. Like you, I remember it in the rain.

I had a post card from Margaret Groves and a funereal card from Patsy in Paris, also a letter from Auntie Florrie saying she hadn't seen Jill since last June and Uncle Frank is staying in bed until the warmer weather comes and he hasn't showed for a week. I can't think of any other news except that I have given up smoking as I think it is a waste of money.

Cheerio, God bless, I hope you are both alright and Jill is better.

Love, Chris xxx

While Christine was usually unwilling to express her thoughts and feelings to anyone she frequently wrote of them, very openly and expressively, throughout her life. In her poems she often seems to describe her feelings and experiences with particular lucidity.

Escaping from Reality

Dreams, dreams, hiding in dreams,
Escaping from the people-fears,
The hurt-fears, the thinking-fears,
Hiding my face and shedding dry tears
The falseness has gone,
I switch it on when I must
There's nothing else left, except a shell-crust
They wouldn't let me take my life,
Perhaps it wasn't time,
But the crust that's left is useless
Because I've forgotten what I am
The safest place is 'My Place'
Some would say it's all pretend.
It took me over once, maybe it will again.

I'm sheltering in my dream-place, nothing matters
anymore.

There are other people here,

But they must not burst my bubble.

They shoot false arrows at me, talking, laughing, all
pretend,

I have to hide my face from them.

I can't start all that again.

To be a plastic person, not really knowing why.

It seemed to please them all,

I can't help wondering why.

So I'm hiding in my bubble, being safe from all
demands.

Living with my shadow-people, and feeling very lost,

Not really happy, and not in the least bit brave,

I've given up the struggle, but perhaps one day I'll find

The crust has turned back into me.

I'll suddenly find I'm a person again,

I wonder who it will be, what she'll be like, and when,

or maybe that's just another bubble-dream too

Surrender to Despair

I want to be swallowed by the sinking sands,

No need to struggle, nothing but vacancy.

To be quietly enveloped, such a peaceful surrender.

I know they wouldn't reject me, just open up and take

me.

Take me as their own, and keep my secret too.

The seas would come and bless me,

I'd be their foster-child.

Twice a day they'd come, I could depend on it.

And so I'd be reborn in the safety of the sands.

Sometimes they'd come in peacefulness,

And sometimes in torment,

But their anger wouldn't hurt me.

I'd know just how they felt.

And so I'd be reborn in the safety of the sands.

I'd belong in a place still un-shattered by man.

I doubt if God would want me,

I'm not his child anymore.

But he made sands and sea,

And he'd let them care for me.

There are a few people who care for me I know.

They'd shed a few tears, and wonder why perhaps

But it doesn't really matter because it's senseless to mourn

When a person has found the peace and happiness she sought for so long.

The Switchback

'My life is a circle' so the words of the song go.

But mine is a switchback, with plateaus so high

And canyons so low.

One climbs to the top, way up to cloud nine,

And the land shines with gladness and everything's fine

And instead of storm clouds there are bubbles of love,

Which can never be burst by sadness and strife.

All that mars the sweetness and spices it with discontent,

Is knowing that one can never stay.

A life-span there is never meant,

For any one of us to have.

The tumble down is quick and cruel,

a sudden flash then down one goes,

Mind bruised by jagged rocks of hatred,

Through blackness to the canyons of despair.

And in the canyon of such sorrow,

There dwells a hurricane of fear.

There are other such tormented spirits

But loneliness keeps them apart,

Each one suffers their own burden,

Never daring, never caring, to turn back a corner of the curtain

Of their terrors, lest this death should be worse.

To move a little in the darkness is a chancy thing to do.

One might be swamped for ever, there are so many fears.

So one wanders for a little, crushed inside and unconnected,

Groping for a foothold to climb back up again.

It doesn't really seem to matter,

Yet somewhere there's a thought,

A memory, crumpled midst hatred and fear,

Of a foam padded land where the sun always shone.

There's no simple stairway to get back up there

So one takes out that memory, irons it flat, looks close and remembers.

And one pushes just a little, just a very little, first

Because it's a long, hard journey back.

'Lead kindly light, lead thou me on'

Above the crags, the jags, the tortuous struggle back begins.

And all the time one's moving but never seems to get anywhere.

Sometimes the struggle's too much.

One folds back, back again into that deep dark canyon where it's so easy to despair.

It's easy to give in when the going's very hard.

To excuse oneself and wade in the slough,

Forgetting even to care.

But one struggles up again, and the bruises aren't so bad.

The tumbles hurt a little less, and when you're going up.

The storm clouds aren't so choking, and the batteries in
that tiny torch-light recharge themselves to brighten up
the clefts of safety.
And suddenly it happens – you've reached foam mattress
land again.
Life would be very boring without the switchback,
But I just wish it would slow down a little, and move
just a little more gradually.

*

Fairfield had just fitted itself with a spanking new Electroconvulsive
Therapy (ECT) unit and was keen to use it to the full. Every new
admission got ECT every morning for a week. And that was the
minimum you could get away with. For me, there were more
frequent doses. One morning I decided to hide. I hid first in the
broom cupboard and then behind an armchair until, at 11 o'clock, I
deemed it safe to emerge. They wouldn't give ECT at that time,
surely? It was always over by that time.

I was led to a side-room and a lot of equipment was brought
and people came. The electrodes were fitted to my head. That was
the only time I ever had ECT without an anaesthetic, and without
even knowing I was having it. The forgetfulness that ECT brings
with it immediately is merciful in such cases. When, that afternoon,
a nurse told me I had had it, I didn't believe her.

Several times, whilst at Fairfield, I was put into the Pad – the
padded cell. I managed to rip some of the padding off the inside of

the double-door with my teeth and nails. One is put in there naked, and there is a gutter in which to urinate, and no bed. Like being inside a box. Completely silent. Completely un-stimulating.

I took to attacking the other patients in their beds at night. "I want to know what it's like to kill someone," I said. I was speaking truly. A weird curiosity led me to want to take a life with my bare hands. When, years later, I very nearly did just that, I was surprised and puzzled by the severity of the punishment.

"Care for a walk with me, Christine?" So I went. "This is F6. Your new ward." All the wards in that place were locked, but this was the worst ward – the Refractory Ward. I gave up every attempt at civilised behaviour as the other patients on that ward had apparently done the same before.

And I now made frequent attempts at running off. A trip into Hitchin with the occupational therapist meant a chance to leap off a bus and make a run for it down the high street. I have no idea where I thought I was going, but am still surprised by the speed at which the Police car appeared beside me. It was around this time that I sat in bed one night and wrote a letter to Doctor Ford, the superintendent. I think it may have been the reason for my removal to F6. He interviewed me, and unbeknown to me, set things in motion for my removal to Broadmoor.

One afternoon a Dr Mc Quade came to see me. I had no idea why at the time. He told me that he worked at the Tavistock Clinic, and also at Broadmoor. I thought he was asking for sympathy, and gave him some.

"How would you like to go to Broadmoor?" he asked me.

I thought this was a rhetorical question, a conversation filler. "That's where dangerous people, and people from prison go, isn't it?" I said. I had vaguely come across the name in the papers. I forgot him as soon as he had gone. Or would have done if my parents hadn't regularly brought him into their conversations when they visited. "Where was he from?" They kept asking. I couldn't recall, only that the hospital had a famous name. They had been to see him. I assumed they had seen him at Luton and Dunstable Hospital, but I wasn't much interested. Until one night, on going to bed, I saw that the clothes had gone from my locker. "There are clean clothes there for you to wear tomorrow. The rest are packed. You're going to Broadmoor tomorrow morning. For six weeks observation and assessment."

This stretched to four years and later another two years, even though I have no criminal record at all. I have never even stolen a bar of chocolate from Woolworths, or parked on a double yellow line. These days terrorists are given a chance to have a voice in law, not to be locked up indefinitely with no trial and no charges, but then nobody wanted to know. You were just a loony.

So that was that and off I went.

*

Jill

It must have been early in 1971 when my parents were asked to go to see the consultant in charge at Fairfield hospital. I went with Dad to this appointment. He and I usually went together, Mum rarely went. I sometimes saw doctors alone if Christine asked me to.

The consultant told us that he had asked a psychiatrist who specialised in working with potentially violent patients to come and assess Christine. This was because of the letter she had written in which she said she wanted to set fire to the hospital to see the patients burn. Christine had by now been diagnosed with paranoid schizophrenia because of the compelling voices she was often experiencing telling her to harm herself or others. He informed us that he needed to clarify whether there was a real possibility of her doing this, because he could not keep her there if she was a risk to other patients and staff.

The visiting consultant would be from Broadmoor. A couple of weeks later, the consultant, Dr Mc Quade, came to my flat in London to meet with my father and I. He told us that he had seen Christine and that his assessment was that she did constitute a real risk and that the only place where she could be safely further assessed and treated was Broadmoor. We were absolutely devastated and appalled by the prospect of Christine being sent to such a chilling place. We tried every which way to suggest and explore any possible alternative. We couldn't bear the thought of it. This place was renowned as the prison where all the most heinous of murderers were sent. He kept telling us that Broadmoor was now designated as a Special Hospital. Now that Christine had had such a damning assessment, Fairfield couldn't keep her and no other ordinary psychiatric hospital would consider admitting her. We knew Christine wasn't well enough to come home. Our hearts were filled with dread and disbelief. How could it have come to this? How could they possibly suggest no option but to send her to this infamous institution for the most criminally insane and murderous members of society. She was a slightly built young woman of twenty two. After the doctor left Dad and I sobbed and hugged. "Surely to God, there must be somewhere else?" I had heard of Broadmoor, it was the place where the very worst people were sent. It was a high security prison.

Chapter Twelve

BROADMOOR

Christine

Walls within Walls

They took away my liberty,

I shrivelled up inside.

I couldn't see beyond the Walls,

I had no choice but to hide.

The world beyond was just a dream, a mirage and we spoke

In awesome tones about 'The World' and somebody would choke

Upon their tears.

As memories came flooding back,

Of places, families, loved and lost, of happy days and

sad.

We lived a desert-island life, it wasn't all that bad.

The torment came from the Walls and bars.

We were birds in a gilded cage.

They gave us all we needed, but something is very wrong

In an isolated fortress, where so many don't belong.

We didn't belong to 'The World Outside' and were well aware of it.

And each of us made our own escape, an inward sanctuary.

And so we built up more walls, but in mine I was free.

Not free in the sense of being 'out there' but just free to be me.

I forgot about walking down the street, and travelling home in a train.

It was there in the past and I'd seen it.

I'd seen it on TV, just forgotten how it felt.

So I stayed within my fortress, my land of fantasy.

And the solid brick-built fortress didn't really bother me.

Because I couldn't see beyond it, so I began to forget.

And my land was the land of dream-pictures

But to me it was so real.

Like a plant that's forgotten how to grow

I shrivelled up and died.

Until one day they transplanted me to the Great World
Outside.

They peeled off all the layers,

I shed tears of fear inside.

At last I could see beyond that wall, to see how people
live.

I wasn't sure I liked it, although it was all mine,

Like Eve I had a fresh new world, created just that day.

Blinked and gasped and grasped at it.

I felt it couldn't last.

Like a spirited horse who's been broken in,

The damage was done and I'd never fit in,

Except to other people's way of thinking.

They've shattered all my barriers, my land of fantasy.

So there's no walls left, no bricks, no dreams,

Just a world that frightens me.

I recall, with a wry smile, my arrival at Broadmoor. I was given a stack of clothes, bedding, and towels. Out of my greenness I said, "Thank you, but I can't take them. I don't have my cheque book with me." Of course they weren't handing me a gift, these were uniform dresses or galateas as they were known. They had in fact been worn by previous patients who had perhaps been discharged, or had died. I remember they had rubber buttons down the front of them. There are probably stacks of them in the cellar too, along with the dishcloths we used to spend our time making.

The brick walls, the barred windows, bore silent witness to the time capsule, to the hell, where we were encased in amber. There seemed to be one vital omission in the set-up – where was God? Not here surely? Was He at the gate and waiting to be invited in? Or had He turned his back on us as lost causes? God loves a sinner. But if He loves us why does He give us so much pain? The walls of Broadmoor have witnessed so many years of pain of so many of the hopeless and helpless. If only those walls could talk. Because inside those walls the rules and laws of society are not applied - basically once you are in there, the law will not protect you.

If Walls could talk

If I could have one wish, one craft,

Beyond mundanity

It would be the ability

To hear the whispers of the walls.

To listen to their tales of by-gone days,

And by-gone people,

Their passions, their secrets, their ways.

I have sat, in the past, entombed by walls

Who's every brick weeps for the misery it has seen.

No history-book can tell me of the woman

Who lived out her terrors in this room

One hundred years ago.

She has passed into the oblivion of the Unknown

Lunatic.

Other buildings could tell me merrier tales

Of battles fought and won

Beside the hearth or in the lover's nook.

There's no such honest witness in any history book.

*

Dishcloths and Dreams

I have this theory – about knitted dishcloths. Week after week, sack-full after sack-full, we knitted our broken minds and private pain into the 6x6inch dishcloths. Who on earth buys knitted dishcloths these days? One day, I'm sure, Broadmoor will be opened up and the jurisdiction as well as the media will witness the opening of a large basement, or cellar, crammed with thousands of black-plastic bags crammed with hand knitted dishcloths. Where else could they all have gone? Knit one, purl one, knit another dishcloth. Women patients silently knitting their grief and pain into this week's required bag full of dishcloths. I wonder where all those sacks of dishcloths went?

"I have measured out my life in coffee spoons," wrote TS Eliot.

"I have measured out my life in knitted dishcloths." (Me!)

I have this theory. This dream. That one day society will turn its heart to the fate of the criminal lunatics – God's forgotten people. A kind of Martin Luther King representing us. Broadmoor will be opened up and will surrender its secrets, and its dishcloths. And when that day comes, when people are no longer afraid to speak up, when punishment is replaced by actual treatment for illness, and the place can be staffed by nurses, by caring people – no more prison officers, no more Heavy Mobs, then the patients will no longer say, "Where is this God of yours?" "Look around you." "Has He written us off?" What answer is there to that judgement? Okay, so God loves a sinner. But why does He allow so many of us to suffer so much?

"Eli, Eli, lama sabachthani?" ("Lord, Lord, why hast thou abandoned me?")

*

York House, Broadmoor

June 22, 1971

Dear Jill and Andy,

I am writing to tell you the great news that I have been released from Lancaster Zoo and am now back in the Infirmary. When I went to occupational therapy, I drew a picture of one of my Horrible Hobbits and they are going to give it to the Doctor. They are not a bit like Tolkien's Hobbits but I call them hobbits so that people can understand, but they are all so ignorant that they don't even know what hobbits are. They are all hairy with lots of arms and claws and swords and they have spikes and tails too, like strange people with and big teeth and huge crossed eyes and they come in swarms on the backs of dragonflies, because dragonflies can get in anywhere even when the shutters and door are locked. But when I call out to the nurses they get angry and give me injections, as well as the injection and medicine I have before I go to sleep. I keep wetting the bed but I daren't tell the nurses.

(Saturday) Sorry I didn't get around to finishing this letter before but big things have been happening. Yesterday they decided to move me out of the infirmary 'through the door' but I couldn't cope and I just dumped all my stuff on the bed and sat on the floor and sobbed. The girls were very kind but I was frightened by the whole thing of having to stand on my own feet so they brought me back again. It is supposed to be a big step forward to go 'through the door' but I just couldn't take it. Thanks Andy for the birthday cards. I sent him the one with a devil on and gave him the false teeth – Jill, I hope you don't mind but I'd nothing else to give him. He sent me two of his curls during the week – I don't know what he expects me to do with them! He has long ginger curls, really beautiful. I expect your exams are over by now, Andy. I hope you got on all right. I'm sure you will be pleased to get back to work. We often get students coming to look at us and this week some came from Chiswick Polytechnic. They were a right queer, freaky crowd. One of the lecturers came up to me and looked at the queer shaped thing I was knitting and asked me what it was. I wouldn't tell her and she was trying to be polite about it, I couldn't help laughing! One of the girls was obviously pregnant and they weren't very impressive at all. Altogether I'm glad you didn't go there Jill! I will write to Mrs Hagen for the address for Chris's archaeological dig. I hope you are all okay and work and college is not too bad. It was lovely seeing you last weekend.

God bless,

Love Chris xxx

*

York House, Broadmoor

July 4, 1971

Dear Jill and Andy,

I am writing to say thank you Jill for the super visit and the fantastic pictures and thank you Andy for your lovely letter. I hope you feel better after your week in Cardiff, exams are so mentally exhausting aren't they? My room looks really nice now with all the pictures up, and a jar of roses on the window-ledge, although Picasso's Blue Period WILL keep falling down! Most of the girls just have fashion pictures up but mine is really different. Did you get all those pictures when you were at college? Anyway it has saved me a lot of money I was going to spend on posters from Camden Passage which wouldn't be nearly so nice. Before my room was like a bleak little nun's cell but now it is really cheerful. I even have a portrait of Phil which he gave me on Sports Day which looks really like him – not to mention the picture of Jeff! Actually Jeff didn't turn up on Sports Day, so I was saved an embarrassing situation. I am going to write to him and tell him that I see a lot of Phil but I still want to stay friends with him, but not too close. Anyway if he couldn't even be bothered to come and see me on Sports Day he can't think so much of me. Phil had gone to a lot of trouble to make it a good day for me, even making a flask of coffee and getting some tins of shandy although we had to stay with the nurses and screws we enjoyed ourselves. The tug-of-war was really exciting and Phil was getting so carried away that he was pulling me! Then we had a discotheque last night and I saw him there. Also I am allowed to go to the Free Church religious discussions on the male side and we can wink at each other across the room there, even though we are kept separate from the men! I have had the cheek to ask if I can join the RC choir but when they audition me I'm afraid I will get a polite refusal!

I went into the tea room today to play my records.

The radio was on but nobody was really listening to it so I asked if anybody minded me putting on my records. I put on Buffy Saint Marie and I've never seen the tea room clear so fast! They didn't say anything, they just all walked out! So I had peace to listen without anybody talking. It was lovely to hear my records again. I hope your prison session went off all right and they liked Johnny Cash. I bet you'll be glad to get back to work soon won't you, Andy? I should like to work in a library when I get out of here. You said in your letter that I should dream about cuddly teddy-bears. Well, I spend all day making them in occupational therapy and they have given me one to take to bed, but very often by the morning he is all torn and has to be darned. Well, I have got a list of seventeen people to write to this evening so I'll sign off now.

God bless,

Love Chris xxx

*

York House, Broadmoor

July 11, 1971

Dear Jill and Andy,

It was lovely to see you and Alf on Friday. I would certainly be pleased to see him again whenever he is down this way. I had a talk with the most sensible and understanding of the sisters yesterday and she says I am here until I grow up and it's up to me whether that's a year or ten years but she says they are prepared to help me 50-50. In other words it's up to me to keep on battling on but I can rely on them for support so long as I don't give up the struggle. Also she says that in September she wants me to sign on for the lessons in shorthand, French and English literature. I don't want to tell Mum and Dad this yet, because they'll only start worrying about me studying, but I am writing to ask you to get hold of some books for me so that I can brush up my non-existent knowledge of shorthand and my rusty French. (The eight o'clock 'cow-bell' has just gone which means I have to go and queue up to be checked in, and I've got half-an-hour before I get drugged up to the eyeballs, so I'll have to write fast). The shorthand book we used at college, and which they use here is a bright pink hardback called Pitman's New Course in Shorthand and I would be very pleased if you could get me a copy. Also if you've got any old copies of Paris Match magazine lying around, and a French dictionary, it would be a great help, or any French novels Martina might have left behind. In fact anything which will help me brush up my French, so that I am not the idiot of the class. I think I will be all right on the English Literature because I am reading a lot now and I have joined the travelling library.

Do you remember bringing me a book by Solzhenitsyn called One Day in the Life of Ivan Denisovich? Well, there is a documentary about him and some of his readings on TV tonight, and I have persuaded one of the nurses to watch it for me, as it's on at 10.15 pm on Omnibus. It should be very interesting, although I have not read the book as yet as I think I will find it a bit depressing, being about a Siberian labour camp under Stalin. I hope the wedding went off okay, despite the preliminary chaos. I will go to sleep now as I have had some dope and I can't write properly, but will continue tomorrow.

(Monday) Have just come down from Therapy and am waiting for tea. Phil has sent me an absolutely massive colour picture of Peter Wyngarde, who is apparently on TV in Department S. I have never heard of him but it's such a nice picture of a handsome man that I've stuck it on the wall! He has also sent me some more good underground freaky records and some papers called Sounds – a weekly record paper. I haven't got anything equal to send him. He is very good to me. Margaret and I are sitting in my pad listening to the radio which has been brought in.

(Tuesday) Things are getting steadily worse and I can't cope. I think they will soon move me over to Lancaster House. Last night they put me in the Seclusion Room.

Love Chris xxx

*

York House, Broadmoor

July 21, 1971

Dear Jill and Andy,

Happy Birthday Old Girl! Thanks for coming to see me at the weekend, it was really great to see you and Chris. Hi Andy! What's it like to be one of the workers again? I bet you love it. Chris was telling me about the books you brought home. Charlie and the Chocolate Factory seemed to have made him very happy and he told me the full story to cheer me up. I loved that card you sent. I was wondering about trying to copy it as a painting in OT.

I found out today that last week-end the girls here got

up a petition saying they wanted me sent over to Lancaster House (the block for disturbed patients). Anyway they weren't successful – I'm still on York and I've taken up shorthand again and also crochet. I spend all my evenings in my room alone as I hate to go out and face the glares and turned backs of the other girls. One day a crowd of them gathered in the corridor and told me what they think of me and what they think I ought to do. I expect soon they will get fed-up and find someone else to pick on but they know they can easily reduce me to tears and that when they do that I get locked in my room and they get pleasure from that.

I must sign off now because it's time for my nightly 'fix' and that knocks me right out. I fell asleep writing to Patsy the other night and I still haven't finished the letter!

Love. Chris, x

*

York House, Broadmoor
Sept 26, 1971

Dear Jill and Andy,

I found the enclosed picture in this month's Vogue and thought it would be lovely as a wedding dress for you Jill. It costs £16.50 without the waistcoat but you could wear it afterwards and it really would suit you and it is worth a lot to look lovely for your wedding. Dad saw Dr Do-little on Friday and he says I have improved. He doesn't even know me so I think he's talking through the top of his bald head, just to keep Dad quiet. C'est la vie!

I found a joke for Andy but I've lost it now – it was something about a woman looking in the index in the library and seeing: Sex – see Librarian. Next time she looked there must have been some queries because it had been changed to: For sex please ask at desk. You've probably heard it before, and anyway you wouldn't have that problem in your library. There was a picture in yesterday's Guardian of children in a play group in Camden doing paintings for an exhibition at Swiss Cottage Library so I expect you are saying "Chaos has come again," at the moment.

The discotheque was lovely last night.

Mum and Dad have been decorating a room for me but I don't want to go and live with them and I haven't the courage to tell them. I am going to get the doctor to start telling them it would be a bad thing and then they would take it a bit better. Give Chris my love and tell him I wish him luck in his new job. I hope you get the house and the job you want in Sheffield.

God bless.

All my love, Chris xxxxxxx

Jill

Andy and I were sharing a flat in Kilburn at this time. It was such normal, sisterly advice that I received in a letter from Christine a month before I was due to marry. It was the address heading the letter – Broadmoor Special Hospital – that was not normal. As a family we were still reeling that it could have come to this and we, like Christine, were already beginning to think she would never get out of there.

My sadness that she would be unable to come to my wedding was dwarfed compared to my continuing sorrow at the horror of her plight that had become consequent to her mental illness.

We didn't go in for the big, flouncy white, extravaganza wedding as at the time, these were viewed as old fashioned. We weren't churchy people and had opted for a registry office marriage with only our parents present. Hampstead registry office was my local, and at that time the chosen venue for many a popular star. After the short service the six of us enjoyed a meal in a room I had reserved at the nearby Clive Hotel. That evening we had a big, boozy, party at the flat I then shared with Andy. The next day Chris and I drove to Sheffield where we were to live for the next three years while Chris was employed as a research assistant at the university to complete his Phd. I had given up my job as an assistant social worker with Camden Social Services and soon obtained a similar post in Sheffield from which I was seconded the following year to complete a CQSW Social Work qualification at the university's Extra Mural Studies Department. Living and working in Sheffield made it harder to get to visit Christine very often.

Christine Delahunty

York House, Broadmoor Hospital,

Crowthorne, Berks.

October 22, 1971

Dear Professor Tolkien,

I am writing to tell you that the creatures you write about in the Lord of the Rings have frightened me very much. I know the hobbits were intended to be gentle, friendly creatures but they torment me and talk to me when I am on my own. The creatures I see have the magic of Gandalf and are as horrible as Gollum and are partly orcs but they talk like the hobbits. I have asked one of the nurses to get rid of my copy of Elevar because I and two friends, who are also familiar with it, find it a really horrible book. I love fantasy books because they take me away from the hospital into a magic world but I hate being on my own now because of the hobbits. They pull faces at me and put their hands around my neck to try to strangle me and I push them away and scream for the nurses and when she comes they say 'kill her, kill her, kill the nurse' and sometimes I try to hurt the nurses. Please can you do or say something to make Bilbo Baggins and his friends less horrifying.

Christine

*

Lancaster House, Broadmoor Hospital,

Crowthorne, Berks

November 22, 1971

Dear Professor Tolkien,

I have spoken to Doctor McQuaid this morning about the hobbits, as he said he had heard from you recently. I must apologise for having wrongly blamed you for the creatures which have been worrying me. Undoubtedly there are parts of 'Elevar' that I find frightening, such as Old Man Willow in the Old Forest, but I was advised recently to re-read your book and I found it fascinating and beautiful and have learnt some of the poems. The creatures I have been calling hobbits are not your hobbits, they are creatures of my own imagination which I have been very muddled up about while I was reading your book and I have got the two things connected somehow. Now that I am a little better I can realise this and not blame it all on your book. Sorry.

Yours Sincerely,

Love and Peace

Christine Delahunty

*

Professor J.R.R.Tolkien c/o George Allen & Unwin Ltd
Ruskin House
40 Museum Street
London WC1A 1LU
Dec. 24th 1971

Dear Christine,

I am sorry that I have not answered sooner your letter of Nov. 22nd. I am away from home, and travelling about. I am very glad that you have read my book again, and have liked some of the poems: and also to hear that you are feeling better. The 'hobbits' of course were meant by me to be just ordinary, kindly human people, fond of food and fun, small in size but strong and brave, and very good at driving away all nasty creatures, and at helping other people that were troubled by such things. There were, of course, nasty and dangerous creatures in their times, but in my story these were conquered , or destroyed by the 'hobbits' and their friends – such as Tom Bombadil who was not afraid of any of them, and when he commanded them to go away they fled at once! I was very pleased to get your letter. If you want to, or wish to have anything explained, write again. It is, I am afraid, too late now for this to reach you at Christmas, but I hope you had some of the love and peace which you so kindly wished me to have.

Yours very sincerely, JRR Tolkien

It is my birthday on Jan 3rd and you may see a picture of me in the Sunday Times on Jan 2nd.

*

York House, Broadmoor Hospital
Crowthorne, Berks
4th Jan 1972

Dear Professor Tolkien,

Thank you very much for your kind letter explaining about the hobbits. The reason I was so frightened by your book was that I wasn't well and I was locked in a room on my own soon after I had read 'Lord of the Rings' (which I call Elevar by the way). The creatures and happenings in the book became so vivid that I was seeing them and they were talking to me and I was feeling them and I just didn't realise it was all imagination. I lived in that room with those creatures for a long while and they became firstly my friends and then my enemies that I was fighting and which no-one else understood about. The hobbits became evil, frightening creatures who were tormenting me during the day and especially at night, even after I came to this hospital which is a good hospital. The nurses tried to explain to me that these creatures would not hurt me and I began to put down food for them to eat, in the belief that this show of friendship would pacify them – I didn't realise that the nurses were moving the food! So gradually, with reassurances, I began to accept the hobbits as being gentle and brave and full of fun and your letter came as the final confirmation that I have nothing to fear. When the doctor told me to re-read 'Elevar' I began to get things back into their right proportions and their right places and now that I am well I can join you in your happy world of fantasy without getting disturbed by it. I hope this will explain to you the reason I was wrongly blaming you for my illness, because the hobbits were involved in it. Finally I would like to say I'm sorry I couldn't get you a birthday card but I wish you many more years of peace and happiness.

Love, Christine Delahunty

P.S. I am in York House now, which is the house for well people – hooray!

(The above correspondence is reproduced with thanks to the Tolkien Trust.)

It was only recently that I realised that the date of our marriage, October 22, 1971, corresponds with the date of Christine's first letter to Professor JRR Tolkien. It was sad that Christine was unable to be with us, but it was just another sadness in an endlessly devastating situation.

Chapter Thirteen

DIARY

Jill

It's April 2019. I have just found another diary of Christine's. The oldest yet. The actual book is A4 size and titled 'A Scribbling Diary'. It's dated 1972. I don't know how I missed it before.

The cover has the remnants of pictures of cats glued to it. It's stuffed with lots of bits of memorabilia that have evidently been pasted in and now largely become unstuck. The first entry is dated Christmas Eve 1971. Christine would've been 22 years old and already in Broadmoor.

*

Christmas Eve 1971

I was dreading Christmas here but it's OK. Everyone is laughing and gay and friendly. This afternoon Chris and Jill came, they are going to spend Christmas at home with Mum and Dad and Auntie Hannah and Nell and Wally are going too. Poor Chris is dreading it. *(Chris and I had married in October 1971 and were living in Sheffield. Mum and Dad had moved to Portslade, near Brighton)*

The Carol singers have just come in so I will listen to them now We all pinched their song sheets and sang together when they had gone.

*

Christine's Resolutions:

TO BE GOOD AND OUT OF BROADMOOR BY CHRISTMAS 1972

TO LEARN TO LIVE IN YORK HOUSE

(The female part of Broadmoor was divided into two 'houses, 'York' & 'Lancaster'. York was the larger, and Lancaster was for those in the most serious states of mental illness, and more restrictive. At this time Christine was in Lancaster).

*

Christmas Day 1971

Have eaten too much and watched TV all day. Santa (Mr C W) brought me a pair of orange pop-sox and some ciggys. (I don't smoke). A lot of visitors came around who I didn't know and the girls from Douglas came up and are all sitting around in paper hats.

'I have always thought of Christmas time, when it has

come round – apart from the veneration due to sacred name and origin, if anything belonging to it can be apart from that- as a good lunch, a kind, forgiving, charitable, pleasant time; when men and women seem by one consent to open their shut up hearts freely, and to think of people below them as if they really were fellow passengers to the grave and not another race of creatures bound on another journey'

'Christmas Carol' by Dickens

26th January 1972

Had a little party in the dining room and had quite a laugh playing kids games like 'Squeak Piggy Squeak' and Musical Chairs and I stood on a chair and sang 'I'm Gonna be a Country Girl Again'

*

27th January

Chris and Jill came again and we had a lovely chat. Mum has given them a lot of junk to take home.

Have made up my mind to be good and get to York House and out of Broadmoor so I can go and stay with C & J.

*

28th January

Terrible day with everyone 'off it' - except me.

*

29th January

Played table tennis with the fellas from Essex House and thoroughly enjoyed it.

Ros Brown gave me a lecture on getting to York – said messy Ann used to be the same. Went to hairdressers and stuck pics in book in O.T.

*

30th January

Sang crazy songs from Cliff Richard on Lancs with the nurses. Everyone laughing and crazy – keeping each other happy – what a crowd!

*

31st January

Had a fantastic New Year's Party with the men from Essex House. Best party since I came here with everyone joining in. Am going to York on Sunday – Ugh!

*

Saturday 1st February

Mum and Dad came. Am dreading going to York on Sunday. Had a laugh with the girls today. They are threatening to do unspeakable things to me tomorrow – Ha!

*

2nd February

Came back to York House. Shed a few tears but am going to stick it out. Wrote card to Mum and Dad. Told them that I've started smoking – hope they bring me some ciggys.

*

3rd February

Good day on the whole with only one small incident of bitchiness. I'm smoking, chewing gum and eating like mad to keep myself from getting silly and hysterical like I did before.

*

5th February

I've been good all the week but I don't think I can keep it up. I feel really on edge tonight and want to be cuddled and spoiled a bit – I'm lonely. We saw the film 'Poor Cow'. It was sordid but I didn't walk out as I would have done a few months ago. It made me wonder what I would be like if I had had to live under those awful conditions and bring up a child on my own. I would hope to have a child of my own but I couldn't bear the responsibility of bringing one up or looking after a man – thank God I haven't got those problems to face – even Phil has got fed up with me, dear kind Phil.

*

Terrible night with a weasel under the bed, a dead toad on the floor and white bones everywhere.

*

Saturday 8th February

Sat in bed and ate a whole swiss role on my own.

*

16th February 1972

> 'May God grant you the sincerity
>
> To accept the things you cannot change
>
> The courage to change the things you can
>
> And the wisdom to know the difference.'

*

22nd April 1972

Retrieved this book at last.

Got a room on Ward one, York and made it homely – great but a bit frightening.

*

24th April

Am making an otter in OT – very complicated. Got my radio and listened to Peggy Ashcroft. Nurse Sewell gave me a photo.

*

25th April

Are they poisoning me? Is there a white devil in me? Why do I get so muddled?

Our Lady of Perpetual succour and love.

*

26th April

All day in seclusion room for throwing a cup of coffee over Christine. I don't care.

Mrs Green has turned against me.

*

27th April

Went to canteen. No money, although we should have been paid. I'm very muddled and I don't know who to trust, who is telling me the truth.

*

28th April

I feel guilty for existing, I'm not good enough for God. I can't live up to the standards set me. I feel guilty when I eat, when I touch the polished door knob.

*

31st March

> 'The body is in prison
> The mind escapes outside
> To bring about great things
> The mind must be large and well tempered'

Ho Chi Minh
17th June 1972

*

Gifts from God

I love God.

He makes good days when I'm sad.

So that I can't feel sad for the wonder of it.

The clear sharp feel of His blues and greens

Trees on the top of a hill

His hands on earth.

I love God

He makes the children naughty, mischievous, quarrelsome

then he makes them laugh and puts pure joy in them

And he shines through their bodies and eyes

So beautiful, so funny, angel-like.

I want to cry out at their fresh sweet loveliness.

I love Him.

He made perfections like leaves.

He startles me with rainbows

And puts funny little plants in the woods for me

To wonder at.

He makes wild, vast storms, rising up shrieking

to tear down his stately makings, oaks and rivers,

And man

Just to tell us we cannot do without Him.

He is Lord.

I love God.

He comes for me as He comes for the intricacies of a

tiny conch shell

On a flat expanse of beach – so very small –

He must have loved it to make it.

I like to believe He had as much joy making me.

He gave me so many god-like feelings

I cannot use them up. But I feel He meant me to.

He made me love a man whose soul shines in his eyes.

I love Him for that.

He gave me laughter to give,

And exhilarant happiness to sow,

And told me it's worth,

By giving me frights and fears and sickness

To make me strong.

He holds my hand

And I know love.

*

1st July 1972

To free yourself from the trap take a good look around your cage.
Stand still in the centre and slowly turn on one foot taking in all
you see about you. Ignore the cobwebs which can easily be brushed
aside – but don't move yet. Standing still let opened eyes get
accustomed to the dark. Take note of the interlacing twigs and
branches which blacken space between the bars. SOMEWHERE

100

beneath the clutter there must be a door. This the only act of faith, so stand there, very still until you feel you know the most likely position for your door to be. Then brush away those cobwebs, toss all those twigs and branches in a heap behind you.

Remember where they land in case you are mistaken and thus save stubbing toes as you search in semi-darkness.

*

When you find your door don't waste energy tearing down the darkness behind you, face it and use all your strength to break the stubborn lock. Then you will be free. It takes time to adjust to the light and it can be disconcerting when you find so few are free and that many have spent their energy tearing holes in their walls of twigs and branches leaving room to talk and look from behind bars.

*

Theologians promise a burning light to flame the twigs and melt the iron. I could not wait in case it were not true.

Psychiatrists know the twigs and branches are there with iron bars behind, but they would have us know the shadows and accept failing to accept they will with quietening drugs chill the exploring senses battered on the wall.

*

Analysts would have us take out the twigs, look at them, and then replace in tidy fashion, find open and pass through your door. Then realise you can do nothing. To open the door for other people, for the locks are on the inside. Arms can reach through the bars and clutch your clothing- words hurled will reach your ears. But when you are free the trapped can't hold you against your will, and those who are trapped would not presume to trap.

*

5th August 1972

A thousand things I see in the night- Hobbits and orcs and dragonflies and creatures howl and bark outside my bedroom window. Are they foxes or wolves? Are they hungry for man? Are they coming in? I bay and shout for attention. For someone to share my fears. But the nurses turn deaf. And then they scorn and scowl at the creatures that are strangling me. If only there was some escape. If only there was a place where I could gain some peace .Is there peace in death? The devil seems to possess me at nights. And at times in the day when I want to destroy and kill. Is that God's will? The shouting of the nurses puts me in mind of school where everybody laughed at my uselessness and timidity. One cannot escape from people, only go apart and cry lonely tears. In years I am twenty-two – I feel a child. A child could conquer these fears. But I cannot.

*

21st May 1972

The Happiness Man

There was a tap, tap, tap on the door
Answered it, and on the floor a tiny, chubby man,
no taller than a tub of jam.

I said 'Do come in, seat yourself on the biscuit tin'

He said 'My name is Happy and I've come to protest

about the Happy Bar'

I said 'Do sit and try not to frown. Here's a cup of tea

and I ask you

not to down'. Now tell me what's your trouble'

He said 'The price attached to my existence is that I am

never sought.

Along with Health & Wisdom, Happiness is never

caught'

He sighed, slurping tea from saucer, dropping spots

upon the floor.

With all these people in hot pursuit

my feet are very, very sore. I want to lodge a strong

protest.

I DEMAND a little rest and I'd dearly like to know

where the Happiness Man is supposed to go

when the world is chasing him?

Why this aversion to my being must I be forever fleeing

from a grabbing hand and running feet

dodging capture in every street?

Please ask the world to just sit still. Watch me as I jump

from hill

to land and prance on window ledge, I play hide and

seek with wall and hedge

to slide down drains with drops pots of rain

and sneak in crook beneath the door

and gaily jig upon the floor

To bubble, bubble in a nice warm bath

Jump out of cracks in a concrete path and slither down a long soup ladle

then pirouette across the table. Do somersaults across the bed

Dance flamenco on the head. Do chin-ups on the brims of hats

Wave batons at wailing cats. Drink the breeze to tousle hair.

Go mountaineering on a chair. This and more can I achieve if only folk would learn to leave the chasing all to me.

With this he paused for breath and drank the stone cold tea.

The worry lines slipped from his eyes

His feet reduced to normal size, stretched his leg and wiggled toes.

Said 'I guess it's time for me to go. Tell the world if you like, the Happy Man is out on strike. Please record my strong upset through folk grabbing what they cannot GET'

With this he slipped down from the tin

And went the way that he'd come in.

All in all a strange intrusion

Happiness, that I'd believed, to be an illusion.

*

12th August 1972

'I was walking in Savana,

Past a church in a cavern den

When slowly through the window came a plaintive funeral hymn

And the sympathy awakened

And the wonder quickly grew

Till I found myself environed in a little negro pew.

Out in front a young couple, sad in sorrow, nearly wild.

On the altar was a coffin. In the coffin was a child.

Negroes sad and spiritual. Preacher at a little wooden desk.

In a manner grandly awkward, in a context grotesque, grandly he said 'Now don't be weeping for this pretty piece of clay, for the little boy

who lived there has gone and run away.

He's doing very finely and he appreciates your love

But sure now the Father wants him in the large house up above.

He didn't give you that baby by a hundred thousand miles,

He just thought you needed sunshine so he lent it for a while

And he let you love and keep it

Till your hearts were bigger grown

And the silver tears you're shedding are just interest all alone.

Now my poor dejected mourners let your hearts with Jesus rest

and don't go criticising the One who knows the best.

He who's give us many comforts, has the right to take away

To the Lord be praise and glory,

Now and ever let us pray.'

*

19th August 1972

The earth is warmed by the kindly sun

but lives are warmed by the deaths of men

And their words of praise when our best we've done

And their parting wish that we'll meet again.

The clouds may blanket the sky with grey

And the earth grow chill as the rain descends

But he shall keep smiling along his way

whose heart is warmed by the love of friends.

It's the glad "Hello" and the handclasp true,

The smile of joy on a friendly face,

that means contentment for me and you

And makes of earth a happy place.

*

The New Year 1974

'Now that you've seen the old year out and let the new in –
remember its only new in yourself within –you renew your mind,
your thoughts, your spirit and your heart-only then can you succeed
and make another start. Let there be a transformation that will
really show- in your face and in your life and as through the days
you go with a greater faith in God and his creative word. Let the
change in you be seen- the song in you be heard. You can work your
own miracle. Its up to you today – to choose the path that leads to
light – or turn the other way – now's the moment, now's the chance
to make another you – to step out of your old dead skin and start to
live anew.'

Patience Strong

*

'Love is very patient, very kind. Love knows no jealousy. Love
makes no parade, gives itself no airs, is never rude, never selfish,
never irritated, never resentful. Love is never glad when others go
wrong. Love is gladdened by goodness. Always slow to expose.
Always eager to believe the best. Always hopeful, always patient.
Love never disappears.'

1 Corinthians 13: 4-8

*

If more people cared about earwigs there would be less people with
bald ears.

Nostalgia's all right but it's not what it was.

*

Julian – 4yr 6m (Julian and Amanda are our sister Anne and Mike's children)

Amanda – 3yr 6m

Cornwall 1971

Chapter Fourteen

THE WING

Shattered (1)

It's strange, so strange - the middle has collapsed

And re-formed itself into a new puzzle-barrier.

It grates all the time like a dentist's drill,

And I don't know how to re-arrange the puzzle

So that it makes a picture

No matter which way you hang it up.

It doesn't have to be a sense-picture

So long as I can understand it,

And so long as they don't expect me

To do it their way.

At the moment it's all shattered,

Some into huge pieces of fear and hatred,

And some into strange unsolvable shapes,

Which will always be there and never fit into place

Because they are changing all the time.

And the problems do too,

But their reasons have been lost

In the secret places of me,

Where none can penetrate,

No matter how they search for the key to it all.

I expect I could do it myself

But it's so long and painful,

And there doesn't really seem to be much point

Because it will only get shattered yet again

The next time around.

Shattered (II)

My safe protective barriers have been smashed,

Smashed by intruders.

There's no other place to escape to.

If they had just crumbled with age and erosion,

Brick by brick, gently and quietly

Then maybe it would have been less painful to watch,

And to experience,

But they had to trample it all into the mud.

They trampled on my feelings, my mind, on every part
of me,

And now I've got to rebuild again,

But this time in plastic,

And according to their mould.

I'm too weak against so many,

And so succumb.

But deep inside there's still Me,

Wanting so hard to fight and be strong.

All day they force themselves on me,

Endlessly, no peace at all.

If I could conquer one single fear,

Then I might find at least a little peace,

But they crashed it all

And I don't know what the hell to do.

A Good Day Lord

I thank you for blessing me today,

Suddenly I'm alive, I'm human, you've remembered me,

Even if it doesn't last,

And I know it can't,

Because I'm not worthy of it.

Yet today you gave me a brief moment of thought

And made all the sadness and fears disappear into
sunshine

And I thank you. I thought you had completely left me

To be lost in the darkness.

The darkness seems to have lasted so long,

It will probably be back to overtake me.

But for one day I have been a human being,

And there's no need to run,

No need to run, no desire to run.

Suddenly I awoke without a fear

Of any person or any creature,

And today has made all the rest of it worthwhile.

*

Question: When they finally open up Broadmoor and begin to look inside, will a can of worms escape? Fat, blindfolded worms who have fed on the silent miseries of a hundred years of mentally ill patients. "History is bunk," said Henry Ford. Or is it the blinding light that hits us when a cover-up which has lasted more than a century is revealed after silent walls finally reveal the pain of tormented beings whose pain cannot lift its head?

The brick in the walls. The horror the rest of the world finds it easier not to know about. I remember pacing the room I lived in (eight paces by five) and thinking about the women who had been incarcerated there over the years.

The walls breathed in the loneliness of them all. Is a table still there if you shut the door on it?

*

The Wing

In Canvas. When I think back now, I can hardly believe that they were allowed to treat us like that. I hope so much that it is a thing of the past – that it does not still happen. Who knows? Who cares? To be in canvas meant being locked 24/7 in a small cell with a stone floor. There was a small window, up high, but it was permanently shuttered so there was no natural light. I wore nothing but a canvas gown. There was a canvas mattress on the floor in the corner, a canvas pillow, canvas bedding, a plastic pot to pee in, which would be covered with a piece of newspaper or a bit of old magazine, a paper cup to drink water out of – and that was it. That was my world, for many a long time. There was a slit in the wall which could be unlatched from the outside, so that if I wanted a drink they would poke the spout of a watering can through and pour some in to my paper cup. At meal times they would tap on the door and jangle their keys – that was a signal for me to sit down on the floor at the back of the room – then they, there were always at least two of them – they never faced us alone, would open the door. They'd put the paper plate of food on the floor with a spoon, just inside the door. When they had locked the door again that was my signal to get up and get my dinner. And the whole performance would be repeated when they came to collect the spoon etc. That was meal times.

The weekly bath was another ceremony. They would open the doors and drag me out – I never had the dignity of walking anywhere – I was always dragged. I would be dumped into a bath which would have about five inches of tepid water in it. A member of staff (they called themselves nurses – in fact they were brutes) would scoop a bucket of water out of the bath and tip it over my head – that was the hair wash. There was no such thing as the luxury of cleaning teeth or combing hair. Then dragged back to my cell.

It was a dreary life. I wasn't even allowed a book. Perhaps they thought I would eat it, or hit a 'nurse' with it. I was sometimes allowed a newspaper but as I was not allowed my spectacles that was more a little joke on their part than any use to me. Nobody seemed to have noticed. I was slipping away quietly, and alone, into a smoggish abyss. I had been in solitary for so long I had switched off from any kind of contact, as if someone had taken a large hypodermic and injected cotton wool into my brain. One thought couldn't quite attach itself to the last, or the next. The lights were on day and night and the permanently locked shutter meant that at times only concentrated effort meant I knew night from day. This went on for a long time.

One day, I don't know how it happened, maybe it was my birthday, or maybe I had a special visit, I had some sweets in my cell. Amongst them there must have been a stick of liquorice. I dipped the liquorice into my paper cup of water and used it to write on the wall in large letters, "ELI, ELI, LAMA SABACHTHANI." When they came to the door and saw it they said to me, "What's that?" I explained that it meant, "Lord, Lord, why have you abandoned me?" and is, according to Christian tradition, the last words that Jesus called out as he died on the Cross. They didn't know what to make of that. They dragged me out and made another woman scrub the liquorice writing off the wall. Was that blasphemy? I don't think so. I think God got the message.

Freedom

Freedom is a word understood by few.

It is a concept too hard to grasp.

So you think yourself outside of freedom.

Think beyond the huge and wonderful pettiness

Of a world where you can catch a bus,

Speak your mind, Use a phone, Go into Woolworths.

Forget about those country walks down leafy lanes,

And a swim in the sea, picnics on the beach.

Think yourself outside of these.

Into a world where you have the right to do these things.

You can eat, sleep and breathe.

Your every moment is timed by bells.

Regulated by rules.

Accompanied by keys.

The stone corridors echo the sound of abrupt orders,

Short and sharp scuffles, and keys.

You are locked in a room, eight paces by five.

(How many times have you counted those paces?)

You are alone with your hallucinations.

Just you and them.

Interminably.

You can have a mattress on the floor, made of canvas and straw

To prevent anyone avoiding all this,

By killing them self.

You wear a gown like a potato-sack

For the same reason.

There's just you, the mattress, the pot,

And your fearful fantasies,

In a world where love and kindness

Are not considered necessary for life.

Freedom is a concept too large to grasp.

But once you have lost it you are scarred for life.

Your mind is scarred with bitterness

And with an ever-present fear

That you might lose it again.

To be a free person is a very wonderful thing.

The human mind cannot grasp it,

Until you find yourself in that little room,

Eight paces by five.

And they threw away the key

Another morning waking up in The Wing – no birdsong here but the sounds and smells of my tormented neighbours. I look bewilderedly around me – a mattress on the floor, a degrading canvas gown and a pot to piss in. And that was it. Period. The Wing was for people who 'They' had given up on. There were five of us locked in cells which were a prison within a prison – this was officially a Hospital for the Criminally Insane. I hadn't had a conversation or left the cell for months – summer had passed me by.

Every day, every day, the routine of isolation and craziness went on – except that today was different. *Today was Christmas Day –*

wasn't it? I heard the rattling of keys and knew that breakfast was on its way. It had to be bacon and eggs. Christmas Day was the only day we had bacon and eggs for breakfast. All greasy and congealed because they were cooked overnight. Ah, I was right, here it was. 'They' opened the door – there were always at least two of them – one to watch the other's back. I raised a question. "When Father Donnely comes to see the other Catholic girls – can I go to pray with them?"

"Father Donnely won't be coming today – it's Tuesday."

"It's Christmas Day," I said. "Father is sure to come."

"No, it isn't Christmas Day – that was yesterday." They were laughing at me. I'd missed Christmas. I picked up the plate of greasy breakfast and threw it at them. It missed them and landed in a greasy lump. Damn. No breakfast this morning. I sat on my mattress on the floor hopeless and helpless – hopeless because of my illness, and helpless against the cruelty of the 'nurses'.

I used to pass the hours by trying to remember the plots of books I had read - the 'goodies' and the 'baddies' and all their names and actions. I wasn't allowed to have books. How do they expect you to get well if the only companion you have is your own madness? I had lost track of time until suddenly, the cell door was opened, by a German nurse called Wally. She had brought with her – who? Yes, it was Father Donnely. He came into my room carrying a small wooden chair, and put two lighted candles on the chair, making a little altar in this Dungeon of Despair. I knelt down with him and we prayed together, and he gave me Holy

Communion. And as we prayed, I felt the months of confusion and illness drain through me to be replaced by a kind of peace and calmness. I can't remember or explain how it happened, only that by the time Father Donnely had given me his Blessing, I really did feel blessed and peaceful. So, on that Christmas morning, after months of isolation I was allowed to get dressed and go into the Day Room for a few hours. I had Christmas lunch with the other patients on the ward. I think that Christmas I found out what Christmas was all about.

('And they threw away the key' was previously published under the pseudonym of Anastasia in 'Threads of Hope, Learning To Live With Depression' alongside the work of Wendy Cope and the recollections of Alistair Campbell. Published by Short Books in 2003).

Chapter Fifteen

A REGIME OF FEAR

Christine

Nowadays the care of psychiatric patients is a political issue but when I was first put away the people in the bins were the forgotten people, even it seemed, forgotten by God himself. The massive improvement in medication to control mental illness since the 60s has changed the more punitive aspects of the system. We have a moral duty to protect and support those who are sick and vulnerable.

But the memories which I recall must never be forgotten or forgiven. In those days the high walls protected the staff from the prying eyes of those who might have spoken out about the abuse of psychiatric patients particularly, but not solely, of those in Special Hospitals. There was a fear of retribution if you spoke out. If you dared to speak out for yourself, or anyone else who was intimidated, you knew that whatever chance you might have had of being discharged had now disappeared out of the window – for a very long time. In a regime of fear the strongest restraint is that the patients dare not speak out, on their own behalf or those around them. When you saw another patient being abused you said nothing because you would be next. If you tried to tell your visitors when this was going on you knew you would be called a liar and a troublemaker and your stay extended indefinitely- the only way to get out was to keep your head down.

Prisoners in a regular jail at least can see the end of the tunnel. They have a release date, even if it is a long way away. In a Special Hospital you know that the only way to get out is to keep your mouth shut. Even now, all these years later, I wonder if I am putting my freedom at risk simply by writing all this – I probably won't dare to sign it.

*

Restraint of Psychiatric Patients – mid 1960s-80s

The staff are trained in Restraint. That means the greatest beating with the least obvious signs or proof. The male nurses' uniform includes heavy boots. All the better to kick you with.

Liquid Cosh

One of my memories of the liquid cosh is of a drug called Paraldenyde. It was the most painful drug I have ever had forced on me. The whole ward knew when a patient had been given it because it had a distinctive smell which you breathed out through your skin for days afterwards. A particular memory is of Jan and Sue – both of them had struggled during restraint and had been injected into the sciatic nerve, which had left them with permanent limps. Ann had been a ballet dancer, and clever. Eventually she took her own life.

Padded Cells

Another memory to be re-lived during long lonely nights is of the padded cell. Unimaginable these days. For those who suffered them they are an unforgettable memory, something often relived during long, lonely nights. When I was in a Hertfordshire bin, which mercifully no longer exists, I remember being naked, frightened and alone. I recall scraping the padding off the inside door with my fingernails and my teeth. In Broadmoor, when the padded cell on the female ward was already occupied the staff would drag the woman, naked, with arms bent up her back, into the male ward and throw you into the padded cell there. Psychiatric patients were allowed no dignity, no respect, not treated with any humanity.

The Heavy Mob

When any woman was admitted to Broadmoor they very soon learnt a hard lesson: when the Heavy Mob are giving you a good thrashing don't attempt to fight back. They are skilled in giving you a thrashing with the least amount of obvious bruising and injuries. It soon became second nature to just go floppy that way you got hurt less. If they're banging your head on the wall you were less likely to injure your neck if you simply went floppy.

Wet Towel

But sometimes a woman did try to fight back. If you fought back you got the 'Wet Towel Treatment'. A wet towel was held over your nose and mouth and then you had to stop fighting because you literally stopped breathing. Then they would pull the towel away and crowd out of the door – laughing. Always laughing. The patient couldn't fight back because they couldn't breathe, sometimes they went unconscious. The staff would then pull it off and run for the door. Sometimes, not often, but sometimes, they left the wet towel on the woman's face too long – she didn't get her breath back. They had smothered her, she was dead. When this happened the staff would close ranks and tell the family that the woman had committed suicide. And who was to know any different? The other women always knew – but none of us dared say anything. We were too afraid. If you did, you would be next. And how could we tell anyone anyway? Our mail was censored. Our visits were closely monitored. We had no access to phones or computers. We had no way of telling anyone what was going on. And who would have believed us anyway? Every word of this is true.

Special Constables

Any time that a patient made a complaint and insisted on involving the police, you were on to a loser. Some of the hospital staff worked part-time as Special Constables on the local police constabulary, so they were matey with the police and there was always a cover-up – no evidence etc. The patient who made the initial accusation would pay heavily for it.

Danger Money

The staff get DM, but it is the patients who are in danger from the staff, not the other way around.

Female Patients Being Raped by Male Staff

During the time that I was in Broadmoor there was one incident which did reach the courts, but certainly in this case there were no winners. We arose one morning to see that three of the sickest girls in the Special Unit were bruised, battered and shocked. During the night a male nurse had raped and beaten all three of them. Apparently half a dozen male nurses had witnessed this performance, laughing and cheering him on, and enjoying the performance. Two female nurses had also witnessed it. They had been too afraid to intervene, obviously afraid that they would be the next victims. But the following morning they went to the local police station and insisted on making sworn statements about what they had seen. It takes a lot of courage to be a whistle-blower in a place like that. They were given a very bad time by the POA and by their colleagues. There was a huge cover up. The two female nurses concerned had worked there together for many years. They lived on the Broadmoor Estate, where many of the staff lived. But after that incident many of the staff who had been friends with them for years refused to speak to them, or to work alongside them. The treatment that they received was worse than that received by the rapist himself. By the time the case was over, both left their jobs, and both, I believe, had breakdowns themselves.

In a case like that, the main priority for those who worked at the hospital was to keep it quiet, for it not to get out to the media or the public. Leading up to the court hearing everybody who had visitors had a member of staff sitting in on the visit. We knew that if we tried to break the code of silence, to get word out about what had happened, we would pay dearly. It was never a good idea to be a heroine. During this time we did not socialize with the male patients. The regime at Broadmoor had a kind of paranoia. Silence was paramount. They knew that there were some things that the media would make headlines about. And so the case came to court. Obviously, a case as serious as this should not have been dealt with in the local Magistrates court but should have been brought before a judge and jury. But the POA manipulated the system. The case, three very sick women, raped and physically assaulted for the amusement of a gang of Broadmoor male nurses, should surely have gone to a higher court or at least reached the newspapers. In fact it was dealt with by a local magistrate. The male nurse concerned was found guilty but given a nominal community service and a small fine. It was revealed that he had been dismissed from several other Special Hospitals for proven cases of arson and extreme violence to patients, and each time he was quietly transferred to another hospital. So he started his job at Broadmoor with a criminal record, worse than most of us. Clearly he should have been in prison himself.

If it wasn't for the huge security blanket which kept all these awful goings on from reaching the press, the outside world would have been horrified to hear that a man who raped and assaulted very sick women, with an audience of other men, received similar punishment to a shoplifter or a petty criminal. The hospital management were compelled to sack him.

Some of the female nurses collected money for him between themselves saying, "This poor man has lost his job." But the thing that shocked us, was that the male nurse concerned was more amoral and dangerous than most of us. This case, for me, displays the position of psychiatric patients in Special Hospitals – that they were nothing, they did not deserve any respect, any protection, any worth. They simply didn't count. One can only hope that these memories are simply that – of the past. But are they? Do psychiatric patients now have more protection by the rest of us? Drug therapy nowadays makes it different, but do we know what goes on behind the high walls? People who are ill, or vulnerable, need protection, or are the rest of us still just turning our backs? I relive some of these traumatic memories during long sleepless nights.

While I was in Broadmoor, the POA called a strike. For over a month the 900 patients in Broadmoor had no visitors, no airing court (outdoor recreation), no work or occupational therapy, no school, no socialising and no mixing between men and women on any wards. And nobody gave a Damn! The strike started on November 21st – my birthday. I remember that because, Patsy, a family friend, had called to see me. They gave me a cake she left, but I didn't see her. A month without any contact with the outside world is a long time. It ended on December 23rd. Christmas pretty much passed us by that year. It was hardest on those amongst us who had children, who would have been brought to visit their parents in the weeks leading up to Christmas.

The reason behind the strike was the POA seeking to manipulate the criminal justice system. If they didn't win the outcome they wanted they would call a full strike and the army would be brought in to look after us. It had all started because a male patient, who had been assaulted by a male nurse, had insisted on the case being brought to court. The male nurse had initially admitted this. So he was guilty wasn't he? The male patient who had insisted on the case being brought to court, was moved to a prison. It seemed to us that the powers that be were afraid that this would open the door for every case of rape, violence or mis-treatment to be brought to Court and then people outside really would have to sit up and take notice of what was happening behind those walls. And so, two days before Christmas the case was resolved, by the Crown Court. The male nurse was found not guilty.

To make up for the fact that we had had no Christmas festivities at all that year we were each allowed one phone call, lasting five minutes, to our family, listened to by a senior staff member. Unlike people in prisons, the patients in Broadmoor do not usually have access to telephones, so this was a first and caused great excitement. So for the first time for over a month we went out into the airing court and had some fresh air. We all learnt a hard lesson from the strike, that no matter what the staff did to us, it was no good calling for the police. When the media insist on human rights for terrorism suspects, whether in Britain, or in Guantanamo Bay, I think back to the forgotten criminal lunatics in Broadmoor who have no protection of human rights.

The Stigma of B

A fortress of hatred, of horror, of fear.

Don't let them near us, we don't want them here.

Experiment on them for medical science.

Do what you will, but don't give them a chance

To embarrass us with their sickness of mind.

"We are normal, normal, normal, every one of us out here."

We'll swear it till the day we die.

Our plastic minds don't want to know

Of those in torment and in fear.

Our world is black and white,

And although many may be lost in a grey world of terror

Let's leave them there for ever

Because we don't want to know.

Our world is pretty, with flowers and woods and trees.

There may be other worlds we'll never reach,

Where only the tormented dwell,

But it's pleasant to forget that.

Let's leave them to their hell.

Bolt the doors and bar the windows,

And let's not seek to find them in the land where they get lost.

It's not pleasant to know, one can never understand.

So leave them there for twenty years.

And then be all kind.

Shed salt false tears for so many lives wasted by an empty, blind society.

Let's be kind, let's let one out and See what happens,

One gets so bored with Crossroads.

Or of the European Courts because

Nobody Gives a Damn

Chapter Sixteen

A HARD PLACE

Inside Broadmoor, my only friends and companions were the people society described as evil. They were murderers, rapists, arsonists, and criminals, the people who normal people envisage as a cross between Elephant Man and Hannibal Lector.

But when I sat and shared a pot of tea with one of these monsters, my eyes were opened to the fact that they too are God's creatures, the same as the rest of us, struggling through daily battles, misunderstood and many of them very lovely.

I find it very easy to believe in goodness, but very hard to believe in evil in humans. We are all simply weak and frail beings. I'm not arguing that murder is not wrong, just that it is often beyond the understanding of most of us.

When I see a small child, or a young baby, I think they are so beautiful that only a God of Gods could have created such a precious thing. I seem to be out of step with the rest of humanity – perhaps I am emotionally numb. I just don't understand why we make such a big deal about sending our loved ones back to where we borrowed them from – to God in Heaven.

I remember sharing a pot of tea with a friend who had beheaded her mother. She put her mother's head in a shopping basket and travelled by bus to the nearest police station and handed the head-in-the-basket over the counter to the policeman on the desk. We laughed when we heard this appalling story – well what else could we do?

Yes, I agree with the commandment Thou Shalt Not Kill except if you are an abortionist or defending your country in the Armed Forces. God chooses the time for our earthly lives to start and finish. Perhaps the problem lies in the fact that He gives each of us Free Will but does not tell us how to use it.

*

Love in a hard place

Paul

We met at a table-tennis evening. I couldn't hit the ball, but his patience didn't run out. He was labelled a Psychopath, and I was labelled a Schizophrenic, but our labels didn't weigh heavily on us. I loved the bones of him and he waited patiently for me. He lived in Essex House and I lived in York House – we were separated by the rule book. But each meal time as we filed out of the dining-hall I would look up to the distant window where a red-and-white spotted handkerchief would be waving frantically at me. I would wave back. I couldn't see him, he could see me through bird-watching binoculars. I had given him that kerchief one Valentine's Day and it was special. In appearance he was a Mills and Boons hero – fit and brown and muscley, with brown curls and deep brown eyes. But I wouldn't have minded if he'd been bald and fat with acne. Through many ups and downs Peter was always there, writing me letters through the internal mail – and the letters always had little cartoon drawings and verses to make me smile. Peter was the producer of the hospital dramatic society play the year we did an Alan Ayckbourne play. I was the heroine. There was a bit of nepotism in the casting! He always fooled around when the show was on and made sure his wig fell off. We didn't have a very good write-up in the local rag, but we weren't short of laughs.

Susannah

I will call her Susannah. She sat all day in an armchair, gently swaying and singing over and over. "Raindrops are falling on my head." Just the one line, over and over. Susannah had been given a lobotomy, supposed to cure depression. But by removing part of the brain, the brain is damaged. It's as simple as that. Her parents came down from London every Wednesday and Sunday and sat with her in the visiting room but she couldn't hold a conversation with them. They gave her sweets and cigarettes. That was all she wanted – sweets and cigarettes. As soon as her parents left, the nurses would take them away from her. I never understood why the nurses hated poor Susannah so much. Susannah's mother carried with her a photograph. She showed it to all the other family members in the Visiting Room. "This was my Suzi," she would say, showing a photograph of a slim, beautiful young girl, smartly dressed and smiling. "She was a secretary," her mother would say. And the visitors would struggle to find the right words to say, as they looked across at the little, overweight, brain-damaged young woman.

The staff used every opportunity to vent their spitefulness on Susannah. Looking back, I am ashamed that none of us ever spoke up for her. But you didn't. It was self-preservation. See all, hear all, say nothing, or be the next victim. It was as simple as that. The morning I am remembering was deep winter, with the snow coming down heavily outside. We were all supposed to jump out of our beds as soon as our doors were opened at 7am.

But Susannah didn't like getting out of a warm bed in the morning. "We'll teach her," the staff said. Always the same: "We'll teach her." So they dragged her out of bed. She was wearing nothing but a thin cotton night dress. Nothing on her feet. No dressing gown or coat. Just a thin nightie. And they put her out in the airing court in the snow. The snow was coming down heavily and was several inches deep underfoot. And they left her there. We went through to breakfast and we could hear Susannah out in the airing court, crying with the cold. Nobody spoke up. After all, we didn't want to be the next one, did we? When we were finishing our breakfast one of the nurses said grumpily, "I suppose we had better give Susannah something to eat." So they opened the window and put out a bowl of porridge and some tea. And then they left her there longer. I can still hear her crying with the cold. Eventually they brought her in. It's a wonder she didn't have frostbite. In fact she quite possibly did. But who would have noticed? Who would have cared?

Matti

I will call her Matti. In writing this I am not defending the crime of murder. That cannot be defended. But when I hear people arguing in defence of capital punishment, I think of Matti. The pain of Matti. When I hear people say "An eye for an eye", and other glib reasonings, I want to tell them about Matti. Capital Punishment was only repealed in England in the mid 1960s, so when I first went to Broadmoor there were a small number of patients there who had been given the death sentence by courts, and then had it rescinded for them to be sent to Broadmoor for life. Matti was one of these people. She woke up every morning saying, "Are they going to hang me today? I can't wait any longer." That was all she said. Over and over during the years I knew her. I don't know the details of her crime. In there we never asked people what had brought them to this place. If they wanted to tell you, then okay. If they didn't, then okay. Obviously, Matti must have committed a terrible crime. But when Matti had been told that she was to be hanged for her crime, it had broken her mind. Completely. Every morning when Matti awoke she would say, "Are they going to hang me today? 'I can't wait anymore. Ask them to hang me this morning." Matti's whole stream of thought, all day, every day, her whole conversation was, "Are they going to hang me today?" Matti died eventually, of natural causes and old age. When I hear people saying, "Bring back hanging" I wish they could have known Matti – the pain of Matti.

Petition

The speaker crackled: "For any of these workers who support the re-introduction of the death penalty in Britain there is a petition in the canteen which you may like to sign." I watched in disbelief as my colleagues made a dash for the canteen, leaving their brains behind them on the conveyor belt. I watched until they had all returned to their places on the line, then I went through, picked up the petition and tore it up in little pieces. Long live Tolerance.

Whether the killer is mentally ill, politically motivated, or just plain evil the result is the same for the victim. But only God can see into our minds and know what leads each of us to such evil action. When I am ill I hear voices telling me to attack, kill, destroy and nobody can know the bewildering struggle of these times. As only God can look into our minds, so surely only He can really forgive me.

Madness equals badness? It's simple arithmetic, isn't it?

A criminal commits a crime, is given a jail sentence, is released and gets a new start. A mentally ill person has scary fantasies, is locked up in a jail and punished with no release date in sight.

Isn't it wrong to punish mentally ill people by treating them the same as criminals? If you say, "No, they're hospital patients," well okay, but then surely the point of hospitalisation is to treat the illness. Do they? No, they just sedate you and you learn to hide your dreams because you are now living in a reign of fear. But they can't imprison a criminal without proof of a crime being committed, and proof of guilt. They tried it in Northern Ireland didn't they? Locking up suspected rather than proven terrorists. They soon had Amnesty International on their backs. If a person is a criminal they have rights, and the law still protects them. But if a person is chronically mentally ill they have no rights. Society should protect the vulnerable. The strong in society should protect the weak – that's natural law isn't it?

I'm still looking around for the existence of a caring institution. Is there such a thing? Isn't that a contradiction in terms anyway? Oh yes, I know about supposedly caring institutions but the ones who make the suppositions are the ones who have never been the victims of the supposed carers. Don't blame the nursing staff, they say.

Don't make the comfortable conclusion that such nurses are now of the past. These nurses enter employment as young, idealistic and desperately caring people – maybe some of them even wear their hearts on their sleeves. The portrayal of them in Stephen Frears' TV play Walter in which a mentally ill young man loses his parents and is placed in a psychiatric institution, was a true one. Yes, many of them do behave like that. No, it doesn't signify a lack of caring (I don't know why I loathe that word so much), they probably care very much, but have armour-plated themselves emotionally in order to do that work.

I wonder how much people realise that the nursing staff are

very often the victims of the patients, not physically but by losing touch with their own humanity. At the end of the film, one of the nursing staff refers to his "59 babies." He wasn't sneering at them. Babies, once you get over a fear of them, usually have some endearing qualities, don't they? Especially if they belong to you? So, I say to anyone who found this play harrowing or heart-wrenching, throw these adjectives on the rubbish-tip, where you seem to think the Walters of this world live and go and find your own Walter. He'll teach you a thing or two!

Exhaustion

Where does a hurricane go when it has worn itself out?
Does it turn itself into a person and shed tears of sorrow
For the damage it has wrought
When it was furious and dangerous and distraught?
Yesterday I was a hurricane.
Filled with anger for no reason.
Today I am a drooping flower crushed by the hurricane of yesterday.
Nobody wanted the hurricane, it was hated.
But it had to spend its anger somehow
Because that's its nature
And it's always alone and fearful of itself
The crushed and broken flower never reached the perfection it sought.
And now it never will.

Although it strove to make a contribution

To a world where it went unnoticed

Gas

The clouds around me are heavy and grey and dull,

And I too am cloudy with sadness.

I carry the cloud on my back.

It is a great burden.

A burden which has no beginning and no end,

And which I try to disguise with the false sunshine of

my pretence of humanity.

The rain cloud will burst into tears which will sweeten

the earth and bring fresh life.

The cloud of my bitterness is a choking, smothering

gas.

It weeps for itself and I am lost in it.

I dream of a life outside the hospital walls.

I reach out to grasp it and sink further back into the

mists.

Perhaps I retreat into my cloud

Because it is a familiar cloud

No matter how painful.

But I am alone in it.

I have been alone for a lifetime.

I will be alone for a lifetime.

A Discussion

What shall we do with her?

Oh, leave her where she is she's all right there.

But we need the beds.

I think we ought to give her some kind of chance.

Okay, okay, we'll sort something out in time.

Yes there's plenty of time yet.

What about dumping her on her parents?

Mmm, But what if, Yes what if?

We can always bring her back if it doesn't work.

Her sister said she'd take her if necessary

She's having a baby – you can't expect her to cope with that AND Christine.

No, no we can't do that.

What does Christine feel about it?

Oh look, keep to the point will you?

And what about the question of her working?

She'll never get a job with her record.

Of course she won't but don't tell her that, we must be kind.

What on earth was she doing in Broadmoor anyway?

They didn't know where else to dump her.

Perhaps we could find a hostel for her – one where they'd keep an eye on her of course.

Of course. But what if? Yes, what if?

A flat on her own in Brighton?

No her family wouldn't stand for that.

After all she's been very sheltered – and we don't want to take any chances.

Hasn't she got any friends we can dump her on?

No, it seems all her friends are in Broadmoor.

I think we ought to discourage her from keeping up those friendships you know.

Mmm – not very suitable – I wouldn't like to mix with them myself.

Look, time's getting on, it's nearly time for tea.

But what are we going to do with her?

Leave her where she is for the time being.

She's all right where she is.

She's getting restless about it all.

Well, be nice to her, tell her we'll do something soon.

Supposing we meet again in a few months and try and sort something out then.

Okay, we'll do that. Good afternoon.

Have Patience

I am in a concrete yard. Circular, with walls reaching so high that the clouds have to dodge around them. The little, skipping clouds can do that easily but the heavier clodhopping clouds often get stuck and scowl down at me in the yard far below before thrashing their way out of the trap. The walls have a name. They are called Time Without End and they echo day in and day out. The echoes go up and down and around me all the time and they say over and over: Have Patience. And there is no break in the fog of monotony, and I can see no door anywhere.

But I know only two things. Firstly I know that when I begin to understand the meaning of the words Have Patience then I will have grown, and I know that some place there has got to be a way out, but only I can find it. Perhaps I will never find it until I have grown in every direction possible so that the walls begin to tremble and crumble around me, allowing me to live.

There is one tiny, tiny flower pushing its way through the concrete and that little flower has more courage than I have, for it is determined, against all odds, to grow. It fights hard for its survival and I draw courage from watching it fight and grow. I don't know where the flower found the ability to grow, for it has little sunshine, no more than I have had myself. If that tiny weed can grow where growth seems impossible then I too can grow and find my door and turn the handle.

Perhaps I have misunderstood the name of the walls and they are not called Time Without End but merely Time. And I am a captive of Time. I don't know the name of the flower. I wish I did. Perhaps it is called Hope.

Lies

The inhuman power of the lie
Is a mind-crusher.
A stroke of cool cruelty

To people who have drifted into the shadows.

When you think you see the dim, far light of hope,

And grasp onto it,

Like a drowning man onto drift wood,

You know how futile it is.

And yet you cannot help putting belief in it.

And then – crash – they sullenly admit that you have been misled.

They deny they lied to you.

It is cruel, cruel, cruel to lie to a struggling shadow-filled person,

For he will take a cobweb as his shroud

And gently, knowingly, go back to his shadows

Knowing there is no return.

I am a thief

I'm living on charity. My clothes are all stolen because I haven't paid for them by working. My family buy them and put my name on them to prove that they are mine but really they are stolen from my family, so I have no right to them. I have no right to the food I eat, nor the bed I sleep in. It is all charity because I haven't worked for them. I am stealing all the time so I have to be punished. I am punished by being watched and when I am being watched people's eyes grow big and their hands grow big enough to choke me. I will die by being choked, maybe by the snakes or by people's big hands. Charity begins at home and ends in a hospital bed. Christ has died,

Christ has risen, Christ will come again.

Chapter Seventeen

LOSING HOPE

Jill

Sometimes it was a relief to know that Christine was safely in hospital because whenever she was out you would never know what the next phone call might bring. She might go missing for some days and then we would get a phone call from the police, maybe she had tried to kill herself or maybe she had been on her way to visit me, and got lost and distressed. There weren't mobile phones then of course.

At other times I would be trying very hard to get her out. Particularly from Broadmoor. She had committed no crime so was not on a sentence with an end date. As the months turned to year after year it began to seem she might spend her whole life there. Broadmoor was a grim place even to visit. It used to take me hours to get there and back especially when we lived in Sheffield. They had very fixed visiting times from 2-4pm.On one occasion because of trouble on the trains it had taken me five hours to get there arriving just before 4 o'clock. I was only allowed to see her for a few minutes. You had to sign the visitor's book when you arrived. One time I happened to pull a green biro from my bag and signed with that only to be told that only the Director signs with green ink. The staff were officious and so petty.

You were then led through, by a nurse jangling many keys, to the visitor's room with its closely set together tables and chairs. One or more nurses were always standing nearby to watch and listen. It all had much more the semblance of the prison that it was, and is, than its official designation of a special hospital. When Christine was least well she would be transferred to Lancaster Ward, a prison deeper within this maximum security prison. In Lancaster she would mainly be in solitary confinement, in a small, bare cell empty of all but a bunk and a pot. While visiting her there we were led through to a further, smaller visitor's room. You couldn't take children there. Inmates in Broadmoor had no access to a telephone so apart from visits her only contact with the outside world for years was by letter. She became a prolific letter writer as receiving them was important to her. There was still no such thing as privacy as letters in and out were opened and read by staff. From Christine's letters it is clear that something she particularly enjoyed was the periods of socialisation permitted with the men's ward which afforded some opportunity for forming some friendly, if limited relationships which she never seemed to find threatening. It is probably a loss for the men currently in Broadmoor that it is now a men only institution. In her letter Christine describes her day to day activities, and tries to stay cheerful. They illustrate how much of the time she was remarkably normal.

York House, Broadmoor

22, 1972

Dear Jill and Chris,

Thank you for your letter. I'm sorry you're not coming down but quite understand the difficulties. I look forward to coming to see you in Sheffield when I regain my freedom. I am doing very well at the moment and have been on York for about 10 weeks. I'm afraid I don't know any quick ways of making money. If I did I wouldn't be rolling my own cigs as I am now, and hustling off Mum for every little thing. Life is quite fun at the moment despite the restrictions. Our swimming-pool has been opened and the next item on the agenda is: why haven't we got a golf course? I go twice a week and love it, but tonight it was raining and a girl kept having fits and we had to have hot baths when we came back, as it was so cold. I have been to volleyball, played bowls, and listened to the Jay Strings group in the last few days. They are a Sally Army pop-folk group – in fact a bunch of Jesus freaks. I think they were on drugs, but that is only my opinion.

I go to lessons in poetry and history and have been writing some rather bad poetry which I am entering for the Koestler Award which is a competition for people in prisons and LAs (lunatic asylums), so perhaps I'll get you that £500 yet!

My boyfriend might be moved to Moss-side, which is the same as Broadmoor, but worse. I haven't seen him since November because first I, and then he, was in the back block (he went on the roof at Easter) but we have been writing to each other nearly every day and he might be coming out soon. Can you get me a funny birthday card before June 23rd for him please. He is a communist, hippie and will be 20. I would be very grateful as they only have awful flowery things in the canteen here. Haven't heard from Auntie Florrie for about 3 weeks. Well, I'll close now as I'm getting sleepy now.

Much love to you both

Chris, xxx

*

York House

Wednesday Night, April 17, 1974

Dear Jill and Chris,

Thanks so much for coming tonight. You've no idea how much it meant to me. I nearly cried to see you go. In fact it angered me very much that I wasn't able to have a few minutes alone with you both afterwards and to offer you a cup of coffee before you started on your long journey home. It angered me because I know that other patients are allowed to take their people into the hall for a while instead of three minutes on the corridor with matron on guard. But this is a small part of the general bitchiness and pettiness which is one of the tools they use to make our lives a misery, because they use it so much and there isn't a damn thing we can do about it. I'm crying even as I write to you, because I want to be out there with you instead of with all these phoneys. I'm sorry if I'm getting emotional and I know I tend to moan and be self-pitying when I talk and write to you. I don't mean to, but who else can I talk to about it? Certainly not Mum and Dad.

Jill, when I saw the prices of that food you brought I nearly dropped through the floor. Honestly love, I wouldn't have asked you if I had had any idea how much food costs these days. I thought Mum was being mean, when she goes on about the price of food, but now I can understand her point of view. Anyway, thanks love. It was really sweet of you. It must be about 11.30pm now and the other two in the dorm are both snoring. I'm glad you enjoyed the play. It was quite good fun doing it. I was a bit self- conscious of the fact you were both there. Again, thanks very much to you both for coming. It means a lot to me to be able to show people that I'm not just a useless lunatic who people are ashamed to be connected with because of the filthy name of Broadmoor, but that I can do something and carry it through. Good luck Chris on your interview. I hope you're successful. I'll be thinking of you.

All my love to you both,

Chrissy xxxx

*

Lancaster House, Broadmoor

30, 1974

Dear Jill and Chris,

I hope you had a nice birthday and got something nice with the present I sent you via home. I've changed my address again as you can see. I'm not sick, I was just a complete fool. I lost my temper with Dr. Levin and asked to come over here. I've lost so much, and yet strangely enough I don't feel like I've lost anything at all. They've told me so many lies about getting out. I got really sick of the lies. For so long I've played the game their way and really believed what they said. They said the kitchen job was a responsible and trusted job and you could learn to cook in there and that people who worked in there got out quicker. I took the job and found I was just a washing-up drudge, and they give you all the flannel about it because otherwise they can't get anyone to do such a lousy job.

The ward they call Semi-Parole, which I worked so hard to get to, has the most hopeless atmosphere of anywhere here. In the four months I was up there nobody left, and nobody up there even expects to go for ages yet. There are girls going from other wards but the Semi-Parole ward is the biggest cheat of all. I'm not telling you all this out of self-pity, but simply so that you can understand it all. I won't be on Lancaster for very long, and when I go back to York I won't give up after 16 months. I'll keep struggling on until I do get out – however long it takes. I'll have to start from the bottom again, but I don't mind even that, so long as they don't cheat me any more with their lies. I won't go back to Ward 3 – I know now that it was a mistake for me to have gone up there at all. Despite all that Le Couteur told me and you about a transfer, he didn't do anything about getting it started. That was just one more lie.

Mum and Dad came on Saturday and I had only just come over so I was in Douglas. Mum had a face like a wet Monday and I was sure she was going to turn on the tears but fortunately she didn't. I tried to cheer her up but I don't think I managed it very well. Patsy came up last Monday – she always turns up out of the blue. I think she's a bit fed-up because Bill spends all his time working on the house and they don't get out very much. I'm pleased to hear about Chris getting that job and that you are moving down. Good luck in your house-hunting.

All my love to you both,

Chrissy xxxx

*

York House
July 30, 1974

Dear Jill and Chris,

Thank you very much for all the visits which made me very happy also for the lovely flowers. I thought Patsy's bake was super and was also very pleased to see Patsy. I am still knitting busily at Jill's cardigan and am also going to dress a doll for the Best Dressed Doll Competition when Mum brings one in. By the way did you give Mum's baby coat to Patsy? She asked me but I couldn't remember it being mentioned. The difference between a minster and a cathedral is that a minster once had a community of monks. I asked Mr F and he went on for ages and said he would bring me a book on architecture tomorrow. I have knitted two coat-hanger covers today – what a waste of a life! Be good, God bless,

Love, Chrissy xxxx

P.S. Have just heard that Tom is out of the security block and back on the roof! POWER TO THE PEOPLE!

*

Broadmoor Hospital,
6th August 1974

Dear Mr Delahunty,

Christine DELAHUNTY

Thank you for your letter of 17 June detailing the hospitals in your area. Unfortunately, Christine appeared to be first under some tension regarding the thought of being transferred from this hospital and in July she certainly became more resentful of being placed in a dormitory and finally demanded that she be returned from Ward 3 and insisted on returning to Lancaster House. Since that time we have discussed this set back and she now is sufficiently settled to return to York House. Consequently, I hope she will again soon be in reasonable remission when I can effect her transfer.

Yours sincerely

N B Le Couteur

Consultant Psychiatrist

*

York House

Nov 1, 1974

Dear Jill and Chris,

Hi! Hope things are going okay with you and that Chris likes his new job. I guess things must be pretty rough for you both at the moment but I really hope they'll work out for you. I've really no idea about it all, as things like moving house are as remote as things on another planet now, but I just want it all to work out because I'd really hate to think of either of you unhappy because I love you both. I haven't heard the date of my Tribunal yet – it's taking a very long time coming.

There isn't really much news from this end. Cousins Michael and Gerard have both taken to writing to me. There have been drastic changes on York which have brought general gloom, as we seem to have lost a fair bit of freedom and gained very little, but I guess we'll survive it. I was given the lead part in the play again this year and it was a very big part, but I've decided not to do it, as I don't want to crack over a play and I think it's better to opt out now than to let everyone down later. Patsy still comes regularly with her friend Rosemary and both their children. Billy is suddenly much better behaved. Perhaps it's because he's getting older, and more used to coming here.

I'm trying to catch up on all my letter writing. What a

task! I wish I wasn't so lazy because it means you have to catch up on it all in a rush. I'm sorry I forgot your anniversary − actually I was too broke to buy a card and I thought it was a bit pointless sending one later. I'm still plodding on with my English studying. I only do it in fits and starts now though as it's harder than ever to get a bit of peace and quiet now that we are not allowed to sit in our rooms at evenings and weekends. (New Rule No. 1,259!!) When Uncle Matt told me that he and Auntie Ena and Philip had visited Anne, I had high hopes of them being able to persuade Mum and Dad to do the same, but have heard no more, so I guess it didn't work out. I'm making a rag-doll in OT and quite enjoying doing it. She's a real old fashioned rag doll and her name is Lucy. All for now.

Keep Smiling.

Chrissy xxxxx

*

York House

December 30, 1974

Dear Jill and Chris,

Please excuse the ghastly writing-paper – I got it for Christmas. It was lovely to see you both last weekend and the jumper is beautiful. Your doormat has come – it has got Welcome written on it in the language of Malayalam, which they speak in Kerala, in India – so if you should ever meet anyone who comes from there I'm sure it will make them feel at home!

I saw the tribunal doctor today, which was a bit of a surprise as I hadn't expected it just yet. I was really shattered by the things he read from my case-notes that I'm supposed to have done and said. I have no recollection of any of these things but they must be true because they have got them written down in black and white. As you know my first two years here are pretty well a blank – and I prefer to leave them that way and think ahead. At least now I can understand why they have kept me here so long. I really think you might all save yourself a journey on the 14th, as they are not likely to let me out. I didn't lose my temper with him. I just sat there calmly and rather shocked saying, "I've no recollection of that, Sir," to each thing he said. It was like hearing someone else's story. I just couldn't think of myself as ever doing or saying such things. And no doctor here has ever spoken to me about it. I asked the ward sister about it all after tea and she said I was acutely confused at that time so naturally it didn't make sense and I can't remember it. But then what's the point of them writing it all down to go against you in years to come? Anyway I'll forget about it now and settle down for a few more Christmases in here. There isn't much other news. Life has settled down again as usual and all the houses are having Christmas parties at the moment – we are celebrating Christmas a little late this year. Hoping to see you soon.

Much Love,

Chrissy xxxxxx

*

York House

January 19, 1975

Dear Jill and Chris,

Thanks for the card – did you notice that if you hold it upside-down it looks like horses legs?! I haven't had my refusal letter yet. I was surprised that you got yours. I'm not disappointed because from the beginning I hadn't really expected anything else. However I must have had a good report from them because on Wednesday, Le Couteur called me in and started talking about a transfer. He asked me whether I would prefer Sussex or London. I said I didn't really mind but that I wouldn't plan to settle permanently in London, it's too big for me. I suggested somewhere in between the two and he said no'because that would still leave me in a "welter of indecision." I don't really mind if he sends me to the Outer Hebrides, so long as I'm well away from here. He said that as soon as the tribunal's decision comes through he will get things moving. I think he means it this time so I'd better mind my P's and Q's.

We've just been out in the airing court and my mates and I have been playing hopscotch and daft things. On Friday evening Larry Adler, the harmonica player, came here and did a one-man show. It was pretty good. He played the piano as well as his mouth-organ, told jokes, and the music was jazz, classical, blues – you name it he played it. I'm finishing this letter on Monday, having started it on Saturday – that's how I get so behind with my mail! The post has just been given out but I still haven't had my refusal – very odd. Am going to a party this afternoon – it's nearly the end of the big Christmas parties now.

I'm very annoyed that my group therapy is going to be held on Monday evenings from now on, as that is the best evening for socials in the winter and volleyball in the summer. They've made a new rule about locking the rooms. They have previously been open from 4pm until 5.30pm for us to get changed for evening functions. Now they are going to be opened after tea, 4.30pm. I don't see what they gain by it all. Never mind. I had a letter from Auntie Florrie. She spent Christmas with Tony's family (the lodger). She has to walk with a walking frame now.

Much love to you both.

Chris xxxx

*

York House

January 29, 1975

Dear Jill and Chris,

I don't know if Mum and Dad told you, but I went to Lancaster for five and a half days after I lost the tribunal. I got really screwed up with my disappointment – but I didn't do anything wrong and I'm back on York now, thank goodness. I lost 5lb in weight in the five and a half days I was there – after all my futile attempts at dieting on York I at least made a start when I was in the health farm.

I have started writing a letter to Peter again .He sent me a lovely wall-hanging with a poem on it, all about love – very romantic! We did an hour's keep fit in

Lancs yesterday and my old bones are aching and my muscles complaining. I have written to the tribunal to ask them what conclusion they came to, and will let you know in due course. I'm in the dormitory now, as I lost my room through going to Lancs. I don't mind though, as they're a nice crowd in there and there is a washroom and loo attached. Trouble is, the heating in the dorm doesn't work. Still I've got plenty of blankets and it's not that bad. I forgot to thank you for coming to the tribunal. It was good of you to come and speak on my behalf. You didn't seem at all cheerful that day. I wondered why. Had you had a row with Mum and Dad? I had a lovely story from Amanda, all about a poppy, and I sent her a poem in return. I have made her a Belinda Bear as a mascot – it is a little bear in a flowery dress with a bonnet and lacy pantaloons. It is from a kit – you've probably seen them in the shops. I quite enjoyed doing it. I had a crazy letter from Andy in Spain today. He received the hat I sent him but the guards had ripped open the lining to see if there was anything inside it. He is wearing it anyway. One of the Basques pinched his kitten. And when Anne visited him she got caught smuggling vodka in. He's got a job washing plates and he gets a day's remission for every day he washes plates. I'd do a bit of washing-up if I thought it would get me out any quicker! Well, I'll close now as it's time I went to sleep.

All my love,

Chris, xxx

*

March 1975

Dear Jill and Chris,

I have been accepted by St Francis Hospital and will be transferred there quite soon. Isn't that nice? It doesn't sound too bad at all there, judging from the sister who came to see me and from a girl here who was there. I hope you are getting a bit more settled into the house now. Have you got your furniture out of store yet? It's Anne's birthday today. Did you remember? I don't know what is going to happen about Bell, Book and Candle. I will certainly be here for the beginning of the season and if my date comes through – well, they'll just have to find someone else to finish the season. By the way, let me know if you want any tickets for it. I am going to send most of my gear home when Mum and Dad come next week. I'll only take the minimum of stuff with me. Beauty will have to go home too, at least until I have found out what the place is like. I started packing last night, or rather throwing things into a cardboard box! We had a parole dance on Friday and instead of the usual sandwiches we had mini-steaks, and chips and grilled tomatoes and peas. Very nice. I'll close now.

Love to you both.

Chris xx

Chapter Eighteen

TRANSFER TO ST. FRANCIS HOSPITAL

Broadmoor Hospital

11 March 1975

Dear Mrs Bolton.

Christine DELAHUNTY

I am writing to let you know that arrangements are being made for the transfer of your sister to St. Francis Hospital, Haywards Heath, Sussex, on Tuesday, 18th March 1975. Christine has reached a stage where she no longer needs to be treated under conditions of maximum security and it is thought that she will benefit from the greater personal freedom offered by an ordinary hospital. She will be nearer to the homes of her relatives and friends and it is hoped this will facilitate visiting.

Yours sincerely,

N B Le Couteur

Consultant Psychiatrist

(They got my name wrong!)

*

It was a great relief to us all when Christine was eventually allowed to leave Broadmoor on the March 18, 1975. She had been there for five years. Our parents were by this time living in Hove so Christine was transferred to St. Francis Hospital, Haywards Heath. This was to become her base for the next few years with the aim of working towards rehabilitation. Their revolving door policy meant she was increasingly allowed out for days, weekends, or occasionally to work, during the periods when she was judged to be well enough. At other periods she would end up back in locked wards, and secure rooms. It was during this period that Christine devised and commenced an optimistic longer-term plan for her future, which involved her starting to study for examinations with the aim of working towards becoming a librarian.

During this time there seemed to be signs of Christine's recovery and she was increasingly allowed out for weekends. Chris and I had moved back to London in late 1974. He was working as a researcher for London Transport, and I was a Social Worker in Lambeth. We often invited Christine to stay with us for weekends. After a while these seemed to be working really well so we agreed to have her to come and live with us. She was delighted and we were all optimistic as she had seemed to be doing so well.

The day came and I booked the day off work to go to collect her from the hospital. When I arrived I was dismayed and in disbelief when the nurse told me Christine wasn't well and that I couldn't see her.

"But she's been so well for months," I said. "And she's so looking forward to coming to live with us."

I insisted on seeing her, sure that she must be okay. The nurse took me through but as soon as I entered the room Christine flew at me and grabbed my throat. All I could feel was a terrible sadness. I couldn't even lift my hands to pull her off. The nurses did it for me. I stumbled out into the grounds and wept. After some time I went back and talked with the doctors. Christine had obviously panicked about whether she would be able to cope with the hugeness of the move. It was a big setback and the only time she ever attacked me. She sent me the following letter shortly afterwards.

Hamsie Ward,

St. Francis Hospital,

Haywards Heath,

1975

My dearest Jill and Chris,

I don't know what to say except that I'm very, very sorry to have let you both down so badly after you have both been so wonderful in helping me. Also Jill I can't say how sorry I am for what happened when you came on Friday. I think it was partly because I was very agitated that day, but also because I couldn't face you because I knew I had let you down so much. I had begged the nurses not to let you come in, not because I wanted to hurt you, but I was in such a state and I knew what would happen. You have both been so wonderful in sticking by me for so long, I don't know how you've done it, but believe me it matters a helluva lot to me.

As for what happened on Thursday, well I'm better now, physically, and also much calmer, although still feeling pretty low. I had all my bags packed up ready to come but when it actually came to it I panicked. I was very frightened to leave hospital. I guess I'd been kidding myself along, trying to be all big and brave and confident, but rushing myself along too fast. The people here are being wonderful, trying to help me untangle the problems and feelings that have been there so long and that I never understood. This is something that they never did at Broadmoor and that I hadn't really given them a chance to help me with here, until now. When we've got it all untangled then I guess I'll be able to start again, and on much surer ground, however long it takes. For the moment I am mostly staying in my room away from the other patients, having a break from being the big false confident me that they've all come to know, and just slowly getting myself sorted out until I can face it all again. Don't be hurt my darlings if I ask you not to come again for a while. It doesn't mean I don't love you, I care for you both so very much, it's just that I feel I must have a break from everyone for a short while to get over all that has happened and to sort myself out before I begin again. I know you want to help but you are helping at the moment by being two people who I know care for me, and that matters a lot. Well, I guess I've said what I wanted to say, although whether it makes sense I'm not too sure. I know you'll understand.

My love to you both.

Chris

Chapter Nineteen

FACING THE WORLD OUTSIDE HOSPITAL

Christine

Q: What do you see as the difficulties of rehabilitation for ex mental-patients?

A: I would divide them into three quite separate categories:

First, practical skills – the obvious things like shopping, cooking etc. Also things which the rehabilitators don't foresee and couldn't remedy anyway, like having no sense of direction. If you never go out you lose your mental map-making process. I spent my first year continually lost, not only on my first visit to a place, but also second and third. This can be quite distressing.

Second: social skills – not just things like keeping your voice low in restaurants, and not slurping your tea. People outside play by different and more complicated rules. Until you begin to grasp the subtleties of these you are very much an outsider.

Third: fear of freedom – very much the longest and toughest to tackle. Getting to the point where you no longer see yourself as an ex-mental patient, and you expect to be able to fight all your battles on equal terms with the others, and to think of yourself as equal and of equal worth, no longer different.

Fear of Freedom

We went through the crowded streets, to the crowded fair.

So many human units buzzing together.

All ready to sting an intruder who shouldn't be there.

I hid all my fears in Asha's hand,

So long as that small piece of strength was tied to me

The rest didn't matter because it was only a dream anyway.

I didn't trouble to untangle it all.

To work out whether I myself was real,

Or whether all the other people were,

It's their world, not mine, but I dared to trespass

Because I was safe with ones who know and care,

And that's what matters, not the whirling, swirling fair.

Not the buzzing people whose eyes I couldn't meet

In case they reproached me for not wanting to compete

With them in their vast, fast land.

I'm supposed to want to be like them,

And so I made a try,

Although it still puzzles me just why I should want to

buzz and sting. But it pleases people,

And it wasn't so bad

With Asha and Linda there.

Up Hill

Getting better. It's an uphill struggle. That old cliché really says quite a lot. The long, stony, seemingly insurmountable path up the hill. So many of us. Each carrying a burden, each of a different shape, a different construction – all seemingly impossible to carry and refusing to be dropped – and all invisible to the rest of the world – even to the other people journeying up the hill. Perhaps especially to them – because each has their eyes on the ground and their thoughts on the burden on their backs.

Will I ever even make it to the top? Or will the weight of it crush me first? Sometimes I'm so tired. Can't I just stop trying to find my way up this hill and let the burden crush me? Why is the road so dark? Sometimes we glance sideways and see – or think we see – the others: family and friends standing comfortably around the hill jeering at us, or maybe with their backs turned. Is that an illusion? Why don't they help me with this unwieldy load? But they're jolly well not going to. You're on your own. Or are you? If you can lift your head for a moment – and that in itself takes courage – then you are surprised to notice the others battling up the hill. So, I'm not alone. Can they help me? Or can I help them? Well, burdens is burdens.

Help

They sold me help, the price was high.

I bargained fruitlessly;

It was too fragile for my care.

I reached for help with my fingertips,

It crumbled into dust.

They sold me help, it was a precious jewel.

I was unworthy, couldn't grasp it all.

The Storm

A thundercloud consumes me, blots my mind.

I'm drifting in a starless universe.

All life is drifting on.

The raindrops are my tears of deep despair.

No glimmer of light can filter through the depths.

The claps of thunder echo cries for help,

But none can hear, none lives within my cloud,

For I'm alone, my cloud is called Despair.

The moon shines only on those filled with love.

He turns his face from me.

I drift on through the dark, lost in the cloud.

The storms are shattering, but there's no escape

For one consumed in darkness,

Blinded by fear.

Violent Feelings (November 15, 1976)

My soul is frostbitten

If I do not keep moving it will perish

It has only my conscience to warm it

And that sleeps.

The icy flames of violence flare within me.

There is no warmth, for winter never ends.

I carry my violence like a gunpowder keg

Which any chance spark could set off.

First day in Woodingdean Ward (November 19, 1976)

I am hooded in failure

Blinded by its dark folds of loneliness.

It has enwrapped me as suddenly as mist.

I didn't notice it

Until I couldn't see beyond it.

I turn, and turn again, but cannot see.

I cannot see the sun for I am trapped,

Crumpled into despair.

None can reach me in my depths

For the hood of failure is a heavy barrier

And searchers cannot find me, lost within it.

Thirst

I am suffering from a deep thirst.

It is a thirst of the spirit.

The drought goes on and on

And others seem able to survive without refreshment –

even to flourish

I thirst for love.

I should love to be loved,

And to be able to love.

I read of love.

I read of life,

Of people who have drunk deep of the liquors of

experience.

I exist.

I exist as an inessential skeleton.

I need space for thought,

wine for inspiration,

white flesh for experience.

I hate clocks,

and television;

they are vultures of the spirit.

Bite into a grape

And what do you have?

Succulence.

Wake up after a drugged sleep,

And what do you have?

Another day to be frittered into dreariness.

God gave me today –

He might not give me tomorrow.

I have not returned his gift with interest,

Only with stagnation.

God speaks to me (7 December 1976)

God speaks in many tongues, in many tones, in anger as well as in peace and love. He loves me and so He makes use of me. He makes my life difficult in order to continually test my faith. He alone knows what is right and wrong. Men judge only by the things that make their lives comfortable. They sit in judgement on me and cannot understand that I must do God's will alone, not theirs for they are close only to their own gods not to my God. They judge me to be a thief but I must do as my God instructs me, for no man knows God's will except as God tells him personally. I love my God and try to please him, but I know that by doing that I am incurring the displeasure of the people around me. There are many things which God tells me which I have to hide from the people around me, for they are unable to comprehend their importance. I live a double life, on the surface being what Man expects from me, secretly praying and talking to my God, for He alone understands what is right and wrong and the difficulties of the tests he puts me through. The reason He uses me to impart bad to others is to test me and when I fail in his tests He punishes me. He punishes me by making me aware that I am different from other humans, their gods talk only to deaf ears. They remain ignorant of the trials of faith and love.

The Clown (July 23, 1977)

Deep seated loneliness behind a brilliant smile.

The smile is for the world.

The world accepts the smile

And rejects the ocean-deep plea for understanding.

The corpse smiles.

It has escaped.

I envy it.

I ask only for silence;

Silence from ignorance.

I wish they'd all shut up and leave me alone,

I can't think.

Escape is in sleep,

But I awake tormented.

Tormented by twisted dreams

Which are beyond my understanding.

Nobody knows me,

All they know is that phoney, artificial smile.

The Lane

I walked alone down the lane.

The same lane I trod when I sought a retreat in which
to kill myself.

The same lane I trod on summer mornings of beauty

When I rose early to dream through a world that was

mine,

A world of calm and warmth

That didn't last.

I slid down the rainbow

And then it faded,

And I crashed down, down, down

Through a whirlpool of ice cold treacle.

And the treacle was the problems from which I had fled

When I walked down the lane.

But there was no escape now,

Just confusion and problems that trapped me every way

I turned.

So I must open my eyes

And search out a way to be free permanently.

To reach out my hands for help is futile,

For who would want to be encased in my trap with me

When the escape route is only a lonely lane that goes

around in a circle.

Thoughts (August 8, 1976)

I'll burn into a pile of fleshy ashes.

I'll watch the flames devour my body whole.

The clouds of smoke will make my sail soar higher

And all my fear of life will drift away.

I'll gain my peace through fire pure and holy.

Freedom will come to me as ashes pile.

The flickering flames will never scream at me.

The muddle will be gone forever more.

Chapter Twenty

SHAKY STEPS

Jill

Christine remained largely in St Francis hospital, Haywards Heath, from 1975-79, with occasional weekends out to stay either with our parents in Brighton, or my family in Camberwell. Our parents and I would often confer, usually by phone, with many periods when our spirits were optimistically raised only again to be dashed with disappointment and distress.

It was becoming clearer that any prospect of rehabilitation would have to be some form of semi-independent living although at this time people seemed to be either fully hospital inmates or fully discharged. The roller coaster of Christine's mental health condition was difficult to keep abreast of and during the periods when she was housed outside of the hospital with no follow up support, she would sometimes stop taking her medication or be going downhill without anyone realising until some crisis occurred leading to her being returned.

My first child, Louise, was born in April 1976 and I have a lovely photo of Christine gently holding her as a very young baby – a far nicer photo than any of me holding her, perhaps because I took it! During some of Christine's stays in our home, Christine was fine. Other times she was not and we knew we were walking on eggshells of unpredictability. She could appear cheerful and all right and then become distraught and unreachable.

I was relieved one weekend that I had long decided never to have a sharp knife in the house, fearing Christine could use these on herself. When she did try to cut her wrists one weekend, she could do little self-harm with the rather blunt bread knife I regularly used to hack our weekend joint. She then tried the alternate of an overdose, but fortunately then told me, leading to a harrowing night's struggle to get her to King's College hospital to have her stomach pumped. The next day she transferred back to St Francis via the Maudsley.

I never mentioned to Christopher, or to my parents, the potential risk to Louise. One weekend I had just gone to the kitchen to fetch us a cup of tea. Christine was sitting on the settee in the lounge, seeming okay, and Louise was crawling around, gurgling contentedly on the carpet. Before the kettle had boiled Christine came down to me in the kitchen and said, "I think you'd better take me back to hospital, Jill. The voices keep telling me to smash Louise against the wall."

"Okay," I said, and I took her straight to the Maudsley from where she was returned to Haywards Heath. You simply never knew what was going to happen next. From then I was always inevitably much more cautious about having her to stay never daring to leave her alone for a moment with my children, Louise, or even many years later with Amelia. I knew she loved them, but her illness, possibly merged with some underlying jealousy either of me, or of my love and care of them, made this unsafe. I had no way of knowing when she was being affected by the voices which she found so compelling. Christine always loved her nieces but that didn't mean she wasn't sometimes liable to harm them. I always had to be on guard. I could never risk leaving either of them alone with her, particularly while they were little, even though there is 13 years difference in their ages. I had come to realise that they were at risk, more than anyone else, from her erratic moods and behaviour. Christine could turn very suddenly from everything seeming fine one minute to a nightmare the next. I couldn't know when she was hearing the voices although sometimes her face would glaze over and she would become very edgy.

We continued visiting Christine in hospital and sometimes would take her out from there. One time, while she was having a bad spell, I arrived and found that she was locked in a single room just off the ward. She was in distress and told me she had been in there in solitary for weeks, with nothing – not even her glasses or anything to read. I went to plead with the nurse and in frustration found myself screaming, "This is supposed to be a hospital. I would not treat a dog this way." Usually we did not feel able to complain on her behalf because as friends and relatives we were very aware of the vulnerability of the patient and didn't dare risk making things worse for them by annoying the staff.

I have never been a regular diarist, but I did write the following in September 1977: "Chrissy has been confined to a room on her own for a month, by the authorities at St Francis hospital, because she has attacked another patient. Her future looks very black. Louise is with me. She's pretty chirpy. Just had to stop to change her. She keeps performing for my attention, in between exploring everything in reach; finding it easier to climb onto stools and chairs than off. She's standing well now – her first solo steps are sure to be soon.

I went to see Chrissy yesterday. She was very depressed at the prospect of what almost inevitably lies in store for her now. She was feeling very unlovable because of her badness in attacking someone and kept asking for reassurance that I still love her, and that Mum and Dad do too. She said they left very soon after she told them last week and she felt this was because they were angry and no longer care. I tried to look realistically with her at how they may have been feeling. I was there about three hours talking with her, and with the nurse who has known her for some time. She told me how bad the attack had been, and that Chrissy had written a letter describing the feelings she sometimes has, and has difficulty controlling – that she could attack Leyana – and Louise. Although it was the first time I had been told by the hospital of the latter – it was no news to me, as I had always known it, sometimes wondering – even hoping – that this may be an irrational fear of mine. It seems that is not so. I said that I would phone Peter to let him know the situation. Also that I would phone Dr. Stead to discuss this with him and see if there is any alternative possibility for Chrissy other than being condemned back to that awful place (Broadmoor). She feels now there is no hope for her, and no point in trying. I don't think she's left me much of a leg to stand on in pleading for her.

Spent this morning decorating the hall. When Louise woke from her nap, I went to clean my hands before fetching her. By the time I went to get her out she'd gone very quiet, the little monkey was happily engrossed in stripping the new wallpaper off in her bedroom! Dad came over to lunch. He's pretty down but I could do and say little to cheer him up. Partly I'm annoyed with him and he knows it. I told him we'll go down to Brighton on Sunday to see him and Mum. It is hard to think of much else at the moment with Chrissy's ever worsening plight weighing so heavily on my mind, leaving me feeling drained. Louise provides me with a continual chain of little distractions – amusements and the aggravations of never having a moment to myself. I must have had to jump up a dozen times already today, while writing this, to rescue her from things, or things from her! Time to take a little lady for a walk. She has tired of playing peek-a-boo and wants more full attention from me now.

Still trying to contact Dr. Stead, so far without success. Funny how I resort to recounting facts at times when feelings are strongest, too hard to face, even to myself. So what do I do with them then?

Create distractions for myself, and busy-ness. Enormous relief to hear from Dr. Stead that there is no plan to send Chrissy back to Broadmoor and no likelihood of this at present. Strange how evasive some of his directness seemed, but in essence I felt he was frank, considering Chrissy's situation, which is tragic in its hopelessness even after all the years of concentrated medical care and effort. He recognised her awareness of her situation, how really sane she is when sane, and at other periods how uncontrollably mad in spite of hers and others' efforts to control these worse times. He indicated that the present month's detention stems more from a need for justice to be seen to be done than any imminent danger, reckoning that following an attack such as the recent one, is probably the time she is least likely to so behave again. I would consider this true if it were not for her present desperate hopelessness.

When I phoned Dad to tell him this good news, he sprang in first to relate to me how he and the hospital staff have worked out between them how to collect Chrissy's things from the flat. I was pleased to hear of his renewed cooperation with them, having been angry with him on Sunday for expecting them to do it all. I am sure Chrissy will be pleased at this practical sign of their caring.

Now Christopher, hopefully I will have time for you again. I know it's hard on you when I get wound up or depressed over these things. We don't talk of them much as I know you hate to discuss matters that you know are distressing me, and probably you, and that you feel helpless to repair. We are all pretty helpless in this situation. Instead you show your care by nurturing me. We have a funny relationship really, but I guess on the whole we keep each other pretty happy. I wonder how far the things I am writing about are really things I should be talking about with you.

Dad phoned. He saw Chrissy last night. She seemed a fair bit brighter and was enormously relieved to hear what Stead had said. Tomorrow we're going to Haywards Heath to see Chrissy. Dad's picking us up at the hospital to go on down to Brighton. Christopher will come back in the evening, but Louise and I will stay down till Tuesday as Mum hasn't seen Louise for about three months. We haven't been able to make it down there since Christopher has been ill, and Mum doesn't come here.

We found Chrissy much brighter on Saturday. She is finding it an effort to keep that way but deliberately busying herself and taking care in her appearance. I found the visit rather arduous because of the potential threats to Louise – not from Chrissy today – but from a couple of the other patients who Chrissy warned me about. I found it hard to keep having to guard her from women who approached her in friendliness but are potentially unpredictably dangerous.

Chrissy had received her manuscript of children's stories back from the publisher with a very encouraging note. I borrowed it to read. She gave me another cardigan, knitted by one of the elderly patients, Peggy Parker, from Hassocks ward. I was very touched by this lady's gifts, which I know must have taken her much effort. I wanted to take Louise up to see her but didn't manage to as Mum and Dad had come to collect us. Chrissy's stories were delightful. I am sure she has real talent at writing and hope she will continue. It is a field in which I am sure she could be very successful.

I found it difficult to talk to Mum except on a household level. This saddens me. We have so little in common in terms of what is meaningful to either of us that there now seems little basis for communication. I have lived away from home for as many years as I lived there. Dad and I had a good conversation over a drink in a Brighton hotel. Christopher will be 31 tomorrow. Unbelievable to think he was 19 and I was 18 when we first met.

This morning I collected some odds and ends into a toy box for Louise's room. She played happily with the toys in there for much of the morning and selected a dish and spoon as favourites, perhaps because she's just learning to use a spoon. She carried them downstairs to the bathroom when I changed her and took her first few solo steps towards me clutching them. Shaky steps, but she shared the thrill of knowing that she had done it.

Chapter Twenty-One

SIREN VOICES

Christine

Suicidal Longings (November 11, 1976)

Death calls in Saccharine Tones

And I listen.

The battle cries of life's conflict make me turn.

I need a spine of steel

But I am weak.

If I could retreat from the continuous nagging voices

Into a cocoon of silence

Then I could have the beauty and freedom

Of a butterfly.

But a butterfly soon dies.

It is weak.

The simplicity of escape whispers and beckons

But I must turn my back

And hold my head high.

I must build an armour plated will

And join the army marching forward

For butterflies are fragile

But I must be strong

And deaf to the call of escape.

To the Doctor:

This week I have felt a real urge, a real need to hurt someone. I have continually been listening to the screaming of a hurt person. As well as the screaming I have been listening to my own voice say words over and over about hurting people, all about hurting people but not chained into sentences or making any sense. The only way I can describe it is as if a giant jigsaw puzzle of words all about the same thing has shattered and had to be put together again before it made any sense. All my thoughts were like this and every time someone approached me I wanted to hurt them and while I had my mind on that I was trying all the time to figure out what they wanted. Every little thing became a problem on its own, like opening a letter or eating a meal. As well as this I have felt very depressed. Now the talking has stopped and so I know I will not hurt anyone, but still I cannot help thinking about it. I hope you can understand this so that you can help me again if needed.

Trees

The land is black. Only the sound of screams. Where do the screams come from? From inside every living, breathing tree – for these are hollow, they are grotesque. Inside each tree are captive humans – when they are skeletons the tree spews them out. I walk on. There is nothing else to do but wait to be captured. The branches of the trees are burning arms, weaving and twisting in the darkness, casting a glow on the forest of hopelessness silhouetting in the dark the eye-picking vultures. I am waiting, not resisting, for there is no point – there is no future and the only way to 'belong', to feel wanted, is to succumb to being swallowed into the trunk of a tree, to take sides with the monsters. I will not scream. I am past that stage. What happened to God? Oh, he lost interest and gave us up for lost. It is very dark. The flames are high. Giving in is easy. It's only the stupid ones who think they can get out of this forest. They can't. It's the end.

Chapter Twenty-Two

SELF-HARM

Jill

From 1977 to 1978, Christopher was off work for about six months. He had contracted hepatitis from the blood change he needed for a wisdom tooth removal. He had low factor 11, a clotting agent, akin to haemophilia. At that time, UK hospitals were importing blood plasma from the United States. Blood there was purchased from volunteers who tended to be down-and-outs or drug addicts. The blood products were not tested. Just as Christopher was recovering, we saw that Laker was offering cheap flights to the US and that children under two could travel free. We decided an extended holiday there would do us all good, so Christopher mapped out a six week holiday plan taking us to Los Angeles, San Francisco, Chicago, Ann Arbor and New York – a holiday of a lifetime.

Before we left Christine, who was still in St Francis Hospital, was very down and endlessly tearfully on the phone to me. We needed that holiday. But almost the minute we walked back through our front door, the phone went. It was my father informing me that Christine had set fire to her nightclothes while in a locked room in hospital. Her very serious burns were now being treated in East Grinstead Hospital. Christopher and I were devastated by the news. The horror of it was unbearable and I blamed myself for having gone away when I knew that for many weeks Christine had been distraught and depressed and pleading with me to get her out of hospital. Not that this was an option as she was clearly far too unwell to be discharged. I think it was some years later that she sent me some pieces of her writing that included the following somewhat accusatory poem that she had presumably titled later.

Written the Night Before Burning Myself (April 1978)

My hands are twitching with unused violence.
The screams from the TV are bouncing out of my eyes
Like beams of sightless light.
My sister is far away and my heart is with her
Crossing the ocean – mine's a sea of tears for her.
I am encased in a cocoon of fear and loneliness.
I fear that I am feared and my fears are not found-less.

*

Christine remained in the specialist burns unit at East Grinstead hospital for some months. She had set light to her highly flammable nightdress while in a locked room. By the time her screams had been heard and responded to by nurses she was in a serious condition and scarred for life. She was reluctant for us to visit her while she remained in East Grinstead, presumably aware, and not wanting to face, how upset she knew we would be. She wrote the following poem:

In East Grinstead Hospital –
Poor Little Rich Bitch

Plink Plonk

It's raining tears of charity

On the roof of my thin robot-ish nobody's house.

They're all so kind.

"But we won't come in today, thank you very much."

Won't anyone shuffle forward towards me a little?

Won't they come and just feel what it feels like to be me?

To be on my side of the barrier for a moment?

"I'm lonely."

"Have an apple dear."

"I'm lonely."

"Nice cup of tea?"

"I'm lonely."

"Here's a nice jigsaw for you dear."

I'm screaming my soul into deaf ears

– is it me who has switched off from life, or them?

If only I could rouse them enough to be honest enough

to stop

being kind.

Bloody hypocrites.

*

By the time Christine was returned to St Francis Hospital we all realised that the prospect of her being transferred back to Broadmoor was on the table. Christine was adamant that she didn't want to go back there, and we shared her horror at the prospect, although we knew she had put the writing on the wall. Dad and I assured her we would do all we could to resist it and this became one of our most desperate battles.

Christine and I were in contact with the charity Mind which was at that time managed by the ardent campaigner Larry Gostin. Having got no joy from writing to the hospital, I wrote to Tim Sainsbury, of the Sainsbury family, who was the local MP for where Mum and Dad then lived in Portslade, near Brighton. He gave me an appointment to meet with him at the House of Commons. Larry Gostin and another solicitor from Mind accompanied me. Mr. Sainsbury led us down to a meeting room in the bowels of the Houses of Parliament. It was evening, and winter. We had just all sat down around a table when we were plunged into pitch darkness by a power cut. It all seemed rather surreal when one of the staff brought us in a lit candelabra which served until the lights were fixed.

Mr. Sainsbury listened and agreed to follow up Christine's case with a letter to the hospital which he did, to no avail. I think it was at this time that Dad also wrote to the Secretary of State for Health, who held decision making powers concerning discharge from Broadmoor, pleading that just because Christine had been there before should not make it easier for her to be sent back there. We were to address the Mental Health Tribunal on Christine's behalf.

When the day came, we were joined by two solicitors from Mind, as well as Christine's A Level tutor – Terry Johnson – who was the head teacher of a local school. Dad and I were to go in, Mum stayed outside to look after Louise.

For my part I knew I needed to present the strongest and most reasonable case that I could to the tribunal both in writing and at the hearing. My first drafts were all written by hand and literally cut and pasted, or full of scribbled margins rearranging the text since these were the days before we had a word processor or computer. It was all typed on my dining room table on the electric typewriter I had purchased for my ongoing studies. Finding the time and space to write also depended on my work schedule, I was part time, and also the times when Louise was having a sleep.

I showed Christine a copy of the report I had drafted, and also sent one to Mum and Dad. I tried not to raise Christine's hopes unrealistically. She was frightened of going back but almost resigned to it, realising the precariousness of her situation. I sent the following to the tribunal in advance of the hearing which was held in December 1978:

Christine has been an in-patient at St Francis Hospital since 18th March 1975 when she was transferred here from Broadmoor following the recommendation of a tribunal. During her first few months at St Francis her progress was remarkably good so that in July her discharge was arranged. Unfortunately Christine panicked on the day she was due to leave the hospital after having spent seven years constantly within institutions. Since then her progress has been more erratic, with periods of being very well, and of being very ill.

During January 1976, Christine was allowed to work outside the hospital in Mac Fisheries in Haywards Heath. In spite of the freezing cold at that time she worked well for several weeks and the manager was so pleased with her that he kept the job open for her for a considerable time after she had stopped because of illness. In November 1976, Christine was transferred from the admissions villa, where she had been under the care of Dr Stead, to Woodingdean, which is a locked, long stay ward under Dr Wheeler.

From May to September 1977 Christine was allowed

to live out on extended leave from the hospital in a flat in Haywards Heath. During this period she was returning daily to St Francis, spending the mornings working on one of the wards and the afternoons attending occupational therapy. She has in fact worked daily on the wards since being in Woodingdean, helping with bed making, cleaning and mending.

In February of this year Christine had a discussion with Dr Wheeler during which he told her he was agreeable to her shortly being discharged on extended leave if accommodation became available for her at a house in Haywards Heath where Father Martin, the local Catholic priest was hopeful of arranging a room for her.

It was during March that the two incidents occurred which have led to Dr Le Couteur's current proposal to return Christine to Broadmoor. The first was attacking a nurse, and the second was burning herself, details of which incidents the hospital will doubtless have given you. Christine was in a state of severe depression at this time and heavily troubled by the auditory hallucinations to which she is at times prone. Her medication had been increased to an even higher level than usual. We make no excuses for her. She would not want us to. Christine was both shocked and dismayed when she realised that she had hurt the nurse. It was very frightening for her and for us, and doubtless also for the hospital staff to recognise that she could on occasion be capable of such action.

The staff at St. Francis have been constantly both tolerant and caring of Christine and we are grateful to them.

It is evident to us that it is because of these two incidents in March that the question of Christine being sent back to Broadmoor has again been raised. Initially she was sent to Broadmoor in 1971, from Fairfield's Hospital near Luton. We are unhappy that because she has in the past been a patient in Broadmoor it now seems very much easier for her to be sent back there. We find it hard to believe that she can really be considered the most violent, or difficult, patient in St Francis Hospital at present as we are aware of many incidents of as bad, or worse behaviour by other patients, for whom no such transfer is suggested.

Since the incidents in March Christine has been allowed to go home for weekends, and to go in and out of the hospital, with or without company, without undue concern being felt. When I visit, she is still permitted to accompany me through the town to the station and then to go off on her own to the local library and shops before returning to the hospital without giving cause for anxiety, so that it seems very inconsistent to assume that it can really be considered necessary to place her in such a totally restrictive institution as Broadmoor from which one never steps outside a locked door and can never have a private visit, or make a phone call, or even write or receive an uncensored letter.

We are familiar with the punitive containment that would be her lot there and cannot believe that this dreadful step is necessary in Christine's case for either her well-being or the well-being of others. For much of the time I believe the hospital staff would confirm that Christine is a model patient as she is normally pleasant, helpful and intelligent. During the past year she has been successfully working on an A Level English course, and attaining very good marks. Her tutor, Mr Johnson, has been seeing her weekly and is so pleased with her progress that he is encouraging her to proceed to an Open University degree course next year, on which she has now been offered a place. She has also been regularly participating in the local Catholic Church, helping as a sacristan, preparing the altar and frequently reading the lessons to the congregation. She has written a children's book and received a very encouraging response from potential publishers.

The doctors can offer little hope of a recovery for Christine in the foreseeable future. In spite of the severity of her illness she is much of the time coping successfully with pursuits in and out of the hospital. A transfer to Broadmoor holds no hope of improving her psychiatric condition but only the despair of worsening her surroundings and social condition to its most extreme limits. We believe the punishment too great and the prospect too dreadful to be either necessary or just. We hope and trust that you too will find this and that the staff of St Francis will be prepared to continue offering Christine their care, support and tolerance as we, her family are, in as far as we are able.

Gillian Delahunty

*

Louise and I stayed with Mum and Dad in Portslade the night before the tribunal. I packed a bag with all that Louise was likely to need. Mum would look after her in the car while Dad and I went in.

It's nerve racking having to face any kind of quasi-judicial proceedings, with

an appointed panel holding important decision-making powers. By this time I had been a social worker for several years so was fairly used to having to present a case – but this was different, this was personal, and we were Christine's best hope of avoiding return to the hopeless and dismal total institution of Broadmoor from whence we feared she may never be released.

We all seemed to talk in hushed tones while waiting to be called in. The panel of three, chaired by a woman, were all of sombre appearance. We too had dressed smartly conscious of the importance of making a good impression. When permitted, the solicitor gave an outline of Christine's circumstances in the context of the then current Mental Health legislation. The chair then asked me a series of questions referring to the document I had sent in advance. She also asked Dad for his views. Their questions were exploratory, and they did seem to be giving the matter their serious consideration. We were all clear that we didn't consider it necessary, just, or helpful for Christine to be sent back to Broadmoor. The impassive demeanours of the panel gave little away. We knew that without a positive recommendation from her consultant we were not in a strong position. In fact if the doctors had been in agreement, we wouldn't have needed the tribunal.

*

It would be some weeks before we would be informed of the outcome and we were all still feeling a bit tense as we departed. We agreed to go and have lunch at a nearby bar-restaurant. I exchanged a few words with Mum and Dad and went in the car with the solicitors to give directions to our venue. As the car went to pull out of the hospital drive another car came hurtling along the road swerving to avoid hitting us. It careered further down the road ending up in a ditch. I got out of the car and ran down the road to check how the driver was.

A young man who appeared rather dazed but otherwise okay, got out. I had a few words with him as other passers-by stopped. I returned to the car I was in. I was surprised they hadn't come too. I guess as solicitors they were wary of the potential prospect of becoming involved in litigation.

We drove on to the restaurant. Mum, Dad and Terry were already there. The solicitors stayed briefly saying how they thought it went, and then departed. We ordered food. As it arrived I asked Mum if she had changed Louise.

She replied, "No, I had enough of that when you were all kids."

I was incredulous but knew there was no point in saying anything to Mum. Terry looked askance at me. It had been about four hours since we left home. I took Louise from her pushchair and changed her nappy before returning to my meal.

After lunch Mum and Dad dropped me off at the Haywards Heath station. We hugged and as I said goodbye to Mum and Dad we were all relieved that the ordeal of the day was over. Dad said he'd let me know if he heard anything – we were hopeful but not optimistic. I found my way home to Camberwell with Louise. I was exhausted and told Christopher about the day while he made tea.

A couple of weeks later we were informed that the outcome of the tribunal was unsuccessful. Christine had been informed directly through the hospital and they had sent a letter to Dad who then phoned me. We felt absolutely desolate. Christine was promptly returned to Broadmoor for a second time. We were fearful about how long she would be there this time.

*Right, Christine and Jill
at Woodford in 1951.
Below, Christine in
happy Bideford days,
aged 10, in 1959*

Professor J. R. R. Tolkien
c/o George Allen & Unwin Ltd
Ruskin House
40 Museum Street
London WC1A 1LU

Dec. 24. 1971

Dear Christine,

I am sorry that I have not answered sooner your letter of Nov. 22nd. I am away from home, and travelling about. I am very glad that you have read my book again, and have liked some of the poems: and also to hear that you are feeling better.

The "hobbits", of course were meant by me to be just ordinary, kindly human people, fond of food and fun, small in size but strong and brave, and very good at driving away all nasty creatures, and at helping other people that were troubled by such things. There were, of course, nasty and dangerous creatures in their times, but in my story they were conquered or or destroyed by the "hobbits" and their friends — such as Tom Bombadil who was not afraid of any of them, and when he commanded them to go away they fled at once!

I was very pleased to get your letter. If you want to, or wish to have anything explained, write again. It is, I am afraid, too late now for this to reach you at Christmas, but I hope you had some of the love and peace which you so kindly wished me to have. Yours very sincerely

JRR Tolkien.

It is my birthday on Jan 3rd
and you may see a picture of me in the Sunday Times
on Jan 2nd.

The letter Christine received in 1971 from

JRR Tolkien, author of The Lord Of The Rings

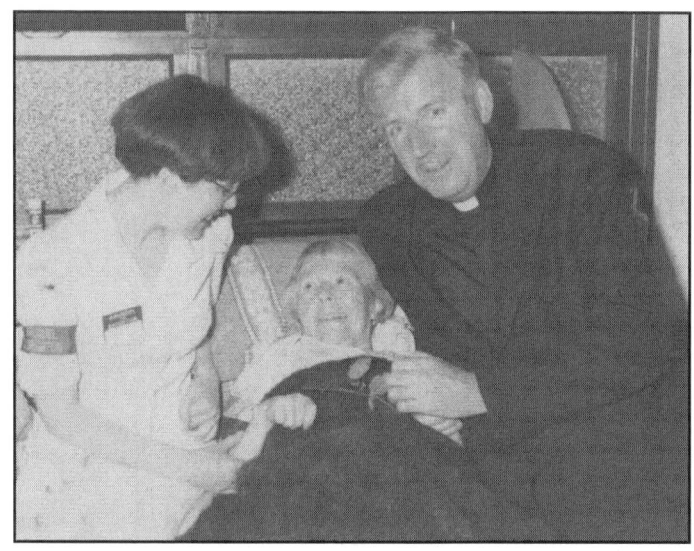

Christine (left) at Lourdes in July 1982 helping patient, Cathy, with the then Bishop Cormac Murphy-O'Connor, who later became Archbishop of Westminster

Mum, Dad, Louise, Christine, Jill, and Anne nursing Amelia at Jill's home in Brixton in May 1989. It was the first time Mum and Dad had seen Anne in 25 years

Christine's notebook, in which she kept a remarkable and detailed account of her life throughout her illness

Above, Christine (left) and Jill (second from right) pictured with Amelia and Louise
Below, Christine on a P&O cruise in December 2011. When she told the family she was dying of cancer she said, "I don't want anyone to cry – I just want to go on a cruise

Chapter Twenty-Three

BACK TO BROADMOOR

Christine

Written After Return to a Hated Place.

I looked up at these walls from the outside

And saw them as the perimeter of a battlefield

Where the battle is too long and sordid for the world to

know about.

If they knew they might begin to feel guilty,

Which is an uncomfortable feeling.

Or they might feel obliged to try to understand,

Which would be even worse.

So they built a great wall

And left the untouchables inside

To fight unarmed

Against the ghosts of warriors such as Despair, Guilt,

Degradation, Rejection.

And they blocked the escape route

To all but a chosen few

Who had wandered in by mistake

And left, singed and scarred by bitterness.

And I went back, through those walls.

I re-entered the battlefield

And sought out my old comrades

Who still fight half-heartedly on

Because there's nothing else to do.

And that's what it's all about.

I looked into the eyes of Joan

And saw that she had been thrown to the bears.

For screws get bored,

And that's when it's dangerous.

But what does the outside world know about bear-baiting?

In this battle there are no rules.

And no weapons.

So they use each other as weapons.

I looked into the eyes of Joan.

They had taken a high-spirited animal.

One who used to have a fiery, friendly spirit

And your eyes Joan were the eyes of an animal

Beaten into submission.

Exhausted by the never-ending battle for survival.

And I listened to tales of petty skirmishes,

And tales of horror.

Of Jane's strange, horrible death.

And of corrosive hope.

For there is nothing so corrosive

As to put a lifeline in front of a drowning man,

But just out of reach.

For he will wear himself out fast

In such a struggle and then go under.

Which is what Paul is doing now.

In another year he will be lost forever.

What a victory for society, and for ignorance.

Futility

I look out and up to the clouds

And there's all that air, that space, that nothingness

But it's a good nothingness

Because it gives all life a breath.

It gives the world a chance to stretch and grow.

But I lie here a solid lump of nothingness.

 Weighted down by my body, but more useless, more unfeeling

Than all the airy nothingness outside.

For some reason that I can't understand

I was lumped together and expected to live.

Expected to be a human being.

But slowly, knowing what was happening,

I became a petrified, fossilised crust.

A solid void.

I've turned myself into nothingness

Because that way I don't have to suffer any feelings, any emotions,

Because that hurts too much.

I can't bear that.

So all I am really doing is taking up space.

I don't think I'd mind if I was a cabbage

Because they have a place in the chain of usefulness

And then I wouldn't even have to know that I was nothing.

I wouldn't even have to be aware

That I'm supposed to act out the duty of living.

Oh God why did you take the trouble to give me life

When I don't want it?

A Cry for help

Oh God my heart is parched and dry.

Come upon it like a shower of gentle spring rain.

Sing to me when I am sad and lonely, like the birds on a summer dawn.

When I am tormented by troublesome voices

Take me in your arms to rest in silence.

When my whole self is burdened with fear

come to me like the happy winds of Autumn and blow

away the dust,

the delusions and the despair.

Never let me be frost bitten into losing sight of your

support

and love Oh Lord. Let me be safe at your feet for always

dear Lord,

Then I shan't mind being in hospital.

Thank you, Lord.

*

Ward 2, York House, Broadmoor   ,

January 15, 1979

Dear Jill,

Hi! I had a really good weekend as we had a party on Friday, nothing much happened on Saturday except that I was expecting Lee and Derek and they phoned they couldn't come and behold, on Sunday morning Lee and Derek came, then in the afternoon Mum and Dad and then in the evening I went to a concert on the male side. I'll slow down a bit and tell you all about it all. The party went on for four hours with dancing and grub and I met some men I used to know and also one new one. However I was out of luck because by the time I had had about half a dozen dances with him, and promised to sit with him at socials, I had also discovered that he was someone else's boyfriend, was 23 and had BO! I never was lucky with men was I?! I'm not all that keen to go to socials anyway.

I have arranged to sit at the next parole dance with someone who is also someone else's boyfriend and who I once went with for a while and ditched rather hurriedly, and heartlessly (he seems to have forgiven that – or forgotten – or maybe he's just thick-skinned) and who is about three feet taller than I am. Boy, was I glad when that party was over. I then decided to stick to entertainments where there were no problems involved so put my name down for Sunday night for Music for Hospitals which turned out to be a very pompous 70-year-old pianist telling us his life history as a piano player from the age of five. He got to 1949 and ran out of time and that was quite a relief for everyone as the hall was cold and I for one wanted a smoke and a cup of coffee.

Perhaps I'll stick to TV and letter-writing and give up this socialising lark, only it scores points for you if you socialise. Anyway I enjoyed my visits and had a good gossip with Lee. They didn't make it on Saturday because they overslept after a party on Friday. They would have stayed all day except that Mum and Dad were coming in the afternoon. They saw Le Couteur – I expect you know more about that than I do. Dad told me about the newspaper cutting and when I told my friend about it she knew the girl in Holloway early in December but had never heard the outcome of her case, although she wondered if she would come here.

Well, that seems to be all the news, but what I've been wondering is whether you have found a place in a nursery school for Louise for April yet. Also I can't remember her birthday date, but I expect one of you will be able to remind me in time. I keep forgetting to nag Mum about finishing the caterpillar I was making for Louise for Christmas, but perhaps it will be done by April.

Love to Chris and a cuddle to Louise.

Cheers, Chrissy xxx

*

Ward 2, York House, Broadmoor,

February 3, 1979

Dear Jill,

Congrats for getting the job. When do you start? I bet you're on your head and your heels sorting yourself out to re-join the rat race. I was writing to Patsy today and told her your good news and also mine about passing the exam. Mum and Dad were thrilled about me passing. It was lovely to see you on Wednesday but I'm afraid I was in a bit of a dream as it was my first day of coming off some of my medicine. However I've got used to it now and am back in the groove – as much as I ever am, which isn't very much!

I didn't really take to Sue, although I usually like your friends, but if she's got a car she's worth knowing anyway. It was just that she seemed to think that Louise should be seen and not heard. Anyway I like Eva and Patsy, and Kitty seems fun so don't take offence! You probably got the book I sent, hide it, or maybe it would be better to destroy it, but I couldn't bear that. I sent the copy of the book I wrote to Patsy to illustrate, or not, as she thinks fit.

Love to Chris and a cuddle to Louise.

*

Ward 2, York House, Broadmoor,

February 11, 1979

Dear Jill,

Hi! How's work? Patsy wrote and said how pleased she was you got the job, and also that she has started illustrating my book and is coming to see me soon with Emily. Rosemary, her friend who used to bring her when I was here before, is going to bring her. Also a friend, who used to be in St Francis Hospital, Paul, is coming soon. Also, at half- term, Father Martin and Terry are apparently coming, so I'll have to lay in a stock of biscuits and hope they've laid in a stock of fags!

Lee and Derek came yesterday. Lee is looking slim and fit, having turned into a yoga maniac and health food maniac. She told me about all the super clothes she has been getting from jumble sales and offered to bring me some. She told me all the news and views and came back in the afternoon, so that was lovely. She has put her name down on the council list for a place for the two of them, and also heard of a housing list where bedsits are £2.50, and flats £3.50 as they are trying to get a few young people in, so she's going to try for that. I have been studying hard.

The programmes start this week, did you know? Also in OT I have been painting with inks. At first I made a terrible mess of it, but I'm getting the hang of it now. I've been copying pictures from the Diary of an Edwardian Lady and have now started on one of boats. The knitting is gathering dust and I'm enjoying OT much more now. Poor Auntie Hannah seems to be in a terrible state with the strikes, blizzards, burst pipes and broken violin strings. She said it's so cold in Manchester that the worms are leaving the ground and freezing to death on the pavements!

Cheers. Chrissy xxx

*

Ward 2, York House, Broadmoor,
February 1979

Dear Jill and Chris,

First of all I must apologise for writing on file paper – I forgot to buy any writing paper this week, and can only go to the canteen on Thursdays so I can't get any until next week. I always write 10 letters at weekends, that way I can be sure of getting plenty of mail in the week. I spend every morning looking forward to the time when letters are given out at lunch time. We've just been out on airing court in the snow – it was lovely – I got a snowball down my neck! Now I'm all tingly and having a cuppa and a smoke and watching an old weepie on TV. Your new job sounds exhausting – I hope you're not too tired with all those miles of corridors to walk every day, especially as your workload will be even greater with difficulties caused by the strike. No-one here is striking, fortunately for us.

I've forgotten whether I thanked you for the skirt. It fits a treat and I'm going to wear it to the next parole dance next Friday – that's the monthly one that goes on until 10pm – and at which we get a meal. I hope you are getting your OU work sorted out. Auntie Hannah passed her Social Science exam. I gave in my first TMA this week, I don't know what sort of mark I'll get. I'm onto history now, I've got a very dry looking history text book to read in the next couple of weeks. However, after that I'm onto literature and I'm looking forward to that. Dad sent me Roget's Thesaurus this week, which will be useful for studying. Also I'm reading The Plague Dogs, which Lee sent. It's by Richard Adams and I'm still a bit doubtful about it, but I think I'll like it better when I get into it. Well, that seems to be all the news for now, so I'll close.

Sending you all my love.

Chrissy x

P.S. I wrote to Anne and sent her the photo you gave me of myself and Louise.

*

York 2, Broadmoor,

March 9, 1979

Dear Jill and Chris,

Hi! Long time no news. I understand the social worker from the Maudsley said you're not in her catchment area, which seems odd and is a little disappointing. I understand from Carole it takes in Brixton, which seems strange. I still haven't seen Le Couteur and he didn't bother to answer Dad's letter, so there's nothing new. Think I'll write to him for an interview this week. The play is going well and is generally thought to be very funny and very well performed. We have only had small audiences so far but are expecting bigger. So far we've collected about £45.

Have you started your OU course yet? I'm well into D101 and enjoying it very much. There is a story writing competition which I am hoping to enter, but the story has to be illustrated so I've written and asked Patsy if she'll do it for me. There is another one for Tales of the Unexpected which I thought I might enter. Mum and Dad brought my recorder yesterday, so I have been practising that. I can nearly play Three Blind Mice! However the staff soon tell me to pack it in. There is a choir coming tonight – The London Crusade Chorale – they come regularly and our choir joins up with them and together we make a fair old racket. Brighton tied with Norwich yesterday – my friend Bev's team. We had three teabags on it but as it was a tie we called it quits. I really thought Brighton had it in the bag at half-time as the score was 2-0 to Brighton, but they let me down.

Patsy came to see me on Monday. She's really good, the way she comes so often, especially as she's supply teaching now. Can you give me any clues about what to get Louise for her birthday? I don't have a lot of spare time to make things but might be able to arrange something.

Love to you both and a cuddle for Louise.

*

York 2,
April 13, 1979

Dear Jill and Chris,

A crisis! I can't remember whether Louise's birthday is 15th or 25th. As I haven't got a card and her present hasn't come yet, I'll have to make it the 25th whether it is or not. I expect she'll get plenty of presents and cards anyway. Well, I've lost 8lb in weight so that's not too bad is it? There's another stone to go yet though. I saw Le Couteur the other day and he still wants me to apply to Ealing College and live in a hospital – I don't think I stand an earthly chance of being accepted under those circumstances but still. He's holding a sort of conference about it next week with myself and my tutor. Wish me luck! I think the whole thing's a waste of time and he's building my hopes up for nothing, so I'm just putting it out of my mind.

*

York,
May 27, 1979

Dear Jill and Chris,

I hope you are all well and enjoying the bank holiday. Please would you do some shopping for me? I will send you some money next month and the month after. What I want is a leotard, as I could use it for swimming and the sleeves would hide my scars, which an ordinary swimsuit won't. I hope you don't mind. Lee says hers cost about £3.50. She offered to get one for me but she's up to her ears in debt so I don't like to ask her, and swimming starts soon. She did say however that she has seen them at jumble sales in the past, and if she happens to go to a jumble sale and see one she'll get it and phone you. I know you're busy but I need it fairly soon. Ta. (P'raps if you haven't got time to go shopping Eva wouldn't mind going. I really will send you the money next month, but am broke this month after having had to pay my OU fees.

*

Dear Jill and Chris,

Hi! I hope you are all well and not working too hard. I am wondering if Jill got the job she applied for? Also what Louise is up to, now it's the summer holidays. I'm writing this in the garden on Sunday morning. The sun has just gone in, the weather's very changeable. I went swimming last night but it wasn't very warm. I can swim underwater now, which is something I've always been a bit scared of doing. The next thing is to learn to dive, but being only a shallow pool you have to be careful when you dive, in case you hit your head on the bottom of the pool! Lee came yesterday. She has made me a bead bracelet with my initials and number in it, all worked in beads. I love it, it's fun and she's done it really nicely. She's going to make one for Carole next. I am still studying hard, in the hope of passing my OU exam this year, also getting a better grade at my English. I haven't heard yet whether I passed the music exam I took, but I should hear this week. Also I should hear the result of my religion essay (OU) this week. I'm not very confident about either, but think I should scrape both. Aunty Hannah has been ballet dancing in a leotard! She gets up to everything doesn't she? Our fete and dance the other day turned out to be quite enjoyable. The sun shone. The steaks were just right and there were plenty of prizes to win for everyone. I won masses of chocolate but gave it away, as I had a tummy upset at the time. That's cleared up now.

Well, I'll close now, sending all my love to you both and a big cuddle to Louise.

Cheers. Chris xxx

Did you see the Sunday People yesterday? Another black mark for Broadmoor, just to make it that bit more difficult for people trying to get accepted by counties, or trying to settle down outside and put Broadmoor behind them. I just wish the papers would leave this place alone for a while so that the public's suspicions of us all might mellow a bit. It was all so stupid, and the girl concerned was thrilled to bits and proud of herself. Actually, I used to be very close to her, she was my best friend for a long time. I suppose you've heard from Dad about the social worker from the Lady Chichester Hospital seeing them on Wednesday, and the doctor from there ringing them up. Maybe things are going to start moving soon. I sure hope so. Well, that seems to be all the news for now.

Much love, Chrissy

P.S. Do you think you could get me some nail-transfers before the play starts. Thanks

*

Ward 2, York House, Broadmoor　　　,

October 4, 1979

Dear Jill,

I am writing to tell you, as I have written to Dad that I intend to go ahead with my tribunal, whether you and Dad decide to come and support me or not – that's entirely up to you – I won't blame you if you decide not to. I need your help, but if you decide not to give it to me I will understand and will go ahead on my own. I hate Broadmoor and intend to do everything I can to get out. I cannot wait around for Dr Le Couteur's vague promises to materialise – I don't know how long that will take. I've got a chance of getting out at this tribunal and I don't intend to lose that chance, if I don't win it, well that's too bad, but at least I'll have tried. I haven't heard from Mind, I don't know whether they've been receiving my letters – perhaps they're not supporting me either. I don't for a moment think the tribunal decision will make any difference to Le Couteur's opinion on whether to discharge me or not next year. If he wants to discharge me he will, that's all. But I don't know how long that might take. Please let me know what you decide as I have already put your name forward to the tribunal as supporting me – I'll have to let them know if you decide otherwise. Please apologise to Chris if his birthday card has come too early, or too late – I asked you some time ago when his birthday was but you didn't tell me.

Love to Louise.

Chris xxxx

*

Ward 2, York House, Broadmoor　,

December 6, 1979

Dear Jill and Chris,

Hi! I'm marking the return of my typewriter from captivity by fingering you out a letter, you'll have to ignore the mistakes. Also I'm so slow you'll probably have to wait until Christmas for this letter. Well the news is that I'm likely to be going to the semi-secure unit at Southampton in the next few months. Dr. Le Couteur says that Dr Fawkes of the unit is coming up to Broadmoor in the next few months and that he is going to ask him to see me. Also he suggested I ask Haydn Gott to arrange for Dr Fawkes to come and see me before the tribunal so that I can jump the queue. I've written and told him, and also asked him to agitate for the tribunal to be held fairly soon. It is too late now to get out before Christmas, but I reckon February should see me in Southampton. Isn't it great?

The other news is that I'm going to a fancy dress party tomorrow, dressed as a boy scout. Hope I win something. The party on Tuesday was really good. There was a fire on the male side last week, and there was £50,000 worth of damage. They don't know what caused it. Are you coming up before Christmas? I've got some presents for you all.

Love to you both and a cuddle for Louise.

Chrissy xxx

*

York 2,

December 1979

Dear Jill and Chris,

Snoopy is ready and I will put him in the post the minute the OT receives your cheque. If I say it myself, he looks quite cute. Well, Dr Fawkes and company came yesterday but it was all a bit disappointing. They said that as my name was not in their administrative area they very much doubted whether they will be able to accommodate me. However, they will let me know in a couple of weeks, and then, even if they can accept me, there is a waiting list of several months, so I must be patient. I reckon that news will come about the same time as my exam result – I'll be a nervous wreck that week! They saw another girl here too – her home is in the Isle of Wight so I expect they're more likely to take her. They seemed to quite like me. Went into details about things I'd long forgotten. But they told me to think they couldn't accept me, and then it will be a Christmas bonus if they decide it is possible. So that's that. So, I'll just start nagging Le Couteur about a hostel. If I can persuade him to find me a place in a hostel then the tribunal won't be necessary. I am going to three parties this week. There is one on tonight, but I'm not going as I'm going to play rehearsal. I am taking Carole's part tonight as she is committee woman and has to go. I am helping her make the preparations for it this afternoon – they are having prawn cocktail, Black Forest gateau and heaven knows what else. By the way, don't forget the prawn crisps when you come will you? Your presents haven't come yet from the mail order firm. Hope they come soon – all my Christmas cards are in it, also Louise's Advent calendar, which you'd better save till next year. Well, I'll close now and put this in the post as it's nearly lunch time.

Love to you all.

Chris xxx

*

York 2,

January 6, 1980

Dear Jill and Chris,

Thanks for coming up the other day. I sent the photos off to Southport for you. It was nice to see you all. I am expecting Dr Fry and Haydn Gott this week, also the tribunal doctor. Any idea when they are coming? I have written to Haydn Gott when he is coming, as nobody here is likely to tell me until he is on the doorstep. I don't know whether Lee is coming but I think I'd probably rather she didn't as there's not a lot of future in going to live with her. She's got a lot of problems and also a very small room. Also her housing situation is uncertain. Also I'm not likely to get the job I want in Haywards Heath. Anyway, I'll talk it all over with HG when he comes. Frankly, I don't think I stand much chance at this tribunal, do you?

I had my broken tooth out on Wednesday, and have had neuralgia ever since. My plate is pinching it. Poor me! We went in the airing court this morning and it was lovely. It was sunny and we were watching some hot air balloons on the horizon. I've been dieting madly this week but have only managed to lose half a pound. I am giving all my spuds to a friend who wants to get fatter! There is a social tomorrow evening. I am going to it, with Bob. I'm going to pour myself into my red satin pants. Hope they don't split. By the way, did I tell you, Dr Fawkes can't take me as I'm not in his catchment area. He's taking Diana. So I don't know where I'll go if I win the tribunal. The Christmas decorations are all falling down – they look really tatty. They'll probably take them down tomorrow. Well, I'll close now. Hoping to see you on 17th.

Love to Louise.

Chrissy

P.S. Did you pass your exam?

*

York 2,

Dear Jill and Chris,

This is an urgent letter about Snoopy. I have started making him, and should get him finished by the end of the week but I can't afford to buy him as I suddenly find that I am £16 in the red and so am not allowed to spend any more until I have cleared my debts. The solution to this problem is for you to pay for him. If you send a cheque, as soon as possible for £1.50, and write it to DHSS, then as soon as they receive your cheque I will be able to put Snoopy in the post to you. They said will you do all the usual things like putting your name, address, credit card number etc. On the back, then it will all be okay. Thanks. Sorry about this but it's the only way.

I saw Dr Le Couteur today and he told me that Dr Fawkes is coming tomorrow and he is going to ask him to see me – I hope he will. We had a film on VD today. And yesterday we saw Saturday Night Fever. I didn't think a lot of either film. This evening is the school party and we are having Chinese food –lovely. I'll get this in the post now, and send Snoopy as soon as they get your cheque. Thanks for coming on Sunday.

Love to you both and a cuddle for Louise – hope she

liked her tea-set. Chrissy xxx

York 2, Broadmoor,

February 3, 1980

Dear Jill and Chris,

Long time no news – I wonder why? Do write if you've got time as I love to hear from you. Well, you will know by now that I lost the tribunal, got upset, went to Lancs for five and a half days and am now back in York and resigned to another year in Broadmoor. That's about all the news from this end. Have you seen the recent Mind Out? Also Now! had an article in running down all the patients, which I suppose makes a change from running down the staff and the system. The OU year starts this week. Are you all set to go again? I'm not, not a bit – I've got lazy in the holidays. I have been hearing from Pete P. again. He is living in Forest Gate now.

Jill, what do you think of me asking to go to the Maudsley? I think I could cope with London now, but it would mean me being permanently on your doorstep, which you might not like. I'm just thinking around all possibilities. The play starts on March 1st. I won't be in it as I'm only an understudy. If you would like to come let me know and I will send you an

229

invitation form – I've sent one to Patsy.

A cuddle to Louise and love to you both.

Chris xxxxx

*

February 24, 1980

Dear Jill and Chris,

Thanks for your visit the other day and for seeing Le Couteur for me. It all helps. Have you got any news for me about getting out? Dad said he was going to write to Sainsbury. I don't know if that helps or not. Anyway it was lovely to see you and I hope to see you again beforehand. I've got a Grade 3 Music Theory exam this week. Hope I pass. I don't know if I will though as I'm not very hot on scales. I'm going to learn to play the recorder, to put the theory into practice. I've got permission and Dad is going to get me one. I've been studying hard on Population, Resources and Technology which, surprisingly, I find fascinating. I've been reading all the books I can get hold of on the subject. At the moment I'm reading one called Poverty and Progress by Wilkinson. Did you ever watch the TV programmes for D101? They get crazier. This morning it was on immigration and it brought out the tiny bit of racialism there is in me – and in all of us who were watching it I think. It was a long-haired Rastafarian sociology lecturer from some English university, who was complaining of a lifetime's discrimination in England. The general consensus of opinion among those of us who saw it was, "Why does he stay if he hates the English that much?" It was a really stupid programme and didn't teach me anything.

Our play starts on March 5th, so the rehearsals at the minute are last-minute-panics. Let me know if you want to see it and I'll send you a form for the tickets. It's very funny – a black comedy. We've got a big dance this week – the parole dance. They go on until 10.30pm and we usually have a good group playing the music. I'm getting really fat. I wore my satin pants to a social this week and the zip kept busting! Then I tried on those brown army pants you gave me, size 14, and I broke the zip. I'll have to go on a diet, but the food here is really good, and we get very little exercise. It's roast chicken for dinner today   Well, I'd better close now.

Much love. Write soon. Give Louise a cuddle for me. Chris Xxx

*

York 2,
March 29, 1980

Dear Jill and Chris,

Just a note to thank you for coming up the other day. It was lovely to see you. The flowers have opened up beautifully and I've put one vase in my room and one in the day room. And I've got the pink nail-varnish on. Thanks. And I've put Louise's picture on my wall, alongside one of Billy's. I'm writing this at the play again – it's another full house. We're doing a performance for Jimmy Savile's Stoke Mandeville Fund in a fortnight's time – all the funds go to them. We've got nearly £500 so far. Sunday morning: was I sick last night! I picked the raffle ticket (it was three numbers away from mine) and a nurse who I particularly dislike got the huge basket of fruit and didn't offer us so much as a grape. And I picked the tickets for the national too – I paid 15p and didn't so much as get a horse and a really stupid cow got Ben Nevis and the £5 prize! I'm just not lucky at gambling. I hope I do better with my Easter Bonnet! I'm writing this in the airing court on Sunday morning and it's cold even though the sun's out. They've threatened to bring us out some cocoa in a minute. Dad will tell you the latest on the grand library school plan. What it boils down to is the fact that there's no point in me applying to library school as I don't stand a cat in hell's chance of getting there, and neither do I stand a chance of leaving Broadmoor before 1981. So that's that. I'll think about applying next year, if I'm out then. I can see 1984 arriving and Big Brother still watching me. Well that seems to be all the news. Now we're all set for the holy week jamboree with the Franciscans. They are some really nice people who come for the week and make religion fun – everyone goes and there's a revivalist atmosphere about the place, even amongst the declared atheists. Bye for now,

Love to you both and a cuddle for Louise,

Chris xxx

*

April 7, 1980

Well, after a week in bed with flu, I've just realised I didn't post your last letter so here it is, with a little addition. I got 2nd prize for the prettiest bonnet in the parade – two china figures of a girl and a boy, which I have put in my room. Also I made the costume for the baby half of a mother and baby entry and she came 2nd too, so I was quite pleased with that.

Patsy will have told you that she brought the children up on Saturday. Also Mum and Dad came on Friday morning, and Uncle Matt and Auntie Ena on Friday afternoon. I had kept the cake you brought for them and they tucked into that. The kit still hasn't come to make the doll's clothes for Louise's birthday so I don't know how long it will take me to make them up! We had lovely big juicy pork chops for our party yesterday. Today it's Lancs' do and they've got turkey salad and I'm on the working party so I ought to get a nibble. I lost six and a half pounds last week when I had flu. It doesn't really show though – I'm still fat. I got a D for my last TMA and a B for my last CMA. I think the D was for disgusted and the B for better try harder! Well I've got a lot of letters to write so I'll finish now.

Love. Chrissy xxx

*

York 2,

April 19, 1980

Dear Jill and Chris,

I have made the doll's clothes and will put them in the post tomorrow so that you get them in good time. Well, I'll tell you about the outcome of the big interview on Friday. Gosh that man's fickle. He started off the interview saying he wanted me to apply for college. I put forward my viewpoint and he then said that I wasn't ready to go to a county yet anyway and wouldn't be for a good while. So we decided I might as well re-sit my English A Level in November – that was Rosie's idea. I'm not so keen on it myself. Anyway

Le Couteur said he wants me to go to 3s (the parole ward) later this year, but not yet as I'm not ready for it yet. So that's that. It looks as if I'll be here for at least another year. I wish he wouldn't keep raising my hopes and then bringing them down with a crash. Anyway, I'm glad he's not forcing me to take on more responsibility than I feel ready for. I was worried about that.

It was glorious in the garden today and I picked some flowers for my room and some blossom. I've arranged them in a tidy-tub and they look super. I hope you like the doll's clothes. I did them all by hand except for the small bit which I machined and then had to un-pick and re-sew by hand. I'm writing this at the play again. It's a mad audience tonight who keep clapping at the wrong places. At least they're appreciative. It was lovely to see you on Wednesday. Lee is coming tomorrow afternoon with Terry. Hope I can cheer her up a bit.

I've lost 11lb in three weeks so I'm very pleased. At last I don't look so hideous in trousers now. My satin pants fit a bit better now too. On Thursday I had my hair cut and blow dried so I thought I'd tart myself up and go out. I put on my satin pants. Made myself up and went to table tennis (watching, not playing). I hadn't arranged to sit with anyone so thought I'd just go and flirt. I sat down amongst some empty chairs and by the end of the evening I had five fellas around me. Gosh, I had a laugh. There was a Turk who told me all his case-history and problems, a coloured fellow who talked to his voices as much as to me, a skinhead who had been in Brixton Prison 12 times, an Irish tinker, and an English fellow who was on the lookout for some mystery girl who hadn't turned up and whose name he didn't know. They all told me their problems except the one who was too busy talking to his voices (They were very funny voices - he kept laughing). They're all lonely men and by the end of the evening I felt loved and I think they felt a bit better. Well I'll close now and do a bit of knitting. The fair-isle waistcoat is at last taking shape.

Love to you both and a cuddle for Louise – Chris xxxx

*

York 2,

May 2, 1980

Dear Jill and Chris,

I'm in trouble in a big way. You'd better phone Dad and he'll tell you about it. I can't tell you now, I don't even want to talk about it. I'm tired, tired, tired. One thing I've made my mind up on though is that the next six months are going to be a lot better than the last six months. I'm going to study hard, keep a low profile and make progress. I want to get out of here, and that's the only way I'll do it. Not by creeping. I can't bear creeping, it's undignified. I'll write to you on November 1st and review the situation. And if I haven't got anywhere by that time, well, I'll give it another six months, and so on. One day at a time though, that's the way to do it. Le Couteur has mentioned my name to a Dr McKeith who is setting up a secure unit in Sussex. I can just see it as a Woodingdean-type-hell-hole. It'll take ages anyway. I'm not allowed to join the choral society this year. Le Couteur says it would be too much for me. I've started the peg-dolls. They're not very good I'm afraid. Write soon and comfort me. I've only my prayers to comfort me. Much Love, Chris xxxx

*

Lancaster,

May 10

Dear Jill and Chris,

As you can see from the address above I have changed my place of residence – only temporarily I hope. However I've started a course of ECT, which is helping enormously, all the horrible thoughts and fantasies have flown out of the window and I've settled down again – thank goodness. I don't think I'll be here (in Lancs) for much longer. However if you are still thinking of coming up to see me on 20th I think you'd better phone first as I don't think they let small children into the visiting room on Lancs. It was nice to see Chris the other Sunday. And by the way the fact of my not being able to join the choral has nothing whatever to do with my being tone-deaf (smile). The musical director was quite happy to have me but Le Couteur crossed my name off the list.

By the way, did Dad tell you I passed my music exam? I'm supposed to be taking Grade 5 in June, but I don't think I will as I don't think I'll be ready for it – it's a hard one. I've done four of the peg dolls, but all the gear is over in York so I don't know when I'll be able to get them to you. Also one of the older women saw me doing them and gave me a little doll for Louise, which I'll also put in the parcel. Love to you both and a cuddle for Louise.

Chrissy xxx

P.S. Did you know Auntie Margaret's Mike has just got himself engaged to an 18-year-old nurse. Good for him!

*

York 2,

June 29, 1980

Dear Jill and Chris,

Thanks for coming up on Tuesday – it was lovely to see you. Louise is really growing up isn't she? Mum and Dad were up on Saturday and were complaining because they hadn't heard from you. You know how they worry. I had a letter from Julian last week and thought about giving it to them, but decided against it. They are going up to Southport at the end of July for Anne's (Uncle John's) wedding. Apparently Auntie Hannah offered to make Anne's wedding dress out of an old piece of satin she had, but was politely but firmly told not to. I bet that was an anxious moment for Auntie Eileen! I still haven't seen Le Couteur about my college applications. Do you know, it's a pity women's lib hasn't yet breached the walls of Broadmoor – the boy I did the OU with last year works in the patients' library, a totally male area where girls mustn't cross the threshold. If you remember, I asked for a job there last year and was told that it would be against union agreement. Because he has gained some experience in librarianship, Alain was able to take a correspondence course in librarianship (which he did as well as the OU). He has just taken, and almost certainly passed his part one in librarianship, and will take part two in November. This will give him BA (Lib) without three years at college. It will also give him two credit exemptions from the OU. This means that because I am a woman I have to do five years more study than Alain to get the same qualifications. Isn't life unjust? He is in the study dorm, which means he has good facilities for study, which I don't. Also they took him to a local library to look around before he took part one. So he's got a career all worked out for him. Well, having got that off my chest I'll close. I'll send you a card from Bognor Regis on Thursday.

Love to you both and a cuddle for Louise.

Cheers,

Chrissy xxx

Chapter Twenty-Four

A DAY TRIP TO BOGNOR

Broadmoor Hospital, May 26, 1980

Today we had some knicker-wetting news. Those of us who haven't been out for more than four years are leaving our Carmelite world and having a day trip to Bognor Regis! We all spend time looking at the moors and hills through the windows of this barred and barren place, but we haven't been outside these hate-filled walls for so long. We watch the television news and look at newspapers but that's only second-hand living isn't it? We're going on FRIDAY the FIRST of JUNE at nine o'clock and we're each going to be given SEVEN POUNDS to spend. I'm fancying lamb chops in a posh caff already!

Broadmoor Hospital, May 27, 1980

More news about the trip. None of us knows where Bognor Regis is but we're all dreaming of it through our drug-heavy days and nights. Linda's dead upset because she hasn't been here long enough to be put on the list – what a funny thing to wish you had been in Broadmoor longer. Sister Beryl is going with our group and she's going to take a camera so that we can all have something to remember the day by – it'll probably be the only trip – some eejit is bound to make a run for it. We've been warned in multi-coloured blueprint about that, but someone's bound to try their luck aren't they?

Broadmoor Hospital, May 28, 1980

Well, those of us who are GOING TO BOGNOR REGIS on Friday had our hair done today. Pam usually charges us a shilling each but the taxman paid today. It isn't a shilling though is it, it's FIVE NEW PENCE. Our Dad showed me some decimal coins when they first came out but of course none of us have used them because everything here is done on little pink forms. Pat is terrified and doesn't really want to go – it's actually 24 years since she took an axe to her husband and walked through those one-way doors. Even having her hair done hasn't taken the tremble out of her face but I expect she'll tell it all to her friend Eric the tortoise in the airing court. Elsie hasn't been out for years either, but she's still sitting indomitably knitting dishcloths. I'm dying to tell Mum and Dad about it when they come tomorrow, but we're not allowed to tell anyone where we're going in case it leaks out – the tabloids would have a field day – coach load of murderers, rapists and arsonists being let loose among the green parks and sheltered piers of Bognor

Regis. See ya tomorra, Diary.

Broadmoor Hospital, June 1, 1980

Well, Diary, I've got a lot to tell you today. We went to Bognor Regis for the day and I'm still as excited as I was when they woke me up this morning. Being excited is probably one of the best things because it lasts for weeks before and after a day like that. School kids have nothing on us on that bus today. I wore the suede miniskirt Mum bought me, with the studs down the front, and my yellow twin-set – I was nearly sick down it. I didn't know whether to shout all day or just look at everything and keep my mouth shut. Most people chose to shout all day!

None of us knew what to do with the new money. It's like doll's money compared to the pounds, shillings and pence we're used to, but we managed to spend it all anyway. On the way back we stopped and had real fish and chips from a chippy and we all sang The Day We Went to Bognor until we were hoarse. I felt sorry for Pat – she was terrified and sat on the empty coach on her own all day rather than get off and party with the rest of us. The worst thing (for her) is that they've said they're going to take her out on regular trips to help her rehabilitate, but to my mind there's no point in putting her through that agony because she'll make old bones before they let her out. Anyway, to get back to our day out, they didn't have lamb chops in the posh cafe that Sister Beryl took us in so I had to have pork, but I didn't let that spoil my day. We went on the fairground and Jenny went on the waltzer four times and couldn't stand up after. The ride attendant guessed we were having A Day to Remember so he speeded them up because we were the only ones on them.

Oh yes, I nearly forgot, the weather. Well, Diary, it rained all day and the wind blew off the sea but we didn't mind, it meant we had the promenade to ourselves apart from some bed-and-breakfasters and some old folk shivering in wheelchairs with plaid blankets. A funny thing was that Julie met her aunt in town, quite by accident (supposedly, although I have my doubts). The aunt apparently didn't know that after all the controversy and publicity surrounding Julie's incarceration, she was out shopping on a wet Friday in Bognor. As it happened, nobody made a run for it – thank God. We were all told the number to ring if we got lost, although most of us don't know how to use the new push button telephones. And, would you believe it Diary, they told us whatever happened not to go to the police because the bizzies mustn't know we were in town – in case they panicked, I suppose. We danced along the promenade in the rain singing We All Live in A Red Brick Loony Bin and other Beatles varieties.

We must have made an odd sight to any curious onlookers because our fashions are motley, our dancing from the sixties mostly, and our songs our own: "We don't need no contraception, we don't need no birth control, all in all you're just another brick in the wall." In fact we were a gang of visiting vagabonds in Bognor Regis, but all with awed faces and big eyes to take in the sight of the outside world and take the magic of the day back behind the walls, to be buried in pillows in dreams and tears. Because this was the heartbreak of this day trip – it couldn't last. You should have heard the silence as we went through the gates.

The journey was noisy, electric and awesome. We were worse than French students shouting across the bus, "There's a horse," "I've seen three horses now," "They've changed the telephone boxes," "Oh look, there's a video shop," "What's a video?" Susan has been here for 12 years and she never has visitors and so she never sees any real, live and kicking children or babies. She killed her own three kids when she killed her mother. So for her it was awesome and terrifying to see children again. She spent all day just staring at them with a silly grin on her face and a strange expression in her great blue eyes. I rather think that she's in for a Big Breakdown after this, but I might be wrong – I suppose they know what they're doing, don't they. Christmas is the worst for poor Susan. It's bad for all of us but for someone like her, so motherly and kind but with no family left, it's awful. She says that there's no point in her ever getting out of here and I suppose she's right really.

Anyway, Diary, I was telling you about today. I have to write it all down now because I don't want to forget any of it. Actually, apart from it being our Day Out, I wasn't impressed with Bognor Regis. I mean, I wouldn't want a holiday there under normal circumstances. The beach was nice though. And I would have loved to have gone to the theatre – they were doing Coppelia there and the Sound of Music at the flicks. We went around the shops. It was like fairyland. I asked for a hair ornament but the shop assistant didn't know what

I was talking about, apparently they're called something else now. I was looking for an artificial flower for my hair but nobody wears them anymore. Before we went, I looked at all the hairstyles in a mag in Pam's hairdressing room, to ask for something really up to date so that I'd look like the King of The Swingers. I ended up with a Rasta look – long plaits, called dreadlocks. Everyone said it looked funny with my miniskirt, but to my horror I found that no one is wearing miniskirts anymore and I was a bit of a freak. They're all wearing long skirts down to the ground in Indian cotton. Jill wore one when she visited me last time but I thought it was just my way out sister wearing an evening dress during the day, but they're all wearing them. And I tried so hard to get my legs tanned in the airing court.

Elsie found a shelter on the promenade and spent the day there knitting dishcloths. Some elderly bed-and-breakfasters joined her but they wouldn't have found out anything, Elsie doesn't talk. Anyway, I sent some postcards and bought a calendar with pictures of Bognor Regis and Sussex to put on my wall. Beryl took some photos of the six of us in our group. We all waved and hugged and pulled faces at the camera. Of course, we're not normally allowed to be photographed because of security. I hope the snaps come out because I'd like one with my mates – and they are real mates – although I don't tell them the things I tell you, Diary. It is ten o'clock and they've just turned off the lights so I am having to write this with my torch on. I don't really want the day to end, and I don't want to forget a single thing.

I'm saving the best news for last though Diary, there are going to be more trips now almost certainly. They won't have the gloss of today because this was the first for many years and so it was really special. But I'm going to buy an album and put in all the snaps and when I'm an old lady and have got used to the outside world again I'll open that album, and try to explain to my grandchildren what wonder really is. It's five years since I saw the world, and that was only from Fairfield Hospital on bus trips and walks and weekends home. I read the paper. I talk to my family and friends and I look at the television news and documentaries but today I saw a dog. That doesn't mean anything to people who own dogs, the same as people who have children couldn't see the stars in Susan's eyes. And the flowers in the airing-court are pretty, but the wild flowers in the woods and hedges we passed on the journey today were handmade by God today, just for us. I'm getting carried away so I'll close now and not look at this diary entry again until I'm living in the world and become stale and apathetic, and then I'll remember. Goodnight Diary – and Thank You Lord.

This account of The Journey was first published, under Christine's pseudonym of Anastasia, in Open Mind 115 (May/June 2002).

Chapter Twenty-Five

LETTERS FROM
BROADMOOR

York,

July 6, 1980

Dear Jill and Chris,

I hope you received my card from Bognor Regis. We had a great day, the sun shone and I spent £8.15p, although we were only allowed to take £8 with us! I bought you a little (very little) present for your birthday but I can't put it in the post so I'll give it to you next time you come. I had some photos taken in a booth in Woolworths but they weren't very good, in fact two were more of my neck than my face. Actually we broke the camera between us and had to wait until a bad-tempered manageress came and mended it – true. We had a good day out anyway, and a sing-song on the way back. One of the girls had bought a book of rugby songs and we had a laugh and found a few golden oldies that we knew.

I had a smashing letter from Anne. It's not often that she writes but she sent me a long letter and said she would like Mum and Dad to write to her, so I sent it, with a previous letter from Julian, to Mum and Dad with my weekly letter to them. Maybe if they were to write to her it would break the ice a little.

It's Sports Day on Wednesday – I hope the weather is warm as we are down the field all day. I'm not entering any of the events this year – I made enough of a fool of myself in it last year! There are money prizes but it's a toss-up whether you value your dignity or your cash account. I'll never be an athlete and don't really aspire to be one, any more than I want to go to the moon! I haven't seen Patsy for a good while, which is unusual as she used to pop in when she had a spare half hour. I don't expect either she or Lyndsay has found time to illustrate my book. The entry has to be in by the beginning of August. It wasn't a very good book anyway, so I've sent it in for the Koestler Award as that's easy money. Gosh, I seem to keep writing about money — that's what Julian writes about — he says he used to collect stamps but now he collects money instead! All for now.

Love to you both and a cuddle for Louise,

Chris xxx

*

York 2,

July 12, 1980

Dear Jill and Chris,

Hallo! How are you all? Well I hope, as I am. There isn't much news. We had Sports Day on Thursday, an all-day affair and good fun. I didn't enter anything — won a coconut at the coconut shy, and some sweets at the Hook a Duck — that was the limit of my sporting activities. I made enough of a fool of myself last year! I spent the day with Bob.

The next big item on the agenda is It's a Knockout on August 25th — I am taking part in the OU Team. Carole and I are the only girls in it, but we have got some good athletes in it. Actually the idea of having an OU Team is to send up the others which I'm not sure is good diplomacy, but still. We are going in fancy dress. Rosemary suggested we went as Course Units but we're not sure how to do it. We'll probably go as St Trinians' girls. Also on the agenda is an OU cricket match. OU people from outside are coming to play the students here. I doubt if Carole and I will get there as it's on a Saturday and the girls don't go to the field on Saturdays, but I think Rosie is trying to arrange it. All I want now is a bed in the OU Dorm, on Essex House. They have their own TV in the dorm!

I got my monthly cash statement this week and found that I had the staggering amount of £31, so I sat down and wrote postal requisitions of £33. I've sent for a cut-out-and-ready- to-sew dress from Cloth-kits. It's a full-length pinafore dress in needle-cord, which will look quite pretty for the dances in the winter. Also a padded waistcoat and matching bag. When they come I'll take a week off work and make them up. We've got a machine on the ward I'll be able to use.

Do you remember when I wrote that letter to The Times a couple of years ago, and received some crackpot letters? Well, one of the writers of said crackpot letters is coming to visit me next Saturday with her husband. The only thing we have in common is that we both read The Times, so it could be a pretty hairy visit. Have you heard anything of Patsy lately? I haven't, which is unusual for her. I guess she's dropped the idea of illustrating my book. School breaks up this week, here anyway, so maybe she'll come in the holidays. I've got a smashing torch for Dad's birthday. We can't forget it this year as it's on Queen Mother's 80th birthday and we keep hearing about that on TV. I can't post your pressie so will give it you when you next come. Have a Happy Birthday.

Love to you both, and a cuddle for Louise. Chrissy

*

York 2,

July 25, 1980

Dear Jill and Chris,

I hope you received the lighter okay and realized it was from me. The only way I could get it was through Mum and Dad. Anyway I hope you had a lovely birthday. Did you know Dad is retiring on August 15th? If I know Dad he'll find plenty to do around the house and in the garden to keep out of Mum's way. Did you know they've dug up the hedge in the front garden? It seems an awful shame to me as it has probably been there about a hundred years. They're putting a fence in its place.

Patsy came on Sunday afternoon for a short visit. She says she hasn't time to illustrate my book for the competition, which is a bit disappointing. However I've entered it in the Koestler Award so I'll maybe get a fiver for it. I have got a week's holiday from work and am doing some dressmaking. Yesterday I made myself a quilted waistcoat in sage green, and today am going to make a bag to go with it. The next thing on the agenda is a floor-length pinafore dress in blue corduroy. If I can get that done this week I'll wear it to the dance on Friday evening. It's all from Cloth-kits. The trouble is our antiquated sewing machine is so temperamental that it's quicker, and easier to sew by hand, so that's what I've been doing – and my stitching leaves a lot to be desired! (smile). Did I tell you I've got my name down to play the saxophone in a band which is going to start up here. Should be worth a giggle anyway!

By the way, I don't know if Mum and Dad told you but Le Couteur said the other day he's got my name down for a semi-secure unit somewhere in the south of England. There is to be a central one at the Maudsley and eight satellite ones, all of which, he says, are planned to open in August. He'll have to get a move on, or perhaps the idea is that we go and build it ourselves. After all, they say Broadmoor was built by prisoners. Seriously though, I don't expect anything to happen for about six months. If I tell myself that I won't be disappointed. Did you know Mum and Dad have gone up to Southport for Anne's wedding? They are giving her a table cloth which Mum has embroidered – no comment. Well, I'll close now. Hoping you are all well.

Love to you both and a cuddle for Louise.

Chris. Xxx

*

York 2,

August 1980

Dear Jill and Chris,

Hi! I haven't heard from you for a while. Have you been on holiday? Where have you been? Do write and tell me how you all are. Well, there's very little news from this end. I've got a new boyfriend, as the old one got discharged. This one's gay but he is really gentle and kind. I'm seeing him tomorrow at It's a Knockout. I'm not entering it this year. I'm up to my ears in revision. I expect you are too, aren't you? I've changed my course registration for next year. I'm doing Twentieth Century Poetry instead of drama. It's still a third level but I think I'll find it easier than drama. Mum and Dad came on Monday. They're okay. I'm auditioning for the Broad-Humourists again in

September – it looks as if I'll be here for another play season. Well, that's about it for now. Do write soon.

Love to you both and a cuddle for Louise.

*

York 2,

August 17, 1980

Dear Jill,

Hi! There isn't much news as I'm spending all my free time studying at the minute, revising for the mock in September and of course the exam in October. I'm finding D101 a real hard grind. The patients won the cricket match yesterday – it was OU students against tutors, with the students in clerical gear and tutors in their academic gowns, which were soon shed as the sun blazed down. Carole and I weren't allowed to go down as it was Saturday, despite Rosemary pleading. She was the only woman on the field. We watched from the bottom of our airing court but couldn't really see who was who.

Mum and Dad are coming on Monday morning – the first morning of Dad's retirement. I wrote and congratulated Dad and Mum wrote back saying, "Dad isn't the only one retiring. What happened to Women's Lib?" (smile) I had a postcard from Amanda in Cornwall. She said the first week was sunny and Darren was as brown as a berry but they were coming back early as the second week wasn't so good. She wrote, "I hope you will write soon with a little surprise for me." Cheeky little madam! So I wrote her a poem about a fairy who was a punk-rocker. She'll have to be content with that until her birthday as I'm broke!

All for now, love to Chris and a cuddle for Louise.

Cheers, Chrissy xx

It's a play-rehearsal tonight. I haven't been on yet but my big chance is coming December 15th when Carole can't go so I am taking her place. I had a letter from Haydn Gott. He said the tribunal will probably be in about four weeks. He hasn't had much luck as far as the hostel goes. I am going to write and ask him to make enquiries about the semi-secure unit at Southampton as I have heard from Rosemary that it is very good. She visited an ex-Broadmoor OU student there and thinks it would be just right for me. I think I'll probably write to Dr Le Couteur about it too, see what he thinks about me going there. Also Haydn Gott said that Dr Fry (the one from Guy's who came to St Francis) is coming to see me soon, and after he has received Dr Fry's report about me then Haydn Gott himself will be coming to see me.

*

Dear Jill,

I have had the papers concerning the tribunal, which I am posting on to Kathryn Dunne at Mind. The tribunal is to be held on 30th October at 10.30am – sooner than I expected and only a week after my exam. The papers deal mainly with the dates on which my section has been renewed since 1971, and also my moves between hospitals and the dates on which I have had tribunals and their results. It also says: form of mental disorder, mental illness, statement of reasons why the responsible authorities are not themselves willing to discharge the patient, she is not yet well enough to leave hospital. These of course are the stock replies. I have asked Kathryn Dunne to look into the hostel at East Grinstead. I feel sure that if I can get a place arranged there I will stand a much better chance of winning the tribunal. The social worker here refuses to have anything to do with it. Can you also look into it for me? Perhaps you could phone Kathryn and sort things out with her. I have mentioned it to her in several letters but she has not written back.

Well, that's got the business out of the way, let's see

what news there is. None really. I went to a dance on Friday which went on until 10pm with a group, and a meal – my favourite, pork chops. It was a good dance but the company I was with was pretty ghastly – a boy who was rather young and short of conversation, and who couldn't dance. I've got a new boyfriend in the offing – Barry – I've got a date with him for a social on Monday. He's about my age, blonde, very good looking and rather shy. It's taken him ages to get around to asking me out, although we've been friends for some time.

Patsy is coming to see me on Tuesday with her friend Rosemary, and also presumably Emily. Emily starts full-time school soon so Patsy has given up work to spend the last few months at home with her before she starts school. How's the studying going? I've got my mock tomorrow week, for which I am suitably terrified, and my exam on Oct. 22nd. I don't know what I'll do if I win the tribunal and have nowhere to go!! All for now.

*

York 2,
October 4, 1980

Dear Jill,

Just a note to tell you that I still haven't seen the nurses from the unit, so nothing has been decided yet about if, or when, I'll be leaving. It doesn't look as if I'll be going on 24th October as I had hoped. Still it might be before Christmas. I'll let you know as soon as anything is settled. Well, what other news is there? – Oh, yes, I had my first saxophone lesson yesterday. That was funny. What a racket, about 30 of us learning new instruments all together in one large room. It was terrific fun. I've got a lead part in the next Broad-Humourist production, I certainly don't expect to see the season through.

Have you heard anything from Patsy? I'm wondering if I've said anything wrong as she has stopped visiting me and it's sometime since I've had a letter from her. I hope she's okay. How's the study going? I've given up and resigned myself to being a failed OU student. Did I tell you what I did in the mock? (Don't tell Mum and Dad!) I couldn't answer the questions so I sat and wrote a poem about a wombat and handed that in. Rosemary wasn't amused. I thought it was quite a good poem actually! All for now. Write soon.

Love to you both and a cuddle for Louise. (I'm dying to see her in her school uniform) Chris xxxx

*

York 2,

October 21, 1980

Dear Jill and Chris,

I suppose you have heard from Haydn Gott, or from Dad, that we have decided to postpone the tribunal for about six weeks so that he can arrange about me going to a hostel. I haven't heard yet when it is to be held. If you hear will you let me know please. My exam is tomorrow – I've given up studying now – what I don't know now I guess I'll never know. It's too late to worry now, Dr Levin has promised me that as soon as I've done my exam he'll take me off one of my tablets! Hooray!

I'm dying for a smoke. It's 11.30a.m and I've only had two cigarettes since I got up. That's all any of us have had, the staff say they're too busy to give us a light. It's no wonder people get upset. Also we haven't been in the airing court for a month – I'm longing for some fresh air and exercise. Sorry to grouse, but can you see now why I'm anxious to leave? We got over £112 at our concert last night, not bad for a couple of hours busking eh? I think Patsy and Rosemary are coming to it on Wednesday. I think Lee is coming next weekend. She's studying hard at the moment – aren't we all?!

Think I'll make a cup of tea. Hang on!

After Lunch. Well, we got a smoke and had roast beef for lunch. I'm up to 8 stone 6lbs now. I've never been so fat in my life. There are big changes coming on the female wing on November 10th. There is a rumour that some of the girls are going to get parole – hope I do. I might get my typewriter. I go to typing classes but am only at the elementary stage. By the way, one of the girls had a tribunal this week and won it. She's leaving this week. She's a Section 26 like me. She's the second girl in a short time to win a tribunal – so maybe I'll be the third! One of the girls gave me a long yellow dress this morning to wear to the dances. There's a dance this week, on Friday. Tomorrow night I'm going to a social with Bob – he's my new fella – I met him at Russian class. It's half-term this week, I'll have to go to OT, haven't been for about a month. Well, best of luck with your exam Jill, and please let me know if you hear anything about the tribunal.

Love to Louise,

Chris xxxx

*

York 2

Dear Jill and Chris,

Thanks for your letter, and for phoning Anne. I haven't heard from any of them for ages, not since their holiday in Cornwall. I guess Mum and Dad told you I'm on my way out of here, to the unit you saw on TV. It's not cut and dried yet so I'm trying not to bank on it too much in case it doesn't work out. It's opening on October 21st, a week after my exam, but I don't know when I'll go. It all depends on the nurses who are coming to see me next week. The nice thing is that I might be going with another girl from here – I hope so as it will be really nice to go with a friend.

Last night I went to the dance, wearing the pink dress that Sue gave me and it was much admired. I bet Louise will look really cute in her school uniform. It's good news to hear she's going to school in January. I failed my mock with flying colours so hope I do better on the day. I'm listening to The Cruel Sea on the radio at the minute – it's a really good yarn. Well, that's it for now. Good luck on your exam.

Love to you both and a cuddle for Louise. Chris xxxx

*

York 2,

12 October 1980

Dear Jill and Chris,

Thanks for your welcome letter. I'm glad your eyes are all right now. I saw the nurses from the unit and it sounds as if they're not going to take me until the spring at the earliest and I'm not sure if they'll take me at all. Actually it sounded a bit grim – 15 patients in a locked block with OT, meals, socials etc all on the ward – shades of Woodingdean. I really want to get out of Broadmoor but I want a good start this time and I'm not sure if this will be for me. I've no choice really though, there's nowhere else for me to go. I think Mum and Dad would prefer to see me end my days in Broadmoor where they've no worries about me except for the three-weekly duty visit. They certainly gave me that impression on the visit yesterday. I don't really blame them but it's a bit hurtful. I thought they'd be glad to see me on the move. There is also a lot of jealousy among patients who have been here for a long time and think I shouldn't get a second chance. I sat down in the dining-room the other day and someone had spat on the tablecloth in my place – you can't get more obvious than that.

Sorry if this is a bit of a grumbly letter, I'm worrying a bit about my exam on Wednesday. I fully expect to fail. In fact I can't even be bothered revising any more – I've lost interest. Then, as soon as I've got this one out of the way, I've got to start going over my music for a Music Theory exam on November 8th. I couldn't get on with the saxophone so am going to start on a violin next Friday, on the suggestion of the music director who couldn't bear my decidedly un-musical attempt at playing the sax. I've got a lead part in the play this year – I'm playing a middle-aged hearty, country type woman who eventually marries the bishop! Should be funny. Well, that's about it for now. Tell Sue I'm delighted at her news and will send the blue dress out to her on November 5th.

Love to you both and a cuddle for Louise.

Chrissy xxx

Sorry this letter is a bit miserable.

*

York 2,
14 October

Dear Jill and Chris,

Have you heard the news? I won £20 for the Koestler Award – £15 for a short story (first in the literary competition), £5 for 'The Swevern Swan' and a Highly Commended for a poem – no money for that. In the commentary it said, "Miss Delahunty certainly knows how to write and I hope she continues to write wherever she is." So I'm well pleased at that. I got an average C for my mock exam, F for religion (again!) and C for an extended essay. Out of all Rosemary's 16 students this year Alain is 14th and I'm 15th. Beat that!

Patsy and Rosemary are coming to the choral concert on October 24. I've asked permission to see them in the interval. We're getting average audiences of 150 per night and average collections of £70 so that can't be bad. And we're getting better at singing too! Mum and Dad came yesterday. They are coming to the tribunal, at least Dad is but Mum might have to stay at home if the builders are there. They brought me some lovely roses but unfortunately they are dying in the heat. I've got a new boyfriend – Bob. Barry is still in tow too, also Paul. Might write on Tuesday after I've seen the solicitor. By the way, how did you get on with him? Write and let me know.

Love to Chris and a cuddle for Louise. Chris x

*

York 2,
2 November 1980

Dear Jill and Chris,

I look forward to seeing you and Sue and Louise on November 5. However will you ring Mum and check whether Mike (Aunty Margaret's Mike) and Sue (his fiancée) are coming at the same time. I am expecting them either this afternoon (Sun) or else some time on Weds. They are spending a couple of days with Mum and Dad. It would be awful if they wouldn't let you in here because Mike and Sue were here. So if you phone home you can fix it with them to come at a different time. Thanks. Did you hear that I won £30 on the Koestler Award this year? Not bad eh? I have now entered a competition in The Times and am hoping to win three bottles of port and a stilton cheese. No harm in hoping is there? I had to pretend I was the fairy on the Christmas Tree and write a letter to Santa saying what I wanted for Christmas. It's a bit of fun anyway. I saw Le Couteur this week and he said he hopes to get me into the unit at Beckenham in the next month or two. That's rather a vague way of talking so I'm not banking on anything. I'm still having violin lessons. Next Saturday afternoon I've got to sit the Grade 4 exam in Music Theory. I'm not worried though, I think I ought to pass. I've made a little hair ornament for Louise which I will give you on Wednesday, also the dress for Sue. Well, that's about it for now.

Love to you both and a cuddle for Louise. From Chris

xxxx

*

Dear Jill and Chris,

Many thanks for your visit and for all the goodies you brought with you. Please thank Sue for the clothes she brought, some of which I am keeping and some of which I have distributed. I would write and thank her properly, but I don't know her address. I have made up the giraffe from the kit you brought. It's not all that brilliant but I think Louise will like it – I presume you intended it for her, did you? You didn't say. Also thanks for the undies – how did you know my undies-drawer was in a state of emergency?! I will discuss the Dusty Bin idea with the OT boss, but I think it will work out very expensive in fur-fabric if it is to be a useful size. I think the best idea would be to get a plastic bucket, with a lid, and cover that – but I can't do that as I haven't got a bucket. Anyway, I'll see what I can do, but I might have to ask you to give me a bit of cash towards paying for it. I have withdrawn from the band – I've had to concede the fact that I'm tone deaf (Chris and I had a chat about that one) and that I'll never be a violinist. I'll leave the music-making to the professionals. Well, that's it for now – I'll keep the giraffe until you come, to save postage.

Much love,

Chris xx

*

York 2,

23 November 1980

Dear Jill,

Thanks for your letter. I had a lovely birthday, with lots of cards and presents, but I think the nicest part was when you brought Louise and she was so cute. I've finished making the giraffe for Louise – it's a bit lumpy because it's stuffed with you-know-whats, but I think she'll like it. I have been talking to the OT staff about the toy-box Dusty Bin. They suggested that I measure around a plastic bucket and make it so that you can buy the bucket and lid yourself and fit it on yourself. It wouldn't be strong enough to just put cardboard inside it – so that seems to be the best solution. There is no way I can get a bucket here. Also, I hope you don't mind me saying it, but do you think you could pay for it, like you did the Snoopy last year? I think it will be about £3-£4 as there is a lot of material in it. I don't want to be mean but the Koestler Award didn't pay up – I never got my prize money and so am still living on a shoestring with not much money for Christmas presents. Okay? I'm sure you'll understand. I understand Auntie Hannah is coming to see me on Tuesday, and you on Wednesday. Carole (my friend on the parole ward) made me a birthday cake, so I've saved some of it for her. I'm on my Sunday Marathon Letter Writing Sprint – writing thank you letters to all the aunts for their pressies and cards. I was very pleased to get cards from Anne and the children – it's the first time for years Anne has remembered my birthday. She said Darren is keeping well and his hair is growing again. In my photos of him he is a skinhead! Well, that's it for now.

Love to you both and a cuddle for Louise.

From Chrissy xxxx

Chapter Twenty-Six

BACK IN THE OUTSIDE WORLD

York 2,

4 February 1981

Dear Jill and Chris,

A quick note to tell you that I am being transferred to the Bethlem on February 17. Looking forward to seeing you soon – either here or there – whichever suits you best. I'm over the moon – I thought it would never happen! Bye for now. Chrissy

Christine

"Tread Softly For You Tread Upon My Dreams" – 1974 to 1984

If you are going to have a dream you may as well make it a Big 'Un. I had been in hospital for a very long time. The hospital system is a sort of bionic escalator. You step onto it blindly but trustingly and it rushes on, sometimes so fast it is frightening, sometimes so slow it is agonising, and then every few years it makes an enormous jerk and tosses you off into yet another institution. The only way to get off is to take your courage in both hands and blindly leap off but whether you will fall on your feet or your head, is partly a matter of luck and partly of careful planning.

It was taken for granted by my family and by my doctors that I would spend the remainder of my life 'within those walls.' This was before the days of Care in the Community. "You will stay on locked wards until you are 40. When you are 40 you will burn out and then you will go onto an open ward and stay there."

Yeah. Right. The doctor didn't explain what burn out meant but it didn't sound much fun. So everyone had given up on me. I had a choice. I could accept what they said, and spend the remainder of my life staring at daytime TV, with the highlight of every day being the afternoon showing of The Waltons and the arrival of the tea-trolley. Not an option. I could take the option chosen by so many of my friends in this circumstance and top myself. Not an option. Or I could make a life for myself, build myself a future, however ridiculous everyone else thought me. So what would I really like, if I could choose my future? I would choose to be a librarian. Well, I like people first, and books second, so it's the obvious career isn't it? I've got the syllabuses of all the library colleges in the country and sometimes I take them out and look at them. So, how did one become a librarian? By going to library college. And how did one get to Library College? By studying, collecting a lorry load of academic certificates, by being Top of The Class. So I made enquiries, and wrote off to the National Extension College, to find out about a correspondence course in Advanced Level English Literature.

Where was I? Oh yes, that awful hospital in Sussex. Well I borrowed £20 from the hospital chaplain, (which I paid back at the rate of £2 a month incidentally) and started an A Level English Literature course with the National Extension College. There's only one way to study if you're in a dormitory of chronically sick schizophrenics and psychotics and that is to discipline yourself to do at least two hours work a day, no matter what. My way is to keep a chart and write down every day how much time I have spent studying, then I get a great feeling of smugness when it gets to Sunday and I can give myself a day off. Everyone thought I was being ridiculous. But I had a dream. And I would strive to follow that dream through impossible circumstances in the coming years. I studied hard in the coming months, sent work off to the college tutor and always got A grades or A*. It was a slow struggle but the time I spent struggling with Chaucer, Milton, Keats, and Shakespeare were an escape. While I had my head in my books I had a brief respite from the misery of my circumstances. A regular visitor to the ward was Father Mac, the local Catholic priest. He knew that I was studying and one day he asked me if one of his parishioners, who was an English Teacher at a local school, could come in to the ward to help me with my studies. Of course I said yes and one evening Terry Jones turned up. He became a regular visitor, coming three or four times a week and encouraging me with my work.

Eventually the time came for me to sit my A Level exam in English Literature. It was arranged that Terry would take me to the Catholic school in Crawley where he was head of the English department, to sit my exam along with his students. It hadn't occurred to anybody that I had not been off the ward for months, even out in the garden, or to the hospital canteen. And when I did, on this great day, I was terrified. I sat in the examination hall with the 6th Form Students. I started writing. I answered the first question – it was Chaucer. I loved Chaucer. I started on the second question. And then I freaked. I tore up the essays I had just written, put up my hand and asked the invigilator, "May I leave the room please?" I was taken out. They fetched Terry who took me to his office while another teacher sellotaped together my papers. Terry sat with me in his office and said, "Just write. Keep on writing." He knew that I knew my subject – I had spent enough time working at it. And so I just kept writing, although my head was all over the place and I really didn't know what I was writing.

Terry took me back to the hospital and soon Father Mac turned up to find out how the exam had gone. I told him, "I'm not going back tomorrow to sit the second paper. I can't do it." Father Mac was furious. "You ARE going back tomorrow. You're NOT giving up now." And so it was decided that I would go back the next day and I would be given an extra large dose of Largactil. I was already on enough Largactil to knock a buffalo senseless. So I went back for the second Paper. And the third. Terry took me to a small office, gave me the paper, said, "Just keep writing", locked the door and went away. I was so drugged up that I didn't know what I was writing about. But I did what Terry had said. I just kept writing. I was sent back to Broadmoor on 23rd December and the exam results came out in January. I had passed with an E Grade – just scraped through. I knew that with the work I had done I should have had at least a B or even an A so I was disappointed, but not surprised. At least I had given it a go. Before I had gone back to Broadmoor, Terry had persuaded me to sign up with the Open University, and I had been offered a place, to start a Foundation Course in Arts, in the February.

The media say all sorts of awful things about Broadmoor, and some of them are true, but not many people know that the authorities there spend a lot of planning and money on education and career training. I used to attend some classes simply to get out of the boredom of occupational therapy. British Constitution classes were interesting but a little puzzling – there are all these great tomes by Walter Bagshot and his mates, written about the Great British Constitution, and yet there is no such thing as a written British Constitution. I gave up Russian classes after a while – they clashed with choir practice and I found singing a more congenial pastime than doing battle with the Cyrillic alphabet. To my amazement I passed exams in Music Theory. Well, those pretty pieces of paper pleased my parents and anyway I enjoyed Music Theory lessons. Typing classes were quite fun too, although my fingers have this habit of turning into a bunch of bananas when confronted with a typewriter. But these were only pastimes. The thing I think mattered was my Open University Course. I was doing an Arts Foundation Course. There were a number of male patients in the hospital attempting OU courses but I was the first woman, waving the flag for feminism. Well, I had to pass, didn't I? My next project with the OU was a Social Science Foundation Course. I now have a pretty certificate saying I have a Full Credit Pass in Making Sense of Society. I think that's very funny – I bet Mrs Thatcher hasn't got one of those! In Broadmoor there's no problem in financing one's studies as the patient is only expected to pay 10 per cent and the Hospital Education Fund pays the rest, and also buys the books.

The regime at Broadmoor were very keen on education, and there had been an Open University group there for some time – but only for the men. The women were excluded. But as I had already been offered a place it was arranged that I could do it with our tutor counsellor, Rosemary and a young lad called Alan who was doing the same course. Of course everyone thought I was being ridiculous with all this studying lark. "What do you want to do to do that for?" I got a sort of pat on the head attitude from some of the staff. "Why can't she be like the others, and spend her time staring at the TV and knitting dishcloths?" But I had a dream. I wanted to go to Library college.

I passed my course that year in Arts, and also the following year in a Foundation Course in Social Studies. But I wasn't satisfied with that. It wasn't enough. I figured that to be considered for a place at college my CV would have to be twice as good as any normal student. So I joined everything – academically as well as socially – as I realised that both would be equally important in building my future. I joined a class in Russian Language. I passed Grade 5 in Music Theory. I studied British Constitution and I took classes in typing. Whatever was thrown at me, I tackled. I grasped the nettle with both hands, joining the hospital Drama Group and played the part of the White Witch in Bell, Book and Candle. I joined the Hospital Band and made a disastrous attempt at playing tenor sax. I joined the women's bowls team – another disaster. I just signed up for everything. After all, it would all look good on my CV, wouldn't it?!

By this time I had looked into the matter of colleges of librarianship and found there were only four in the country that did the course that I wanted. The top one was Aberystwyth. It seemed that a student who passed at the College of Librarianship of Wales at Aberystwyth could get a job anywhere in the world. It was the Oxbridge of the Library World. Right. I would go to Aberystwyth. Just one small problem – I had to get out of hospital. By this time Care in The Community were the buzz words. But would it include those of us in locked wards, in Special Hospitals? Would we ever get out into the world? Oh yes. I would. I had a dream, didn't I? To everyone else it was a joke. To me it was an escape. Escape from the horrific situation I was in. A future. I wasn't going to burn out and spend the rest of my life sitting listening to my voices and p--- ing my knickers. I was a fighter. A survivor.

And so, after another two years in Broadmoor, I was transferred to a secure unit at the Bethlem Royal Hospital in Kent – the original Bedlam where I would be from 1981 to 1982. I had to apply for funding for my studies when I moved there. How I hated filling in those forms for The Paupers Fund (euphemistically called Financial Assistance) and having to send official proof to the OU that the Hospital Philanthropists benevolently give me £5.50p a week, and the state won't give me a penny. That sounds like a bit of a chip on the shoulder doesn't it? Perhaps it is. I just hate wearing jumble sale clothes! Where was I? Oh yes, the problem of paying for my studies. What a boring subject. I can usually find somebody to tap for my bus fare when I attend the OU tutorials in Croydon. Yes, that's progress, that's real progress, to go out to the tutorials.

I don't want sympathy. Sympathy, for the disabled, is often a more destructive thing than their illness. Did I say illness? I'm not sure I qualify as an ill person, despite the last 14 years of hospitalisation I have had. You see, my illness is not the kind that draws state handouts and Blue Peter Christmas parcels. I am a patient in a psychiatric hospital – something that I'm expected to be ashamed of. They always say, in hospitals of this nature, that you can't beat the system. But I am beating it, and beating my disability (what a horrible word!) by studying.

It was a small unit, but I found the staff there very hostile to my studying with the Open University. By this time I was on a Third Level course in Twentieth Century Poetry. Staff would put every obstacle in the way of my studying, so that very often I was only able to begin my day's studying at 10pm.

But there was one person at the Bethlem who encouraged and supported me in my studying, an Icelandic Psychologist called Gisli. When he offered to take me out to a monthly tutorial with local students on the same course as me, the nurses stopped him taking me – implying that Gisli and I were having an affair. They couldn't grasp that what we shared was a love of learning, of studying. It was never anything more than that. If Gisli's superiors had listened to those women, his career would have been destroyed. Fortunately they didn't and Gisli is now Professor of Psychology at the Institute of Psychiatry. He was a good friend to me, the only person who believed in my dream. And so I took, and passed, my course in Twentieth Century Poetry.

After a year in the secure unit I was transferred to an open ward, for rehabilitation, with a view to leaving hospital, At last. I was going to have A Life. All the years of struggle were coming to fruition. I would apply to Aberystwyth. I was terrified. During the time I was in the secure unit I had been taken out shopping, learning to cross the roads, to handle money. Decimal currency had come out while I was in hospital. I had to learn how to handle travel on buses and trains, how to use a bank, so many things. The first time I was taken to a shop I was so excited – and confused – I went around the shop picking up things and putting them in my shopping-bag, totally forgetting that they had to be paid for!

And so the time came to send in my application forms for the Colleges of Librarianship. I filled in the long list of academic studies and of social activities. I knew that for my application to be considered my CV had to be twice as good as that of any other student. I had an offer of an interview at a college in North London. But that wasn't what I wanted. I was waiting for the big one, for Aberystwyth. I was asleep one morning when a member of staff came in my room and told me, "Christine, there's a big fat brown envelope in the post for you – and it's postmarked Aberystwyth." I struggled to work out what it was about. I had been turned down for my place at the College of Librarianship of Wales. But I had been offered an unconditional place at the University at Aberystwyth. No interview. No more studying. Unconditional. Mine. Mine on a plate. And I hadn't even applied for a place at University. My first thought was that I would phone my parents. They would be so proud of me. I had finally turned bad into good. All those years, of studying, of struggling under impossible conditions and I had finally achieved something good. For once my Dad wouldn't have to pretend that I wasn't his daughter. He would be so proud of me. I went to the ward telephone and phoned my parents number. "Dad, I've been offered an unconditional place at the University of Aberystwyth." A stunned silence. And then an angry voice, "Who do you think is going to pay for that?" "I'll get a grant, Dad. I'll get a job." I can still remember the pain of that moment. I left the hospital that summer, after nearly 14 years of incarceration. My parents wouldn't offer me a home, so I spent that summer in Southport with my auntie and my cousin Philip. They were very patient and kind. I had a lot to learn. The outside world was a very strange and bewildering place to me. I had done all those years of study. But I had a great deal to learn about ordinary life.

I accepted my place at the University of Aberystwyth, believing that if I passed my degree there I would surely be able to move to the College of Librarianship and do a shorter course. I would be a librarian. After all, I had a dream, didn't I? I signed on, to take my Part 1 in Philosophy, Education and Classical Studies, needing to pass three subjects in year one to be accepted to move to BA level. I studied and passed my first year. But the studying was the easy bit. The bit that I was struggling with was coping with normal life and normal people. When you spend years in an institution, you don't mature. Every decision of every day is made for you. Somebody else decides what you eat, when you bath, every smallest decision of every day, you become a middle-aged child.

Another dream that I had had for so long was of a real Christmas – a family Christmas. For so long I had thought about my first Christmas in the outside world. With my family. It would be so wonderful. The reality was that my parents went to Spain for a month that Christmas and I stayed in my digs on the campus because I had nowhere else to go. That really hurt. I struggled on, in a world where I was confused, bewildered and lost.

It was pure magic to be a student at the University at Aberystwyth – waking up every day to hear the sea outside the window. The only expectation of us was that we studied – and I loved that. The countryside was unspoiled and as the seasons changed so did the wonders around us. Students nowadays complain and demand money and loans. They think they should not have to contribute to the cost of their education. I got into debt and went through the traditional struggle of students – do I spend my money on books or food? But I wouldn't have minded if I had had to spend the rest of my life paying for the wonder of being a university student – it was such a privilege.

After 18 months I became ill again and had to leave university, and exchanged it for a dreary flat on a council estate in Kent. The bubble had burst. I was sick, isolated, and desperate. But my memory of the privilege and wonder of studying at the University College of Wales, Aberystwyth, stays with me. A little verse I wrote, taking the mickcy out of the Town and Gown in the little Welsh town where life stood still, was published in the local newspaper in Aberystwyth. I recall the 10-yearly vote of the local people to decide whether to continue the tradition of Dry Sabbath – to close all the local public houses on Sundays. While I was there they voted to keep up the tradition, but summer holiday-makers did not exactly find this welcoming, while all the local drinkers had their secret boltholes and clubs where they could have a peaceful Sunday drink with their mates, without being bothered with the irritation of tourists. I wonder if the tradition continues?

A look at Aberystwyth happenings

Bamber's is closing

Storms will smash up the Prom,

The students are back

And the visitors gone,

The town settles back to its heritage state,

'Mother, wake me at Christmas, Make sure I'm not late!

O, what shall we do with Park Avenue?

Should we put up grand stores like in Brighton?

C&A would replace an empty car-space,

But the sheep at the mart would be frightened!

Should we build a Marina for the yachts of fine men?

Their own 'Harbour Village' for summer weekends?

It's a lovely idea It would look good on the brochures,

but the wealth that they'd bring would be simply

atrocious!

Should our Festival last for three months, or for less?

Would Poco survive?

What about all the MESS?

Super Ted was a hit.

And those Bretons could jig.

It was good 'til it finished, so long as it did!

Yes, I was there when they launched the new lifeboat,

Pride filled my heart.

I'd a lump in my throat.

There's no argument here.

Tiny boat, mighty men,

I pray that our God will look after them.

But the centre of Summer, the high spot of all,

Was the day they put a cash-point in Lloyds Bank wall,

The choir sang proudly the Welsh anthems true.

And a bank-clerk made ceremony, '£5 for you'

The Police held the traffic.

Tourists stood still in awe.

Except one little boy, who said: 'What's it all for?'

So Summer has passed, to the sound of the till,

Now it's denim and books, for they're back 'Up the Hill'

We love 'em and leave 'em, and go our own way,

Watching coming and going by the cranky Railway.

First published in 'Cambrian News' 14.10.83 under the pseudonym Stasia.

Within Sound of the Sea

I have a desire to walk on the shore,

To visit the caged beast whose murmurings kept me awake.

That I have the power to do this all day long, if I wish to.

I know what thoughts will arise,

What questions.

They have done so before,

Unanswered.

It is in the freedom

To go or not to exist!

To balance all the exhilaration

Of brisk moments upon the sand

With the knowledgeable hours that my books give me.

Between their pages the beast sleeps and never looks out

Through the print bars.

Have I been wise in the past

Letting my nostrils plan my day?

That salt scrubbing left me unclean.

Am I wise now?

With all this pain in the air,

To keep in my room, reading perhaps

Depression

Alone I stand on the ridge top, beaten naked by the wearing winds of depression. Sunlight and Moonlight reach out to me but I am clothed in darkness, engulfed by a soupy blackness. The essence of a laughing, carefree person watches me from a distance but sees only a distortion of myself. Relief comes only in sleep from that Being whose will is our peace?

Driftwood

Safe within the time-hallowed folds of this oaken tree I lie

Protected forever from an alien world.

The tree floats gently down-river,

Down to the sea, which will engulf us.

Gently, gently my armour of driftwood sinks,

Deep, deep into the sea.

I do not struggle – why should I?

I am enfolded in peace and beauty,

Rescued at last from the infliction of life – What a beautiful end.

They couldn't kill us - 1983

They couldn't kill us. They're not allowed to any more. Nor could they kill our joy – quite. Some of us had killed, all in some way had destroyed. But they couldn't kill us.

We were the crazy ones – the ones who saw life lop-sidedly through a splintered/crackled/clouded/shattered prism – which makes it not worse, not better – just beyond the focus of most other folk. So they put us away – Clink-key, Hang. Padlock. They Can't Forgive but Can Forgets. But they couldn't take away Joy. It was harder to find. You had to pestle and sift the misery, here the white-light-in-the-eye degradation and loneliness – and there, a nugget, a so-precious nugget of Joy would pop up – and soon be stolen. But now there's the joy of forgetting it all – but some of it couldn't be forgotten and some of it shouldn't be – because it's all about people and suffering, and worse of all suffering people. I could put a joke or two in here. But jokes about madness are ignorance – half embarrassment, half lack of understanding. The bitterest joke of all was that few of us were crazy – damned few before they locked us away. Only we'd broken the rules – the rules of the sand-blind society. You can't do that it spoils the game for everyone else. Even if the rules don't make any sense – to you, through your crackled prism. One Christmas I'll never forget. Locked up I was. But I knew it was Christmas Day. "No," they said – sneer, jeer. "It's not Christmas Day – it's Tuesday." "I want to see the Father when he comes," I said, "to receive Communion." He used to come and pray with us on Sundays and Days of Observation you see. "No," they said, "It's Tuesday – he only comes on Sundays." Freezer-cold laughs, sneers, crash door, clink key, bolt. I knew though, – somehow. I knew – perhaps someone had told me. I looked at my breakfast plate on the floor – that clinched it. We only had bacon and eggs on Christmas Day. And there it sat – bacon and eggs. All congealed. Telling me I'd lost another battle. So I threw it – what a WASTE. Got to wait another year for a breakfast like that. But they should have understood. I didn't mind staying locked up for Christmas Day – I really didn't, I was used to that. Only I wanted to pray with the others. They came for my plates. Not angry – for once. Threw a little parcel across the room at me. I threw it back hard against the slammed door. It was my League of Friends of the Hospital Christmas Gift. It turned out – much later – to be a wash-bag. Nice. Didn't want it.

Only there was one nurse who understood – who knew why I was wild that day – an old(ish) German nurse – her daughter was a Catholic. She would have got into trouble for it – probably did – but she caught Father O'Berne when he'd finished with the others, and brought him round the wing – where I lived. And an old(ish) nurse called Dolly sat outside. There was just me on my canvas mattress, with my canvas gown – and he brought a little chair and set it up in my room – and we held Christmas. Not mince-pies-and-crackers Christmas. But Real Christmas. After that I was calm as a cucumber – a very warm-inside cucumber. They let me get up for an hour or two with the others. And years later that old(ish) nurse, Dolly, said to me, "I think about you every Christmas, Christine." And I do too.

There are other things I remember – silly things. Knicker inspection. Before we went to 'social events.' There we'd all be – lined up, best skirts and blouses on, hair combed, clutching bags with precious fags in – and they'd say: "Have you all got your knickers on?" And check. They were perverted – those nurses. Honestly, how many people do you know who play Bingo without their knickers on? No socks either. Or stockings. When you went to the male side. Just tights. Perverted they were. Those nurses. But it isn't funny – degradation isn't funny. It's cruel. Only the person who inflicts it cannot see the cruelty in her own eyes.

She's lucky. What's lucky? We used to talk about that. "You're lucky" people said – the ones who always thought their bit of grass was yellow and everyone else's was emeralds. You have to pay for them on a credit card account for a long time before you get them – and then, all the credit's yours again – it's good. Like passing exams. I passed mine – in there. Just because so many people thought I couldn't and shouldn't take them. I had to prove them wrong. Had to pass. I went a bit crazy after the first one – but that wasn't because of the exam. I'd made a bargain with the doctor. "Can I come off one of my drugs after I've sat tomorrow's exam? As a reward for sitting it?" "Okay." he said. So I did. Went a bit crazy. Bad idea. They gave it me back. Reprimanded me for being too ambitious. Wonder why they never reprimand doctors? Perhaps they do – behind closed doors. So now I'm out. Here. At Aberystwyth. Came a long road. Still seeing things through a crackled prism a bit – only now it's called experience – and experiences like that do make you see things differently from the 'normals'. You can't help it. Pity them sometimes, for their jaded eyes. Because if you've always seen dog-roses, and honeysuckle, and foxgloves – then you don't see them any more – I hope I never stop seeing them. Rain, to them, is just wet water and cold – but I can still hold up my face to it and get soaked and saturated with Joy. Sheer joy. They think I'm crazy. Poor them. Only tears hurt – they cause runnels right through me. When I can't share them – and usually I can't. Because they're tears of years of memories. And nobody wants them.

'Keep them', they say. 'I want to share them' I cry. But you mustn't. And they fade. Dissolve. They're going. Which is probably good. So long as I don't lose the knowledge that comes with them. The knowledge about the others. I ought to keep that. And share it. That's my responsibility.

Money became a big problem. I had never learned to handle money because I had never had to. I was deep in debt, and the bank charged me enormous amounts in interest. That summer I found two jobs, one as a daytime cleaner and one in a cafe at a local holiday camp. And so the inevitable happened. I became ill. Very ill. I was admitted to a psychiatric hospital in Carmarthen.

*

Brechfor Annexe

St David's Hospital, Johnstown,

Carmarthen, Dyfed,

27 November 1983

Dear Jill and Louise,

Many, many thanks for the lovely carnations, for Louise's masterpiece of a birthday card, and for all the other greetings. Thanks a million. I hope the visit to Sheffield went well for you both. I expect to return to Aber. By midweek. The cutting I am enclosing will, as you see, enable you to get reductions in the Co-op on turkey and wine. I hope it reaches you in time, as I have little faith in the speed of the postal service out of Wales! And besides I haven't got any envelopes at present anyway, so this won't catch first-post tomorrow.

It's strange how I'm missing going to sleep at night with the sound of the sea and wind outside, as that's my usual lullaby. The students at Aber are planning a rent-strike. I think the idea is that we pay as usual next term, but into a special account to be opened by the union. It seems that the introduction this term of pay-as-you-eat is putting the college into the red for £8,000 (for one term? We don't eat that much, surely?). So obviously, they're putting the meal prices up – from December, which seems a bit mean, as few people have much money in the last week of term. It seems that no-one can win, since both sides have reasonable arguments, and the real problem is that food prices are rising much faster than student grants. And no-one gains if the college gets into huge debts, since that would just mean more cuts in departments. And a lot of Welsh people, and horsey people, have been getting quite steamy about the fact that the college recently sold its horses, which were the Llanarth stud, which nobody really cared much about until they were gone! (Perhaps that was the funny-tasting hamburger? – sorry, silly joke, only suitable in France). Anyway the college has us over a barrel on this one, since there is a long-standing rule that says nobody is granted their degree if they owe money to the college!

I am hoping to come up as arranged, in the vacation, to spend a bit of time with you. I had planned to do some studying during the vacation. But can see now that I'll be spending the whole of it catching up on essays! Must find out which London library I can use that is likely to have the books and papers I'll need to save a mammoth Xeroxing operation before I come. Is it still possible to get day tickets to use the library at the British Museum? It seems that on the strength of my UCW library ticket I can gain access to other college libraries, although obviously not withdraw the books – but where would London University house it's philosophy books amongst all its scattered buildings?

By the way, I won't be a drain on your resources when I visit over Christmas as my bank account is fairly healthy at the moment – I've got about £150 left of my grant, which I think must be either a miracle or a mistake! I think the best thing is for you to prepare a food shopping list for me to buy for you, so that I get what you need, rather than getting the wrong things and wasting money. Suppose I come up to you from Mum and Dad's on the 21st? Will that be okay? Let me know if not. Will close now.

Lots of love Christine.

Nadolig Llawen is the Welsh for Happy Christmas. I thought Louise might like to try that on her friends. *Nadolig* is pronounced as written.

*

When the term started for my second year I signed on to do a Joint BA course in Classical Studies and Philosophy. On paper, I was winning, but I was losing another battle, and before long I found myself back in the Bethlem Royal Hospital in Kent. I had withdrawn from the second year of the course, but I would be able to re-start and re-join it the following year. But I never went back.

The dream had turned into a nightmare. I ended up in a miserable flat in a horrible council estate in Orpington. Alone. And ill. I never returned to Aberystwyth, Never went to the College of Librarianship But I had tried. I had given it my best shot. I had studied my way out of hospital. I still had a lot to learn. But it wasn't for want of trying!

Chapter Twenty-Seven

COMMUNITY SUPPORT

Jill

I was delighted when Christine started to study for A Level English, and I knew that if she was well enough she was capable of passing it. It was good to hear she had found something she was interested in and to channel her energies towards. I was particularly pleased by the encouragement and support she received from the local Catholic priest and school teacher Terry Jones. This was to be a long, rocky route for Christine particularly given the setback of her return to Broadmoor in 1978. She was strongly motivated to become a librarian and to salvage a more normal lifestyle. Having by 1981 additionally gained three Open University credits, I was amazed and thrilled for Christine when she received her acceptance to Aberystwyth University. It was an incredible achievement and she successfully enjoyed her first year as a student.

Unfortunately without follow up support she then floundered, not on the academic side, but with the struggle to cope with the demands of normal life in the outside world. Trying to make ends meet financially led to her taking two exhausting and low-paid manual jobs, which triggered another episode of mental health problems. She had achieved a tremendous amount against impossible odds and so nearly made it to her dream.

After withdrawing from university, Christine was transferred back to Kent. She was allocated a flat in St Paul's Cray, but without community care support she struggled and was intermittently readmitted to hospital. Waddon was a day centre, for people with special needs, aimed at rehabilitation and preparation towards employment that Christine attended for six weeks. Regrettably many such centres have now been closed due to withdrawal of funding. She wrote the following piece there in 1984:

Waddon

Standing at the Clock. Watching. But where do they all come from? Who knotted and pulled the strings that brought them all together here? The limping feet and limping minds, wobbling wheelchairs, wilted faces. A wobble in their lives brought them here. A wander from the straight and narrow. A weariness, a warp in the weave. Look into their faces – is there a lack that unites them, this odd little microcosm of the luckless? Think. The hard face of success, the callousness of climbers, the cheque-card eyes. No, these are the trod-upon rather than the treaders-on. Sorry for themselves? Yes, some –naturally. But all with a little bit of pity to share. Strangely childish, so many. Dependent humans. Just passing through. On the way to where? Who knows? A career? A course? Please point the way to the next refuge, I'm a little lost at present. But did we laugh. We did. Blamed the job situation for the fact we weren't working. Were we shirking? Hiding behind our hobbles? Perhaps it was all just a holiday from the dole? The endlessly patient instructors – how do they do it? Lower their expectations and bury their sighs in the staff room? 'You get blase said one. "Oh, another tin leg?" As if half the world had tin legs, and the remainder tin heads. "And twenty-year-old stories pass me by." But what if you've fought it for twenty years – a wobble in a wheelchair – "I've got an electric one now. It's marvellous, gives me so much freedom." (Silently – but what if you had electric legs instead of electric wheels – where would you be then? Waddon? On top of the world? Or walking to the dole office instead? Wheeling, appealing, dignity. Every time I took her to the loo she sat there and cried. I heard her. And then she came out laughing, cheerfully back to tackle a new skill. "Yes, I've been ill. But I'm better now. You'd better be." "Most of these won't get jobs. No way. They're vacant." And patiently (and less so) he sets them to their tasks. Knowing it won't last. Don't you sometimes want to scream? Yes, every time there's chips and beans for dinner. Every day of the week. Isn't there room for the weak? A niche? Are they all weak? No, maybe exhausted – they used all their strength in fighting their weaknesses, their wobbles, their limps and personality pimples, the spots that the strong will focus on as they race them to the Interview Room. And the reports. A whole set of staff who deal just in Words. Who drown us in sentences, carefully worded statements, assessments – of what? In wages. I wouldn't do it. In soldering. I couldn't do it. Surrounded by little bits of wire, all cut in different, differing, wrong lengths. Amazing. The extent of the failure. About forty-odd three-inch-ish bits of wire. And a lot of over-sized blobs. My God I'm useless. I'll never make my mark on the world. There it is in front of me. On the bench. Look Lord, take a good look. That's the extent of my uselessness. Will it reach to Always and Forever? Give us a break, Lord. It's time I had a bit of success, a bit of meaning in my life. Or a day in bed. Whichever seems easier. Still. I got an A for stapling boxes – can't be bad, eh? Isn't there a niche somewhere for a Box Stapler with a Wobble? And he read me the Final Report. Bog-eared and bewildered, "It's nothing to do with me" Is that what they think? Ten weeks of united thinking, drowning and dousing in words, absurds. Maybe that's someone else's report, he's got it wrong. People do. That's a human failing. And here we all are among the chips and beans, the cheers and tears and fears – The Band of Human Failings – They're playing our tune – soon. Hang on. What's a human failing? Is it the same as a failed human? No, there's no such thing as that – but plenty of those – the world's full of them. Living proof. Human failings. "Not me, I'm perfect." Sorry – wrong door. Try the one marked Gone to Heaven – back soon. "No, closed for business." Everyone's got failings, but they're all chasing success, and some have to come back to the race. What's success? – Little green bits of paper. Of course, silly me. No. It's more than that. It's feeling Someone- not Tin Leg, or Tin Head but Peg or Fred.

And that's what it's all about. No I don't have a job. But the six weeks? Yes, they brought Fred a little nearer the top – of himself, moving up in the world. Upper-crusting, upward thrusting, moving, proving – just making his groove a little more comfortable to sit in. Worth it? Rather! A holiday from the dole. I'll go back to it refreshed, not a new woman, just re-cycled. Shaken and stirred. Thanks.

*

Christine hated being on benefits and when out of hospital would take any job/s she could find to pay her way. Mainly all she could get was the lowest paid jobs –usually as a cleaner – so she needed to do several at once to pay her bills. She had little time, or energy to write. For eight years she worked as a packer, for Pinnacle, a record distribution company in Kent, who were most understanding employers. I would periodically visit Christine, or she would come and visit me and Louise.

*

Broomwood Road,
St Paul's Cray,
Orpington, Kent,
1987

Dear Jill and Louise,

I haven't been able to get you on the phone so am assuming you are coming next Saturday as arranged. I suggest we all go to the Children's room of the local pub (the Partridge) and I'll buy you both a Ploughman's Lunch. Is that okay? I attach the directions. I look forward to seeing you next Saturday then.

Much love, Christine. Xxx

*

Fortunately while staying with me whenever Christine had taken an overdose, or come very close to harming herself, or one of my children, in compliance with the voices in her head, she did manage to tell me in time. Sometimes in the nick of time. And she would ask me, or enable me to persuade her, to return to hospital. I couldn't risk my children. I couldn't have her to stay anymore. I could never leave her alone with either of them even for a few minutes. I could never invite her to join us on holiday. For those suffering from paranoid schizophrenia, as Christine was, the closest and most vulnerable members of the family are often those most at risk.

Throughout Christine's illness, right from our schooldays, the majority of conversations between our parents and myself revolved around Christine, how she was, and whether there was anything we might be able to do to help her. We all felt so helpless. Mum would also tearfully bewail the lack of contact from Anne. They tried their best. They always visited Christine in hospital wherever she was. They were distressed and bewildered by the things she got up to. On one occasion, after they had moved to Brighton they returned home to find she had smashed practically everything breakable in their home, strangely apart from the mirrors. When the doctor arrived she threatened him with a carving knife but he managed to talk her through. Another hospital admission.

Living with Schizophrenia poses lifelong serious difficulties for the individual and their families. It is hard to comprehend the transitions as the person's behaviour changes from seeming fine to unpredictable incidents of self- harm and/or potential risk to others apparently at the behest of voices that may be compelling to the victim but are unheard by others. How best to help remains a challenging puzzle to family and friends as well as to professionals. Christine's accounts certainly indicate some approaches that she found very unhelpful, and that one hopes are no longer prevalent.

How do you cope when someone in your family, or close to you, is suffering from long term, serious mental health problems? I don't know. All I can say is some of the things that helped me to keep going. Actually, when you have children, particularly as a single parent, you have to keep going whatever – although I'm not suggesting that's a reason to have them. They certainly provide a demanding diversion.

I was always fortunate in having many interests and good friends, although over the years I only ever confided about Christine to a few close friends. Her circumstances were just too painful to trouble others with, as I knew they could do nothing to help, however much they may have wished to. My friends always were, and are, a great source of support and joy. When feeling upset for whatever reason I have always tended to divert myself by doing other things so over the years have got myself involved in many local activities –and still do.

Having not travelled abroad until I was 18, I found I loved going to different places, meeting different people and experiencing something of their culture. As work and family life became more demanding a conscious survival strategy became to carefully plan our summer holiday abroad as soon as the hype of Christmas was over and when the travel brochures started to arrive. This was then a recuperative break to look forward to. For some years Greece was my favourite venue but about the time that Amelia was born (1989) I decided there was more of the world to see and that I would aim to go to a different country each year. I have been fortunate in managing to do that which is probably how Amelia has now acquired the travel bug and is currently living in Laos giving me long journeys to visit her.

As Christine's most extreme difficulties appeared to commence at the age of puberty and finally diminish around the menopausal age, I find myself wondering if hormonal factors may be causally contributory. One of the terrible symptoms of schizophrenia is the compelling voices that can compulsively instruct the actions of the sufferer. Christine was often seriously afflicted by voices instructing her to violent actions, sometimes towards my children, particularly in their early years. On other occasions it was nurses or patients in hospital. Later when he was old and frail it was our father.

I never told Mum and Dad, or even my children's fathers, of any of the times when Christine was a real danger to our children, or later to Dad. In fact I barely told anyone. Ever. It always was, and still is, difficult to talk about mental illness in the family. My fears that Christine was capable of harming my daughters were very real, and not unfounded. In fact it was family members who were always at the greatest risk. Christopher and I had divorced in 1981 and I had had Amelia during a later relationship in 1989. Even though there is 13 years between my children Christine came alarmingly close, on different occasions, to harming each of them. While I was always trying to be alert to any mood change that could be cause for concern, I could never risk leaving them alone with her, not even for a few minutes because she could change instantaneously, and unpredictably in those odd moments one's attention is inevitably diverted in any family situation. After incidents like this I had to stop inviting her home for extended periods. It was just too dangerous for my children, even though I knew she really loved them.

Christine has written much to explain to others how she experienced both her illness, and the treatments she received, was for her emotionally, psychologically and in practice. Her hope, and mine is that this will add to the pool of understanding and managing for others who may be suffering from mental health issues themselves, or as family members and friends. Most of her accounts, letters, and poems were written at the time.

I was never a diarist being too busy with the business of living, working and bringing up my children. Over time I have not dwelt too much on the past trying to keep my focus on crossing each bridge as I came to it. That was usually enough! So, perhaps mercifully, I can't recall everything that happened, or always the succession of events. By the 1990s Christine's health, though often seeming better, was still erratic. She moved to Southport to be near enough to help Mum and Dad as they grew older. After staying for a while at our cousin Phil's, and after returning from Aberystwyth University she moved into a one bed flat. When her illness recurred she would find herself back in Clare House, a group living provision for people with mental health problems which maintained an effective focus on support and rehabilitation. During periods when her condition was more serious she would be transferred to the Hesketh Centre. Both were very local and supportive small group provisions.

My younger daughter, Amelia, was born in 1989. In 1990, while on one of my visits to Southport, Christine was living in a one bed flat on the top floor of a four storey Victorian house in Bath Street. Amelia and I were in a bed and breakfast next door but one, and also on the top floor. We had had an enjoyable few hours out with Christine in Southport. A recurring difficulty for Christine was that she could suddenly become urgently tired and irritable. At the first indications of this occurring we always had to turn promptly for home. We got back to Christine's and she invited me in for a cup of tea. I carried Amelia and her McLaren Buggy up all the stairs to Christine's flat. Amelia was tired so I put her in the push chair.

Christine needed something that was in my B&B – I can't remember what it was – only that it seemed important that I fetch it. It didn't seem to make sense for me to carry Amelia and the buggy all the way back down the stairs of the flat, up the stairs to my B&B room ,fetch the article then struggle back down, and up with her when I could more quickly and easily dash up and down to fetch the item. Amelia was fine, strapped in her buggy. So I hurried back and forth but as I came back up the stairs I could hear Amelia screaming alarmingly, sounding terrified. As I came in Christine stepped back and said, "She just started screaming." I grabbed my baby and her buggy and left. I never knew what had happened, but many years later Amelia said to me "Don't ever leave me alone with Aunty Chrissy." I never again had. Amelia didn't know why she felt afraid of her. She loved her aunt, and Christine loved her, but the fear had never left her.

Christine used to visit Mum and Dad most weeks and when she wasn't well enough they would visit her whether she was in or out of psychiatric care. On one occasion, while she was in the Hesketh Centre for a few weeks I was asked to go and meet with her consultant psychiatrist. At this time she was not being allowed out to visit Mum and Dad and they had been told they couldn't visit her. I went to Southport and without telling our parents I met with Christine and the doctor while nurses kept an eye on Amelia for me .The doctor told me he was concerned because Christine had told him that she kept hearing voices urging her to kill our father. Dad was by this time very frail. The consultant talked of how when she hears voices Christine feels urged to attack the vulnerable, particularly in the family. He was seeking my opinion as to whether I considered it safe to let Christine see Dad, and also whether I thought he should inform my parents of this potential risk, which I knew our parents would find hard to cope with. I had been watching Christine's responses and had some discussion with her about it. With some hesitation I said I thought it would be okay for her to resume contact with our parents, but not to tell them. We proceeded on this basis and Dad died of natural causes in 2001. Schizophrenic illness does sometimes seem to include symptoms of extreme ambivalence to closest members of the family and friends. Fortunately for us this never led to the tragic and disastrous outcomes that can sometimes occur.

Much is now being discovered about genes and the mechanisms of the brain. New and better drugs are being developed. Treatment is managed more in the community than through incarceration although much of this progress is again being lost through cuts in health and social care services. Christine describes how eventually she was put on medication that finally helped her, particularly in drowning the voices. She had been told, as I was, that schizophrenia sometimes burns itself out in middle age. My own surmise tends to be that hormonal changes, initially at puberty, and later at the menopause would seem to have some correspondence with the worst and prolonged period of her illness. She was to be prescribed considerable anti-psychotic medication for the rest of her life. Eventually Christine felt the right medicinal regime was found.

Certainly this was helped and corresponded with her allocation to a flat in a provision that was purpose built for people recovering and rehabilitating from mental health problems. Here, with the ongoing support of the community mental health team she was finally able to achieve a considerable degree of independent living. Throughout this later period, Christine was much helped by the various community mental health groups she attended and participated in. These provided support and relief from her loneliness and isolation as well as a range of therapeutic activities from gardening to woodwork and crafts. Also social events, outings and holidays. Regrettably most of these services have now been cut.

For Christine, her religious beliefs were also a feature of her illness, writing: "And the disciples spoke in many tongues and understood each other' (New Testament). Perhaps the disciples had dined on Magic Mushrooms with their bread and wine. Many famous people in history were recorded as having voices and hallucinations – for some of them it was pot-luck between being executed as a witch, or being called a Saint, in coming centuries. The cleverest scientist, or psychiatrist, cannot comprehend what it is like to live with schizophrenia."

Chapter Twenty-Eight

MEMORIES

Christine, 1990

My sister's young baby was crying in her crib whilst Jill was folding the laundry. "Will you pick her up please Chris?" I gently took her in my arms – and immediately I had this huge temptation to throw her against the wall. I loved that baby. I laid her back in the crib and left the kitchen. People who attack babies or defenceless old people are the lowest of the low. I must be a very wicked person.

*

Memories 2005: I loved my Dad. I remember sitting across from him, in Mum and Dad's flat, as he dozed in his armchair. The Voice in my head was screaming at me to "Go for him, Strangle him, Kill him." But I loved my Dad. Yes, I know right from wrong. But what was happening? I put on my coat and said to Mum, "I'm going now. I won't stay for lunch. Goodbye." I walked away from temptation. I was bewildered and frightened. And very alone. If you try to tell someone about this endless battle against what I should do, they cannot comprehend how confusing it is to live with these daily battles. Am I evil? Apparently, my brain must be different from others. But how? Why? From the age of thirteen I danced to a different tune than the rest of the world. Maybe they were out of step with me.

Punishment. I weep lonely tears of fear inside. But none must know for I must be punished. Doesn't anybody ever punish God For all the fears and tears. And all the muddle? He says "Now, choke her, now." And if I do she'll scream and maybe die. And if I don't He'll punish me, He'll scream at me. But He screams only at me. And I mustn't scream. I must smile. I must laugh, For none must know, While I'm all tied in knots, And the knots choke me As I would choke others. I don't understand, and none must know.

The Mystery of Death

"Go on, throw the baby against the wall. Bang her head. Kill her." As the beautiful, compelling, terrible voice echoed through my head I put the tiny baby back into her crib. I looked across the kitchen at my sister sorting the laundry. She would never know how seconds had separated our family from tragedy. Don't you know the difference between right and wrong? I am not at all sure that I do. It's so bewildering. It seems that life can be so pointless. Thou shalt not kill. We learn from the Commandments. All humans have the capacity to kill, to destroy. So why did God give us the capacity to kill each other and then tell us it's wrong to do it. I used to visit my parents regularly and would sit looking at my father dozing in his armchair. Nobody knew how I had to struggle not to surrender to the beautiful voices telling me to kill my Dad.

In the end Dad died slowly, and painfully, in bed after nature had taken its course. If I had done it it would have been over in moments. But that would have been wrong. Only God can decide when the time is up for each of us. But suppose the Voice meant I was actually God's handmaiden, his chosen, supposing he wanted me to kill my Dad, or the baby Amelia. When Jesus was in the desert he was tempted three times by the devil. He didn't give in to the devil – but then He was the Son of God. "Get thee behind me Satan." When my Dad died I watched the tears, and anguish of members of my family but felt no grief. I can imagine him in Heaven, meeting up with his brothers and sister. They had all lived life to the full and it would be quite a party Up There. Okay, so they might have broken a few rules along the way. But God wouldn't have turned them away.

I remember discussing with a friend how she had killed her best friend. "She smiled at me as I pointed the gun at her. If she hadn't smiled at me then I couldn't have pulled the trigger." Pulling the trigger at that moment made her a criminal, a murderer, put her outside society. Right and wrong – it's so confusing. I feel so sure that old lady had a special place reserved for her among the angels. But she had done wrong in the beginning. Another friend had killed her grandchild and ended up putting her under the floorboards. She would say: "And that baby took an awful long time to die." Why does God let us take these things upon ourselves? Where was that baby's guardian angel? I think only God gives us Free Will and only God can judge us. He sees the diamond from all angles at once, sees the whole picture. The rules of a free society in the western world are morals and ethics of the Christian faith as well as the laws of the land. But to kill and to say it's ok to kill is to break the taboo.

Once I nearly killed a woman called Violet. I had my hands around her throat, her eyes were popping and her throat was gagging. A nurse heard and came and pulled me off her. They said that in another ten seconds Violet would be dead. And yet I never felt any guilt or remorse. This whole Life and Death business confuses and bewilders me. Sometimes the Faith is actually an insurance policy, paying one's way into Heaven by prayer and fasting. Does it work like that? I think Faith and Joy in Life come together. God doesn't want us to weep and wail at life. If we have Joy in Life we will have Joy in Death. I think that is why we find suicide and euthanasia so difficult to tackle. They are escape routes but there is no light at the end of the tunnel for people who choose those options. Because Jesus, to me, means Joy. Joy in life and Joy in death. Grasp the nettle with both hands.

Some of my friends and family have chosen to take the route of suicide rather than to fight on. Jeff had been only a teenager when he went into hospital. Being young and untouched the old queens fought over him and he became homosexual. He was well known, and well liked, by us all. I was his first girlfriend, but I was too young to realise that I was playing with fire. He detached himself from all his men friends for me. And I got bored with him and dropped him. He was 21 when he killed himself, leaving a letter in which he blamed me for taking this terrible decision. A girl called Leonie climbed up the ivy that made our prison hospital look so picturesque. She fell off the roof and died. She was 16 years old. They cut down the ivy and hushed it all up. Another empty bed waiting for another criminal lunatic.

When I got to the stage of setting fire to myself, I was too numb to experience physical or emotional pain. I watched the flames moving up my nightdress and felt nothing. When one of us committed suicide, or as happened sometimes was killed by another patient, everything was hushed up and none of us were allowed to grieve or to attend the funeral because in the desperate, hopeless, situation in which we lived one suicide often led to others. Instead of being allowed to think and consider, or mourn for our friends, we were most of us permanently so over-medicated that we hardly noticed when one of our number had gone. Where is God? He isn't here is he? Look around you. We're his forgotten people. Yes, He's here amongst us. We just have to look.

*

But how did you survive fourteen years in a locked mental ward Christine?

Easy – well, not easy really, but my survival technique was studying.

By the time I left those tall grey walls behind I could read Russian, had passed an exam in Musical Theory, had a go at playing Alto Sax, and got three credits with the Open University! But what did you do the rest of the time? Well, I joined the Dramatic Society, and cuddled a cat called Ginger who was supposed to be Pyewacket, the witches cat in Bell, Book and Candle.

But what did you do when you left?
Well, out of that House of Negatives I got one Positive Thing – a place at university before I left. That was a brilliant, but sadly brief experience. So I went back behind the tall grey walls, eating soggy meatballs and drinking tea from plastic jugs; and as I paced that sad little room in my canvas nightgown, I knew that my only salvation was my books and my music. So I found a corner, curled up with Scott Joplin, or Django Reinhardt, and learned miles of poetry by heart. Then, in 1982, I threw a beach party, on the dunes at Ynslas, to celebrate a year of freedom. I wanted to have a party on the same day each year. But by the following year I was living in poverty in a lonely council flat, and I lived there for seventeen years. But I got myself a job, and a mortgage, and a three-piece-suite, and paid my council-tax. I was normal. And now? Now I work as a toilet-cleaner on a fairground. I have my own little room and my own little kettle. That's progress for you. So you see, when locked up in a prison of a hospital I didn't just sit in the chair and pee myself. Not every day is positive or I wouldn't be there – but I read, read, read. Then when they put me in a Pad with no books I just repeated in my mind from

beginning to end each chapter of my latest book. Believe me, it helped me to get the tangles of my brain together and bring a positive future nearer.

But what do you do now that you have that long desired freedom?

I clean the toilets at a fairground. And I've done farm-work, cleaned vans in a bakery, worked in a music warehouse – and at the end of the day gone home to egg and chips and desperation. There's no cure to this mental-illness lark – it goes on and on and has done since my convent school days. But the weapon is my love of books and classical jazz, and that's what brings hope – and hope can't be abolished, it's what brings warmth and smiles and courage to the afraid. So, if they lock you up and throw away the key think of something you'd really love to do and have never done, like embroidery, or chess, or just reading a good newspaper every day. It will be each morning's challenge, something to get up for, and believe me it will help you to survive inside those tall grey walls.

I dreamed for years of studying to be a librarian. It was the plan that carried me through sunless hours in mental institutions. When the going gets tough the tough find a good book, get stuck into it and turn their back on bullies, brutes, and barred windows. At one point in my time in Broadmoor institution the staff went onto a 'work to rule'. This meant that for over a month we were allowed no visitors, no work-time, entertainment, or Airing-Court. So what to do? Most of the women chose to sit glazed-eyed watching Open University – Advanced Chemistry. I filled the time by embroidering roundabout-horses on my best pink jeans, and reading Richard

Adams' Shardik, about bear-worship. That book saw me through endless dreary days and nights.

*

Amongst the muddle of recurrent memories that haunt me during long sleepless night is one that seems to sum up the bewilderment and pain of it all. It is of being naked and terrified in a padded cell and ripping the padding off the door with my teeth and my fingernails. The more ill I was, the more punishment I received. So being mentally ill was a punishable offence, a crime, it was my fault. Since my teenage years, when I just disconnected from the world around me and slipped into schizophrenia, I have been made to believe that I was to blame for being different. That I had chosen the path that my life had taken. It's bad enough living inside a world of voices and psychosis, without carrying the blame for it as well. Perhaps it isn't all my fault. Perhaps it does lie in the chemistry of the brain. I watched a TV programme, by Professor Robert Winston, about how the changes in the physical and chemical make-up in the brain as we mature control our development and personality. I didn't mature during my teenage years. I simply got stuck, not intellectually, but personally. A child's personality in a woman's body. There are some things that marked me out as a loser from the beginning. I was always useless at games and sports, because I don't have any hand/eye co-ordination. I couldn't hit a ball, even a table-tennis ball. This, with slow reactions, means that I could never drive a car. Also, being tone-deaf means I could never sing, or play a musical instrument and am totally useless at dancing. That catalogue of can't-do's marked me out as different from early days at school. So I always saw myself as a loser, a misfit, and blamed myself for it all. I am just coming round to the thought that maybe it isn't all my fault, perhaps it is chemistry.

Chapter Twenty-Nine

POEMS OF HOPE AND DESPAIR

Jill

I am still incredulous to realise that being sent to Broadmoor meant that Christine was judged to be one of the most dangerous women in the country. This was firstly from the age of 22, for five years, then again from the age of 30, for a further two years. Thankfully the only person she ever really injured was herself – and this most severely while in a locked room in hospital. There were certainly times when she posed a serious risk to others, most chillingly for me to my own children while they were very young. I still struggle to comprehend how she could ever have been in such a terrible frame of mind. Christine's poems and writings provide a window into the inner world of her disturbed thoughts and imaginings and indicate the chaotic intensity of her sensitivities and emotions.

Amazingly Christine managed to keep a continuous notebook from 1975-78 finding solace by expressing her frequently tangled thoughts and powerful, if fearful, emotions, often in verse. Christine vividly expresses her sometimes delusional thoughts, and feelings which are illustrative of how her condition of paranoid schizophrenia was impacting on her.

Her poems are both beautiful and awful revealing the contradictions and struggles of her troubled mind where her emotional sensitivities and powerful imagination conflict. They are demonstrative of her repeated personal struggles to comprehend the turmoil of her mind as she battles with the tugs between good and evil, hope and despair, reality and unreality in circumstances where she rarely felt understood. I have shared some more of them here:

High Seas – 20.05.72

I close my eyes and walk dumbly into the icy wilderness
Past the red flag to the ocean of deceitful solace.
Leaving the margarine sands I try to be Jesus,
To walk on the waves and to bravely carry my cross.
Astride the proud stallion of the sea I'm carried
Beyond the sunset to the land of sleep,
Accompanied in my aloneness by my ever faithful self;
We cling together and she is not there
I only dreamed of her in my despair.
My burden's heavy and I am but weak,

Driftwood in a troubled sea I seek

No Utopia for the blessed few

One moment's rest for all humanity.

Dead or alive give them Pax Domini.

Give us release from fear and sin and war.

For this reason I leave the crowded shore.

The seventh wave hovers – a vision of my life,

I gasp in panic just before it strikes.

The sea is just, and justice fair and good,

Tosses me landwards as human driftwood.

With seaweed hair I face the court, and smile

Drugs bring escape, if only for a while.

Reflections

And I looked at the glass

The hard uncompromising mirror.

It surrounded me.

Like being on the inside of a diamond.

But there was no false beauty here,

For it was the mirror-glass of my life.

My past, my present, and my future.

And beyond there were more mirrors, more mirrors and
more mirrors.

And I stood still and looked.

And the mirror of the past shed tears.

It couldn't look at itself.

And it blushed with mist and hid its face.

But when I looked close I noticed

There were tiny spots of reflected happiness.

And they sparkled through the tears.

The rest was mist.

And I looked at the present.

And it looked back at me

And wondered.

It was like a mosaic

And today smiled back at me

And slid gently into its place

And begged me to look no further.

But I made a mistake.

I turned and tried to look

Into the mirror of tomorrow.

And the mirror shattered

Because I wanted to look

Beyond the jewel of today.

Happiness?

Milk curdles. Snails shrink into their shells.

Rabbits retreat to their death in the last stook of corn.

The whipped horse drags itself over the last mile,

Head hanging, sweating with exhaustion,

Walking in blind obedience to the will of its ignorant
master.

The baby that was loved becomes the rejected old man

Sitting alone in the corner despised and unwanted.

What is this elusive thing called happiness?

It is the drained and choking feeling

Of having conquered my yearnings for destruction.

Of having wanted to attack,

And not having done it.

I sit with china-dog stillness

And nobody guesses

The yearning, struggling, churning urges

Which are possessing my mind.

And afterwards I am exhausted.

Screaming inside.

Feeling like one of Dali's cats.

And nobody must know.

And nobody does know.

And that's happiness.

The happiness of overcoming

My own longings to hurt, hurt, hurt.

Snake tormented

At last I can tell the secret.

The deep dark longing.

I've wanted to tell people but I couldn't bear to tell,

Because I couldn't face up to their lack of knowing.

How can they realise that I'm not human. It's Hell.

There are snakes inside of me, crawling and thronging.

In every part of my body they spread their venom.

Their forked tongues sting my brain, my heart.

And when they've nothing to feed on it's a world apart.

But when they're deep inside me that's when I can feel

That they're feeding on my happiness, stinging me to shreds.

And that's when I get lost and frightened,

Because I know they'll leave me nothing.

They cramp me up inside, dig their fangs into my life.

I'm incapable of loving and yet they're not serpents,

More like greedy eels who survive

By sucking up my happiness and leaving me to die.

Because I'm dead inside except for wriggling, greedy snakes.

They wrap themselves around my heart.

They shrivel up my mind.

I can feel them now inside me,

Black and cruel and blind.

And when they're contented, when they've had their fill

I'll have a time of peace, however short, I know I will.

But they'll still be deep inside me.

The serpents of my life.

They've swallowed up my soul.

Spat it out and strangled it.

So I've no chance of goodness, until they've had their fill.

Sometimes they clam together

And there's no escape for me.

But how can I tell the doctors

That I never will be free

From the fork-tongued, squirming creatures

Who kill all my life and hope?

When I despair they're well fed.

But they can't bear to see me in a state of calm and peace.

So they must torment me.

They wind themselves around every living, loving part.

Their venom kills my feelings,

And sometimes I'm even grateful to be dead and shrivelled up with the poison of despair,

Because it hurts too much to feel,

And it hurts too much to care.

But oh squirming fork-tongued vipers of my body and my mind,

Have compassion sometimes, sleep contented for a while.

Because I want a time of freedom, just to be a human being.

But I wonder perhaps if every person on earth

Isn't snake tormented from the moment of their birth.

Perhaps they're not all poison.

Maybe some are free.

But what I want the most is simply to be me.

Cloud Nine

Today I have arisen from the grave of the living.

I have left the carcase of my body

To carry on its regulation duties.

I am the wind and the water,

The moon and the stars.

I am greater than humanity itself

Because I have the freedom of nature

Which is not concerned with pettiness or the dandruff
of life.

Sometimes I will be gentle, soothing, spraying the world
with tranquillity.

But other times I will laugh and toss the seas with a
tantrum

The wind and the water

The water and the wind.

I have the power to bring peace and the wilful anger to
take it away again.

I am their God and they are mine,

Because freedom is theirs and mine.

But it is the wild, wild moors that reflect my passion

They will not bend to the hand of mere humans.

They soothe the troubled mind.

They entrap the universe.

They hold many secrets

Which are understood only by those who speak the language of the wind

And look to it for their wisdom.

And few men are great enough to realise how small they are

Compared to the great old spruce.

Tonight I am one of those trees.

I am the heather of the moors.

I am the seventh wave crashing against the cliffs.

I have the power to destroy.

And I have love for the weak and lonely

So to them I will bring the gentle Chinook

So that they will turn their faces upwards

From the slime of their misery

To a world where peace is theirs.

Each shall have its own bright star.

Just for tonight.

Because freedom is mine tonight

And tonight will never end.

Colours

My life is like a paint palette that somebody ran under

the tap.

The sunshine yellow turned into mud,

And the icicle white swallowed by black.

The soft gentle colours got lost in the swirl,

And all the sweetness was lost in the mourning of purple

It only took a moment to turn the tapestry into smog,

A careless thought, a sudden twist and all the beauty was gone.

And that's how it happens in my mind.

Because the darkness has more power

The sudden thunderstorm can crush the smallest gentle flower.

The flowers show us life is real, they form the tapestry.

The people are intruders, plastic gnomes who cannot feel.

And so they wade amongst the beauty, unthinking, unknowingly cruel,

Because the sunshine only wanted to be left alone to smile,

And the icicle has its beauty,

Like frost on the window –pane.

We need the blackness, darkness, so that we can wake afresh,

And reach out with our finger-tips to love but not to crush.

The darkness of the night is to give all life a rest.

It doesn't swallow up the goodness, just lets the world relax.

But the darkness of my mind is a fighting struggling beast.

You can never win the battle.

You can never kill the beast.

Invisible, intangible, unknown to all but one,

And that's the one who's clasped between the jaws and mighty paws

Of the one who mars the tapestry,

And mixes all the colours wrong.

But when you've won the battle and proved that you are strong

You can wipe the palette clean of all that's past and sad and gone

And begin again to form colours in just the way you want.

You can choose the sombre colours and admit that you've been beat.

Although perhaps to some it's a tactical retreat.

But I think I'll choose the primrose and perhaps a gentle green.

They're nature's shyest colours but there's strength and rest in them.

I don't want a garish tapestry because my life's a dream.

Lonely

Lonely I walked the meandering sands.

The sea spluttered its drink. The sky glared whitely.

Lonely I walked in December.

Lonely the sands swallowed me.

Unresisting I was sucked into

The womb of the world

To learn my lessons

The Misfit

Sometimes I think I was born out of my time.

I should have been one of Hardy's milkmaids.

A peasant girl in a land and a life where changes come slowly.

Or Alice.

I can understand Alice.

And I think I can understand Salvador Dali, sick as he is,

Because he paints the way I see when I am lost.

I should have been born before psychiatrists were invented,

And then perhaps I could have been me.

I'll never fit into this world.

It's too fast and demanding for me.

Too sophisticated. Too pretentious.

Somehow I got left behind

From another era.

I'll never fit into this one,

Because I don't really know how to be a twenty-seven-year-old 1975 woman.

And I don't really think I want to.

They bewilder me.

And so I'll stay as I am.

I don't believe I was ever really sick.

But I know I'll always be a misfit.

And if they'd leave me alone to be a misfit,

I'd be contented.

But they won't.

Apartheid (for Janice)

When God the artist sketched his plans for earth,

Perfect in composition, shade and light,

He used his mightiest gifts upon the land

And every tree and leaf, painted by love,

Varied just slightly in its shade of green.

Each had some beauty, soft or bright and shining,

And none was better or worse, nor lacked God's love.

Then God created Man, greater than Angels,

In like and image of his very self.

He armoured each with spirit for life's battle.

Some strong, some weak, but each His very own

As with the leaves, his paintbrush varied slightly

And Mankind came in many different shades.

He left the choice of Good or Evil to them,

And sometimes Evil took the upper hand.

The primrose or the oak each has its beauty

But neither is the greater of the two,

But blind men build hatred through this small distinction,

And wars are fought, lives ruined by this thing.

Apartheid is a cruel, senseless dogma

Its festering sores can never disappear

Yet strands of hope are strengthened in the vision

Of undiluted love upon the face

Of negroid girl with tiny babe in arms

The child is white but here there are no barriers

She loves the child as if he were her own.

She lullabies it, softly, gently rocking

While in her country racial war draws near.

The strands of hope she wove must now be plaited,

Strengthened by tolerance, made colour-blind by love

And when the rope of hope is strong enough,

Passing all barriers, customs, creeds,

Then we shall have no more apartheid.

It will shrivel up with the ignorance that it leans upon.

Self-Pity – September 1976

The custard sands are empty

The world is far away

Alone I stand In this desert land.

Just me

And a gritty pebble of self-pity.

Beneath my toes

The pebble grows.

It's as hard as my heart,

As big as my head,

And it grows and grows and grows.

I'm standing on a rock now,

It has overtaken me,

This fossil of self-pity.

The sea comes in in a circle

It is streaked with silver and black,

It's vinegar black with cruel Revenge.

But the silver is a promise,

It's a promise of peace of mind,

I must climb down from the pebble

And leave self-pity behind

But I cling to the mighty rock,

For Pride is holding me there.

The savage black sea Is approaching me

Hope is speeding away.

The waves are lashing and thrashing and crashing

At my last refuge so hollow.

I'm surrounded now by the starless black.

I tumble down from my Pride.

The silver water flashes up

And cradles me into the shore,

Gently, gently it lifts me of course

To the sand-dunes of humility and remorse.

Lack of Courage

To live forever in an empty disused coal mine,

Completely alone, and yet never undisturbed,

That's something I find easy to imagine.

I'd fear-dream down the tunnels of my mind.

The terrible darkness and traps would follow me still.

But I'd belong in the darkness

And the tunnels and the shafts would be my protection

Because I wouldn't have to face the people.

There'd be nobody to know or pretend to care.

There would be rock-falls in my coal-pit mind.

They'd come crashing down on top of me.

But it wouldn't hurt because I wouldn't be there.

The cavern-walls would fall in all around me,

But I think somehow I'm getting used to that,

And there cannot be more hurt to come.

My coal-pit would be peopled by hatred and fear,

Because I'm never without them, which is bad,

So I probably deserve it anyway.

If I had the courage I'd look up sometimes,

Far, far up,

To where there'd be a tiny speck of light

Called life –but I don't think I'd be brave enough to do

that very often.

I'd just wander on and on in the darkness.

The fearful darkness where I'd never be safe,

Except from people.

But that at least would be a bit of a relief.

The Pool of Peace

The pool of peace was filled with the last tears of sadness and bitterness of those who made a pilgrimage to it. It was a little secret world of happiness, built in the ugliest of surroundings, but it was a place where problems ceased to matter, as the cares dropped into the pool one by one. There were no willow trees, no ducks and the water was grimy with the dust of human misery. And yet it was an oasis to folk whose minds were clogged with the everyday problems of existence, and especially to those who knew no peace elsewhere. But the developers said 'it's an eyesore' and filled it up with concrete and the tears of the people were un-staunched because the pool of peace had gone. But before long a spring appeared where the pool had been. And the people wept with happiness so that the spring became a waterfall, and the waterfall gouged all the ugliness out of the town and out of the people.

Ice Age Poison

The clammy fingers of the darkness reach out to me.

The fingers spurt poison.

It is the poison of unhappiness, from which there is no escape.

I am the victim of the dark poison.

My body is free but my mind is captive.

The fingers join in a circle around me,

More binding than iron bars or stern words.

The poison freezes.

I am mummified in my own Ice Age.

There is no life permitted, no speech or action,

For it is not possible,

Fear has taken over.

Sorrow

The tears flow until the stream becomes a river.

The river is called Sorrow.

It has burst its banks and become a flood.

The sorrow has flooded my world.

The burial clouds are massing in the sky.

The silken thread will tighten by and by.

I see my destiny.

The road runs clear.

The halter of execution is right here.

I'm cursed.

God's turned his back on me.

The garrotte tightens.

That's all.

My Journey

I've travelled far along the road to nowhere.

My journey takes me through uncharted lands.

The road is rough, with traps and tricks and chasms.

I travel blind, the journey's end a mystery.

I'm all alone, for none can travel with me,

Though helping hands are offered from each side.

This is my road, and many times I've fallen.

Stumble on, there's little chance for respite.

The road snakes on, each corner fearful to approach.

I've clawed my way up mountains, tumbled down them,

Yet sometimes the road is straight and smooth and tree-lined.

I sink into an abyss of contentment.

But very soon the path turns back to swamp-land,

I'm swallowed to my neck in deep depression.

I'm fooled and foiled by the road that seemed so smooth,

It wasn't meant for me.

I travel loaded with concrete blocks of fear and solitude.

I dream of home at journey's end

But it's far, far away.

Fragile

My skin is a shroud, inside it I am withered and lifeless.

The shroud is armour plated, it wears a painted smile like a clown.

No battering ram from outside could dent it.

Keep it polished to impress people, so that none can guess

How fragile it is inside.

Inside is a waterfall of tears for a life which I can't cope with

And of all the things I don't understand.

God – 4.12.1976

He doesn't punish me with whip but with words.

He scourges me until I am a pulp of confusion.

God talks, I listen.

Man talks, I listen.

I bow my head to submit to my punishment

For God punishes

And so does Man.

I need a spine of steel to withstand the temptations

And I am weak.

I try to explain in empty words.

They fall upon the bricks,

For none can know

And none must know

That my spirit is drained with the exhaustion of the fight.

I can't fight anymore.

I am beaten.

What a shameful thing to admit.

Echo – 27.2.77

Sounds echo within me,

I am hollow

And the darkness clings.

Good can come from hollow.

Christ's mother bore him in a stable

Where it was dark and empty

But one star shone

And it was enough.

I must find my star.

Christ was buried in a cave,

A lonely pit.

His light flickered

And the darkness was deep,

But the stone was rolled away

And the shaft of light penetrated centuries.

How can I roll my stone away?

I must push it every day until I die.

And if it will not budge an inch

Then I must drill through the granite of my difficulties

To let in some light

And turn the bad into good.

I must bring life to the hollow

So that the sounds can no longer echo, echo, echo, echo.

The Black Snowdrop – Sept. 1977

The black snowdrop hangs its weary head.

Its roots are deep in the mire of despair,

Tangled into knots of bitterness and confusion.

Its sabre leaves stretch up, looking for light and hope.

And they find none.

The black snowdrop is an enigma.

Few admit to have seen it,

For it grows in only one place,

Deep in the dark, dank well of Utter Hopelessness

And none return from there unscarred.

The black snowdrop lifts its head

Only to sing the song of fruitlessness,

Beckoning to the weeds far above, with a sweet, deceiving voice.

They fall, one by one, deep into the pit

Looking for a safe landing

And turning their faces from the cruel world,

And so they are twisted into the roots of the black snowdrop,

Twisted and tangled, gnarled and snarled.

And there is only one remedy from the pit of despair

And that is the love of true friends

Who reach deep down

Risking their own peace of mind

To pull the unfortunate ones back

And help them find a world

Without black snowdrops.

Sun-Radar – September 1977

The pure white sun beams powerfully

Throwing its rays deep into the minds of the Lost.

Its beams can reach the deepest thought

And illuminate it, to burn brightly like a star

So that all the world knows that thought,

Except the Thinker.

The Thinker sobs, not knowing why

Except that the sun's rays have burned into his mind

Leaving a hole, for the world to look through.

Sorrow

Sorrow is a drooping violet which, after fighting its way through Winter into Spring timidly but proudly shows its fragile face to the world, only to find that it is tramped upon. Nobody notices it because the vain daffodils are blowing their trumpets into the ears of passers- by. That is sorrow, That is grief. There is a disused well and every drop that trickles down the mossy walls into the bottom is a drop of sorrow, seeing the light narrowing as it goes down.

Envy

As a fungus grows from one tiny, unhealthy spot to weaken a whole structure so an infestation of envy in the same way can darken the clouds of goodness. As a daisy will not lift its head on a dark morning, so the light will not penetrate a soul so darkened. As a guitar plays sweet music only when it is in the hands of an artist, so the strains of good music in the soul will be out of tune and warped. As a bee will make good honey from the blessed flowers so a soul that is pure and free from envy will create goodness and purity around it.

Icicle – 21.3.78

My heart is pierced by an icicle
It is an icicle of steel,
Frost sharpened, ice painted.
But who holds the ice-sword?
Is it the hand of God?
Or is it the hand of Fate?
These are scapegoats.
I must be honest,
It is the hand of my own self-destructiveness
That murders Hope so often.
Many times I dance along the primrose path

Towards a New Life,

But the sunlight blinds me.

It frightens me.

And I retreat Into the dark of Hopelessness

Where I'm safe,

Where Despair looks at me and winks its eye

And where I am no stranger.

Opaque – 22.3.78

The sugar-frosted windows of my conscience

Are brittle walls between right and wrong.

I question which side of them I should be,

For my eyes cannot penetrate the opaqueness of a clouded mind.

To smash the sugar-frost would be disaster.

There is conflict I cannot resolve

Between me and my shadow

For without one the other is unreal.

Chords – 1st May 1978

Nature is a pianist.

The sound of soft, sweet, stuttering rain

Plays lost chords to me.

The lost chords reach to the heart of my suffering,

Not to quench the pain but to make it easier to bear

By bringing the feel of Hope a little nearer.

Perhaps the rain-drops are tears.

The tears and fears are a spinning-top

Which spins until it topples with exhaustion.

I love the sound of rain,

It brings freshness to stagnant bewilderment.

Those things that are destroyed by fire

Are revived by the tear-drops of the lost chord,

Which is the whisper of good people praying for those

Who find hope an elusive abstract

The Eye – 11.11.78

Chains of rusty fear held me in the fetid darkness. I was in a well. An eye watched over me. It had not blinked for years. It was pink, with sties. One day it blinked and a tear fell from it. Down, down, increasing in momentum, until it broke every bone in my body, and broke the chains and froze in a round block around me in the bottom of the well. The eye had closed. A strange creature came to the mouth of the well and breathed warmth and strength so that the ice melted and I was re-born, not as a woman but as a bird, a young vulture thirsty for my first taste of blood. In the warm current of air I flew up in vertical take-off straight to the top of the well. I remembered an eye which had tormented my mind for so long and I wished to peck it out. I found it was the body of a chicken with a giants head neatly attached to it with barbed wire. I left it. It was evidently a sign-post for travellers on journeys such as mine. I flew out of the well and paused; all around the well, in the darkness, yellow pairs of eyes shone. They were the eyes of wolves. Beside me sat the creature who had breathed life into me as a vulture and who was to be my guardian. He was greater in stature than any wolf, although he looked like a wolf, yet he had wings and his name was Belial. He had not lost his beauty, although fallen. He swallowed me whole and I lay in the warmth of his stomach gaining strength and inhaling venom. I understood that he would stay with me until I had accomplished my mission. I was to learn much evil from this master of evilness. There was neither day nor night, only warmth. I did not need food. All I needed was to understand the meaning of hate, real hate, and my life in hospitals had taught me some of this, and the way to store up venom like precious liquid and spew it up at my tormentors. And so I grew and took to picking at Belial's teeth and sitting between his ears as we journeyed through the underworld. We came to a forest of steel crucifixes and hanging on every crucifix, alive and screaming, was Christine. I pecked out the eyes of every Christine, ignoring the cries for mercy. I was a vulture, I knew no mercy, only hate. And as I pecked they grew again, shining, luminous in the blackness. I followed the path through the forest until I came to a gate. And at the gate was a good angel. And I could not look at him. I tried to fly back to the crucified Christine's but they were all lined up behind me, watching me and waiting. And Belials led us away from the good angel and into Hell. And Christine had found her resting −place, in Hell, in the belly of a wolf. Inside the belly of the wolf long iron fangs drew and I was constantly crushed, and distorted. I became a shapeless lump of flesh with only one element in me that was solid and that was the hatred of all men, which bound me together. All the time I could hear bells ringing, they never seemed to stop. Finally Belial, the Angel-Wolf spat me out into a dark, dark cavern. The fire that is in Hell does not burn, nor does it consume, it only blinds you and sheds fearsome shadows, outlines of things that you half-remember were once good and wholesome and may still be so if only you could remember how to love them.

Hope

Hope spoke to me and I replied I'll try.
You hold the soul that speaks to me
Although our conversation be as wordless as the windy sky.
I'm fettered now by deep Despair
Its rankling chains are twisted tight
The echoes of silence deafen me
And Hope is gone.
Yet when today has run its course
I'll open my eyes afresh.
With my fingertips I'll reach for the day
And the clouds of Darkness will slink away
And Hope will lead me by the hand
And whisper Come, raise up your head.
The clouds are made of Christ's sweet tears.
So cast off your bundle of nightmares and fears.
He loves you, so, you've nothing to dread.

So remember that and hold up your head

I've lost all sight of Black Despair.

He crowded into a corner far over there.

So sweep him away with the cobwebs and dust.

Forget him 'til his chains have turned to rust.

New life came into my world.

Spring came into my soul,

Through the gloomy months of nature's winter.

Spring came into my soul.

The days were long and light

And the nights soon gone,

The flowers began to bloom.

The birds burst into song;

It was a new beginning for me.

New life came into my world.

None knew the wonder of it,

The old sadness was gone,

Today the Spring is over,

And Winter chills me through.

I'm cold with fear, frostbitten with hate.

The bloody storm-clouds envelop me.

There's nothing left but the long dark tunnel of my winter.

Keeping up appearances

I dream-walk through the days

Bewildered in a haze of negatives

Sullen in my loneliness

Because the haze will not lift.

It is a haze of uncertainty

Wondering which voice is real

And which is fantasy

Puzzling over dream-pictures

Which exhaust me with fear,

And all the time switching on the smiles

Laughing and chattering nonsense

And hoping the veneer will not crack,

Because it is a very thin veneer

Hiding a multitude of confusion,

Hiding the smothered screams

And the too-perceptive eyes,

Pretending there is nothing there,

And all the time puzzling

About what is real and what is not.

*

Christine's symptoms of paranoid schizophrenia appear to indicate that her psyche was frequently thrust into dark, terrifying realms which haunted her. At 15, as a schoolgirl, she was first diagnosed as suffering from night terrors. From her writings these would appear to have remained a continuous feature of her illness that could occur through days and nights for many a year. Often these were evidently compounded by the badgering voices that often instructed her to harm. Christine often seems to show insight into her own condition and to be both sensitive to and perceptive of, the attitudes of others.

From her earlier highly judgemental responses to the psychogeriatric patients she encountered, while a teenager in Fairfield Hospital she later demonstrates more understanding and empathy with those in Broadmoor whom she tends to regard as misunderstood and ill-treated like herself. Christine was for long resistant to talking therapies apparently considering these an intrusion into her personality rather than offering any potential route through her problems. She was conscious of her roller-coaster mentality and at times seems to enjoy the ride and not want to lose it. Her religiosity variously appears to have helped and hindered her progress. There were times when she apparently considered herself called on to aid god's work by speeding people, such as our Dad, towards heaven. There was also the Christmas day in Broadmoor when the priest's visit to her in the confinement of solitary isolation soothed and calmed her better. Whenever she was back in the wider world Christine's own strict protestant work ethic made her determined to work rather than claim benefits. Unfortunately her history meant she could usually only get the lowest paid of jobs and as these were often part time, she would need to be doing two or three at a time to make ends meet. This inevitably led to recurrence of her illness further aggravated by the delays involved in restarting her benefits claims, without community support her situation would rapidly deteriorate and she would soon be back in hospital. Perhaps if policy makers did the arithmetic, they may find it more cost effective, and socially beneficial, to fund mental health support in the community and reduce the considerably more expensive alternate of hospital re-admissions.

Christine's final recovery was slowly achieved, after many setbacks, through a combination of her focused determination to get out of Broadmoor and other hospitals by working towards her dream of becoming a librarian. Her high intelligence somehow always made her mental illness harder to understand, as though she should be able to maintain a rationality that is evidently beyond the reach of someone suffering from a severe mental illness. It was with the combination of rehabilitation, ongoing community mental health support, and suitable medication that she was finally able to achieve almost independent living during what was to be the last decade of her life.

As family members one inevitably questions oneself about whether you were to blame in any way or could have done any more to help. Although some of the horrors that Christine describes were not known to me until after her death there were certainly times when I wanted to protest to hospitals about the treatment of her and others. Fear of the patient's vulnerability to recriminatory behaviour by impervious staff was a powerful deterrent not only to the patients themselves but also to their friends and families and even to caring staff fearful to risk becoming whistle-blowers. All were aware that the patient's own testimony was unlikely to be believed or given the credence it deserved should they reach as far as offering evidence. I hope that those with mental health problems who find themselves in hospital no longer face the kind of experiences that Christine did. One is left wondering how much things may or may not have changed in the treatment of those who suffer from mental ill health. Regrettably the succession of institutional abuse cases that continue to be exposed appears to be on the increase. Perhaps the good news is that they are now more likely to be exposed.

Things began to improve for Christine during the 1990s when her treatment started to reflect the spirit and practice of the NHS and Community Care Act 1990. She had moved to Southport as she wanted to be able to offer support to our ageing parents. Initially her flat dwelling was interspersed with periods in Clare House and the Hesketh Centre, a small psychiatric hospital. These were part of the excellent mental health provision that Sefton Council provided in Southport. Sefton Health and Social Care services proved to have the most enlightened, and effective approach to the treatment and care of people with mental health problems that Christine encountered. The NHS, with their open-door policy liaised and worked in harmony with the Social Services Community Mental Health, Housing Association and Voluntary Services and were responsive to the often changing needs of the individual. Between them these services supported Christine with an integrated, flexible, and appropriate package of care, responding effectively to the up and down needs of service users, maintaining support as needed by Christine whenever she was in or out of hospital, residential care, or living in the community right up to her death.

I share Christine's gratitude to them all and my conviction, that they confirmed, that well integrated provision focused on the changing needs of the individual can effect life changing differences and by reducing their need for full institutional care undoubtedly constitute a more beneficial and cost effective approach to care and treatment of those experiencing mental health problems. If it was possible to do the maths my bet would be that this was costing considerably less than the weekly rate of incarceration in Broadmoor.

Christine was dismayed, both on her own behalf and that of others, when under governmental cuts regimes they were being progressively dismantled. This led to her writing to the local MP John Pugh in January 2011. Unfortunately she didn't have the confidence to follow up his invitation to meet with him.

While Christine still insisted determinedly in trying to achieve independence from needing to claim Social Security benefits, the only jobs she could now obtain were very low paid cleaning jobs necessitating her doing several at once to make ends meet because of the all or nothing nature of the benefits system. The stresses and exhaustion inevitably led to recurrences of crises in her condition with returns to hospital. But hospitalization here in much smaller, local, caring provision, mainly linked to the Hesketh Centre where the staff worked closely with her towards rehabilitation.

After periods in lodgings, and group care and a period of relative stability in her 50s, Christine was most fortunate to be allocated her own one bedroom flat in newly built independent, but supported, living accommodation for people with mental health problems that opened in Meols Cop in October 2001. Her flat comprised a living room, kitchen, bedroom, bathroom and storage cupboard which all led off a narrow hallway.

With essential equipment provided Christine soon set about furnishing her home, largely from charity shops and the boot fairs she loved to visit in the early mornings. Soon besides her collection of books there were collections of puppets, chinoiserie, and much other homely clutter. Like me she didn't go in for minimalism. She delighted in the fact that she could now finally have her own things around her – including her own much loved cat. She took particular pride and joy in the area of the garden she was permitted to develop. Crucially Christine was convinced that she was finally being prescribed the right medication regime. From this time she managed to live largely independently.

Chapter Thirty

REHABILITATION

Christine, 2004

Two years ago, after 35 years of schizophrenia, I was prescribed a drug called Clozaril. It has made me well. I am learning to live a normal life without voices. When they first gave it to me, I was frightened. It seems silly but I couldn't imagine what it would be like to live without my demons. Every day I thank God for making me well. But I don't understand why He made me go through all those years of listening. I somehow got through all those terrible years without harming anyone. One thing I have got that other normal people don't have is an insight into the mind of murderers. When there is some appalling report on the News about an apparently pointless murder of a vulnerable child or old person, and people say How could they do that? I know. I've been there.

Now I am moving forward, enjoying each day, learning to be in total control of myself – and thanking God for the Scientist who invented Clorazil and gave me back my life after 35 years of bewildering, and apparently incurable, schizophrenia.

My voices are gone. The compulsion to attack people around me – often people I love – gone for the first time since I was a teenager. I no longer experience compulsions to attack others and set fire to myself. If one new drug can resolve the struggle between Right and Wrong that I have suffered since I was a teenager, then medical science can resolve an awful lot of pain. All those years of struggle have now come to an end. I can wake up every day and look forward to the day. After nearly forty years of severe mental illness I have been given a newly discovered medication which has totally turned my life around. It is more than magic – it's miraculous. Like opening my eyes after years in the darkness – a bulb opening in the Spring after Winter darkness.

I would say to anyone who has an apparently incurable, insufferable, illness – just hold on, believe in God, and believe in Science – your day might come.

Making Space is our local charity that takes us all on holiday, day-trips, and celebration. Phil-and-Cath, who organise it all, are in their 80s – and they still walk around hand-in-hand! We call them Mr-and-Mrs-Shepherd – with us being their flock of sheep.

*

Postcard of the Kadampa
Buddhist Temple at night,
3 October 2001

Hello! Enjoying my week's holiday in the Lake District. Went to this Buddhist Temple today. Home on Friday – moving flat soon. Love to you all.

Christine xxx

*

Making Space Trip, June 2005, Manchester Ship Canal

It is said that the English people's love of the water is because we are, by nature, an island race. We love to swim in it, sail on it, and travel miles just to spend a day sitting looking at it. Certainly there is nothing to beat spending a sunny Saturday in June drifting down the Manchester Ship Canal with a bunch of friends, just admiring the scenery, listening to a very learned man telling us the history of the places we are sailing through, and just relaxing spending a day on the water.

25.9.05

Sitting-room being painted mauve – Chaos is come again. Swam, early at 9am – the best time, no crowds or kids. Hoping to hear about Central 12 job – no news yet. Andrew Pickup was supposed to phone Gwen. Gwen helped me sort out the front room. Bedroom to be painted on Thursday. Heard on bus – small boy telling his mother about his friend – obviously doesn't know the word sister –

he calls it lady-brother – Wonderful!

26.9.05

Trying to sort out my paperwork and timetable – plans – for Writing Course. Took cat to vets with Gwen. Interview with Mr Pickup. Nice man, keeping fingers crossed that I don't get selected for the job. Museum – group. Tea with Mum.

2.10.05

Mum is poorly again so I have to jump every time she says jump. I know she's an old lady, and when she dies I won't know what to do without being at the end of her piece of string. I just wish that when Jill comes up next weekend she will open her eyes to the situation. As far as Jill is concerned she is the prodigal daughter and when she comes up she expects the fatted calf to be brought out for her. When Mum dies Anne will remember the way to Southport and they'll all come up looking for rich pickings.

Sometimes I am a bit bitter about the times when Mum and Dad shut the doors in my face. I remember times in the flat in Orpington when I would go weeks on end without a conversation with anyone in the world. When I was too broke to buy any food. When I went down the stairs of the flats and saw the big, fat, white cat on the window-ledge and said to myself –There's a lot of fat meat on that. When I walked past the Fish and Chip shop and tears came to my eyes because I was so hungry and didn't have any money for food. When I went into the supermarket in Orpington, to the veggie stalls and bought a carrot, and tears came to my eyes when I saw the loaded trollies of the other customers. I remember a man looking at me – buying just two potatoes and a carrot. I used to cook myself egg and chips every day – it's surprising how far a carton of eggs and a couple of spuds can stretch.

I've gone totally off the subject – I was writing about Mum being poorly – sometimes I see myself as hard-done-by. Other times I see myself as an angel – better and holier than everyone else. All those years locked up – I'm not really bitter about that – only it's a subject that I mustn't talk about – Taboo – it embarrasses people. Because I went through all those years of mental illness I see myself as being nearer to God. I tell God that I have forgiven Him. If I told that to Father Jack, or Father Philip, they would be horrified – to feel the need to forgive God –we're supposed to spend our lives asking Him for forgiveness. But I didn't choose to be schizophrenic. I thank God that I am well now with the Clorazil. I just sometimes feel cheated. When I see a baby, or child now they make me smile and laugh. All those years every time I saw a baby I wanted to strangle it – I thought I was the most wicked person in the world – and anyone I told thought I was wicked and evil. Why did God make me go through all that suffering? I think babies and small children are the most beautiful thing in creation – only a God of Gods could make something as beautiful as a baby – so why do Scientists think they can create a baby in a laboratory?

12.10.05

I have decided that each day's soap TV time (when I normally watch Emmerdale and Corrie) will be my daily time to do my writing work. That way I will have a regular routine and will be doing something concrete for one hour each evening. Gwen came this morning – nothing out of the ordinary to report! I woke up feeling very achey – muscles and bones complaining all through my body. I am wondering if there is a problem down below as the doctors seem determined to carry on poking at me. No news today really. Making Space meeting, very boring. Lots of rain. That's all.

13.10.05

It is 9pm and I haven't stopped today. I have just spent one and a half hours fighting with my computer. Trying to type out and print the diary. I had my hair cut and coloured today – a big improvement. I had a couple of winners at the bookies – a profit of £13.50. It all helps. Terrible news on the TV about the earthquake in Pakistan and Asia. They are very dignified people, and very family orientated. They all clearly love their children. What a difference from Hurricane Katrina, in the USA, the other week when the people turned to looting and letting the people in the hospital who couldn't move just stay there and die. It made me think of the Lord of the Flies – when in a desperate situation the people simply lost their veneer of civilization and their dignity. I have decided to work on my writing each evening when the soaps come on the TV. Soap time is now Writing Time. I am going to keep my diary each night. Also I thought that if each day I take an article from the Daily Mail and write about the person, or the matter, concerned, that would be a good way of improving my writing. But I can't do that tonight –

I'm too tired. I've had enough! Goodnight Diary.

14.10.05

8.25pm – I've just finished my nightly battle with the computer. The most difficult part of my Writing Course is not the actual writing, it is the struggle to put it all on the computer. Tonight I typed out a whole page, and then, in trying to save it I pressed the wrong key and lost it – and had to start at the beginning again! Tomorrow is Saturday and Elaine and I are going to Leeds Market. I have decided that Saturday is going to be my day off from the Writing Course. I'm out on Saturday evening anyway – and I think it's not a bad thing to have one day off each week. I haven't heard back from the tutor about the student profile I posted to her the other week and am beginning to wonder why – whether it is because of the work I sent her – I sent copies of the two pages of work I had published – perhaps she disapproves of the subject matter, I went to the bookies today. But my luck had run out. There's no such thing as easy money! I'm packing it in now – it's getting on in time and I've had a non-stop day. Goodnight Diary.

16.10.05

I have just spent two hours fighting with the computer – and have finally managed to type out The Diary of a Dysfunctional Family. I'm glad that it is finally done. I have filled in a couple of job applications, for part-time work, shelf-filling for Christmas, at Woolworths, and Wilkinsons. I'm not sure whether it is a good idea. Mum will go mad, and I won't have the time to do my Writing

Course. Strangely I seem to have more energy since I have been using the Oestregen –I'm not sure whether this is fact, or just coincidence – whether I'm kidding myself. That's all now – I've had a long, tiring day and I'm going to relax with some TV rubbish, and a bit of Harry Potter. Goodnight Diary.

17.10.05

I have finally got my work ready to send to my tutor – all I have to do now is get it photo-copied. I wonder if Gwen can show me how to copy on my computer. This morning I took my job applications to Woolworths, and Wilkinsons, but I'm not at all sure I want a job. I wouldn't have time to do my studying, and I keep waking up so tired and achey that it is a real struggle to get up in the mornings. I have been thinking whether to ask if I can take over a little bit of the back garden and make it into my own allotment. I could get gardening books and learn how/when etc to plant veggies and flowers. When I got to the Museum today there was no one there. Lindsay had left a message on my phone throwing another sickie. I've never known anyone to have as much time off as she does – even Mike and Andy at the Woodwork couldn't compete with her. That's all for now. It's 9pm – so time to pack and relax with some TV rubbish.

24.10.05

Today I am going to try to turn the beginning of my diary writing into the bones of an assignment. I am still wondering about the reaction I will get from Elizabeth Asworth about the work I have sent to her so far. I am half expecting her to write back saying she can't (won't) be my Tutor because of the nature of the work I have sent to her. I am still wondering what I will do if she does this – I think I will be hurt, but not surprised. Les Carlisle has been working on Stigma and Prejudice against People with Mental Illness. If she does do this to me, I'll phone him and put it in his book. I will work on this piece (towards assignment 2) from today until Mum and I come back from Blackpool. That would cover the trip with Making Space to Bradford – and all the characters and relationships involved in that. And also my relationships, and emotions/feelings/thoughts/deep-down anger/ towards Mum/ Five days will be in the hotel in Blackpool in Winter – plus her 88th birthday – and giving her the sewing picture – that should all cover quite well. Me and them and Me and Mum. That ought to be enough for the piece of writing. I have had all day to myself today. Lindsay phoned AGAIN to cancel the Museum work. I wish she had the guts to say "Christine, I really don't want you here anymore," instead of leaving me every Monday to wait for the phone to ring with her latest excuse.

Anyway, it was a cold, wet day so I stayed in on my own all day. Something I haven't done for ages – and spent all day sorting out my paperwork and my files. I'm actually quite proud to have nearly tackled the job. I've given it a good bash anyway. I haven't done any Lifetimes work since last week, so am going to try really hard to get stuck in this week. On Saturday I had another go at reading Maya Angelou's wonderful book I know 'Why The Caged Bird Sings'. It is quite hard work but is worth every minute spent on it. I will continue with it, and with Kilver's Diary when I have finished Also Ran – Harry Potter 3. That's about it for today really – having spent the day on my own – chucking out a lot of paperwork, and sorting out the list of each months Incoming and Outgoing money through the Bank.

26.10.05

I didn't write my Diary last night because I was too tired, so I'll try to make up for it tonight. I went for lunch with Linda at Jim's yesterday, as we do every Tuesday. BORING, BORING. Linda doesn't help herself at all – we have the same conversation every Tuesday. She eats the same thing every Tuesday – I feel as if I should be paid to be her support worker. Even her poor little cat, Kitty, seems to be permanently suffering from depression. Actually, I think the poor little cat is suffering permanently from constipation – Linda only gives her dry food and she has a tummy like a little hard barrel. Like owner, like cat, miserable, bored –BORING. When I got home Kath and Phil Furnival turned up. I put the kettle on and it turned out that they wanted me to go with them to the Crown at Birkdale for a photoshoot with The Visitor. The Crown has adopted Making Space as it's charity project and we were expected to be presented with a cheque for about £200 from them. Elaine turned up at about 2pm and agreed to join in it all with us. Anyway, when we got there it wasn't quite what we had been expecting. I had never been in the Crown before – it's a really nice pub. There were small groups of people from CAMRA (Campaign for Real Ale) who were supposed to be pushing beer barrels around the pub car- park in aid of Making Space. We all had our photos taken in the car-park, but when we came away, about 6pm, it was dark and raining outside and nobody had attempted to push any beer-barrels around the wet, cold car-park.

When we came away Phil offered to buy us all pizzas at the take-away in Manchester Road. So he got them and we all went back to Phil and Lorraine's flat – a lovely, cosy, snug flat by Hesketh Park. And so home. And so to bed! I have been sorting out my stuff from my suitcase to go away on Friday. I met Elaine in town and we had breakfast in Woolworth's and did a few jobs. Then I left her because I had an appointment with Dr Vessa. I told him that I really want to kick-start my life back again. I told him about Lindsay making excuses every Monday for me not to work in the museum. He told me to speak to Joanne about it. On reflection I think that's a bad idea, as Jo and Lindsay are thick as thieves. Dr Vessa says it is illegal for people to discriminate against people who have been ill – but things aren't always as black and white as that are they? I told him about applying for jobs and not getting any response, and being turned down for the job of cleaning the car park. Dr Vessa said that's because I was over-qualified for that but I actually didn't tell the fellow at the car park that I had a drawer-full of academic certificates. I told Dr Vessa too, about not hearing back from the tutor of my writing course. I'm paying a lot of money for my course and getting no response. If I have not received anything back from her by the time we come back from Bradford I will start to stir things up a bit. They can't just ditch my work and refuse to take me on as a student because I've been ill – can they? Dr Vessa says not. So that's about it for today really. Gwen and I went to Hesketh Park in the rain – I'm going to take my camera there next week – The autumn leaves and the work they are doing on the lake make some pretty unusual photographs. I'm just going to read Maya Angelou's book for a while. I finished Harry Potter 3 last night. The plot is so complicated. It must be pretty strange to be able to think like that, and write like that. All for now. G'night Diary.

Diary of a (very long) Fortnight – Thursday 27th Oct 2005
Well Diary –tomorrow morning begins the annual ghastliness of our two winter breaks. I took Satin to the Cattery – it is quite strange in the flat without her. I have to make sure I get up early. We are going to Bradford tomorrow at 10am. We begin our Making Space bun-fight – this year to Bradford for three days – praying that we all survive that long. We have all spent months looking forward to our weekend away – planning, discussing it, saving for it – and now it's upon us – wondering, and worrying, at the hugeness of it.

There are so many diverse characters in our group that it is inevitable that new friendships are made and old ones shattered – and by the time we arrive home on Sunday night some souls will be rather battered. So – it's bedtime on Thursday and I am just holding my breath until we reach home on Sunday. The thing is, for me, when this ordeal is accomplished, after I have collected Satin from the cattery, and laundered my clothes – it will be time to re-pack my suitcase to go to Blackpool for five days with Mum – God help us! We go each year to celebrate her birthday. She will be 88 next Tuesday. As the years go by it becomes more of an ordeal. I have to look after her, whilst at the same time obeying her and trying to keep her happy – and fighting for survival myself!

I have just watched the first part of a dramatization of Dickens' Bleak House. What wonderful characterisation. I don't think I have ever finished reading an entire Dickens novel, except A Christmas Carol. I don't think anyone does these days. We are all too impatient – it is much easier, quicker, more effortless to simply watch it on TV, or buy the video. I received a long report from my OCA Tutor – Mrs Elizabeth Ashworth. I was very pleased. I had expected her to be hostile to me but she was quite the opposite. I want to spend the next fortnight on this diary making it into a story for the next piece of work I have to submit to her – it will be the story of how I and my friends pass our lives and fill our days. I think that in order to make my story more interesting I hope to open my mind and my ears to what is going on around me. When I was ill I had a very different outlook on the world around me, but being better helps. Or does my being nearly normal mean that I have lost that spark' – that unusual way of looking at the world around me? I need to cultivate it again if I am going to be a writer. In fact I know that my writing is more original if I do not take my medication. I am going to read Maya Angelou's book now. I would like to be able to look at things, remember things, describe things, as she does. I think I need to practice thinking if I am going to be a Writer. G'night.

Bradford, 28.10.05

Well, it is Friday night and it has been a very strange day. It's hard to remember this morning -It seems so long ago! We left Southport at 10am and were headed for Holmfirth. We thought we were nearly there and were itching to get off the coach – but the driver had taken a wrong turning which added about half an hour to the journey. When we finally reached Holmfirth I was getting very twitchy. I just wanted to sit outside for a while on my own. I find a long coach trip difficult and by the time we reached Holmfirth – the village of Last of the Summer Wine, I was pretty wound-up, so I left Lesley and Joanne to go exploring on their own whilst I found a bench on my own for a little while until I felt better. It is usually a bit risky to leave the two of them together for long, inevitably sparks will fly before long. We all had a quick look around the Summer Wine exhibition and then Joanne, Lesley and I wandered around the village looking for a toilet and food. We got some chips and sat on a seat to eat them and then wandered off around the shops. We managed to spend some money in a record amount of time – I bought a couple of things to put on the armchairs in my sitting room. We left Holmfirth at 4pm. I thought it was a very dirty, scruffy village with too much traffic tearing through the narrow streets – it wasn't at all the way it appears on the programme. Apparently they no longer film the programme there. It is mainly filmed on a set in London, except of course the outdoor scenes of the moorland.

We came over Saddlewitch Moor, which reminded me of Myra Hindley and Ian Brady. Finally we arrived at the Dubrovnic Hotel. A beautiful building inside and out. It is hard to imagine that we are in the heart of Bradford – an industrial city. I imagine that these sort of buildings were probably built for the mill owners in the time of the wool industry. Anyway, we found our room. I got showered and changed. We watched the news and Joanne was changing when, suddenly, about 6.50pm, the lights went out! Suddenly we were plunged into darkness. Joanne thought I was larking about but I went to the door of the room and although the corridor light was still on (emergency power) everyone else was standing at their doors saying "What's happening?" One of the hotel staff came up and said, "It's not just the hotel, if you look out of the window the whole area is in darkness except in the far distance. If you go down to the bar, that's where people are gathering. We will bring candles down there." It seems to have occurred at the moment when half the women in the hotel were putting on their knickers, or were in the bath!

So we all crowded into the (very small) bar. The only lights still on were the emergency lights on the corridor and the bar, which was candlelit. So, we crowded into there and the spirit of the Blitz took over – but as time went on and we had nothing to eat except crisps the shilling-in-the meter' jokes faded and hunger took over. Fortunately most of us already know each other, as it is mostly pretty much the same group who come on these trips. We had sat down there for nearly an hour, eating crisps and wondering if we were going to get some dinner. It was a long time since we had had the chips in Holmfirth. Then the Hotel Manager said, "If there is no power in another ten minutes we are going to make some sandwiches." Eventually the lights came back on. Everybody cheered.

With the promise of dinner on the horizon we moved into the dining room and waited – and waited. By the time the first course arrived we had all gossiped ourselves to death and knew the most intimate secrets of our neighbours, and their neighbours. Joanne and I agreed later that the major problems that both George and Ben have is their mothers – who have accompanied them on the holiday. What a beautiful room that dining room is – it's circular, and reminds me of the Pavilion in Brighton. I wondered what it was originally built as – I know the Pavilion at Brighton was just built as the stable for the horses of the Prince. I had chicken liver pate, roast pork and raspberry gateau. By the time pudding was served I had just about had enough. They waited for their coffee, and I wished them all goodnight. It's been a long and eventful day. Lesley is really fed up and grumpy at having to share her room with Beverly – who never stops talking! Its 10.20 now and Joanne still hasn't come up. She will be up soon – I think I'll feign sleep when she arrives – I've had enough for one day! But it has been a lovely day, so I'm ready for bed. G'night Diary.

29.10.05

What a lot I've got to tell you tonight Diary! First of all, I've been thinking about how to work out my assignment 2, to be based on diary entries. I thought I would write some characterisations of some of the (strange) people on this holiday, and would work it out from them, like an artist doing a pencil sketch and then filling in the details and the background to complete the picture. But the artist has to paint the whole composition, based on the original sketches and cartoons. First of all, this morning at breakfast Lesley was throwing her toys out of the pram, grumbling that Beverly had been talking all night. Beverly said Lesley had left the TV on all night! Two grown women acting like a couple of kids. Lesey said she didn't want to come out with us – so we didn't bother begging her. It was her look out if she wanted to miss the whole day's outing just for the sake of sulking. Joanne was getting wound up about it, but I said to her forget it. I didn't tell her that the real reason behind this display of sulking by Lesley was that Lesley is jealous of Joanne and I being friends. Lesley wants me, or Joanne, to herself. Her nose is pushed out of joint by being the third in the group. I just ignore it. When we got back tonight Lesley was still mumbling and grumbling about Beverly. Thank heavens we're going back tomorrow or there'd be war in the kindergarten.

And so we went to Scarborough, and then on to Whitby. Joanne and I walked down the long hill of shops to the beach. We sat on the beach drinking tea and finding this gorgeous sunshine unbelievable – next weekend the Christmas lights are to be switched on in Southport, but today in Scarborough it was like midsummer. The donkeys were taking the children for rides on the beach. Children were making sandcastles. It is half-term but it was like midsummer. Anyway, we had a little walk around the Charity Shops and I bought a nice sweater for £4.95. Then we went to Whitby – I have been there a few times with Mum but had never seen more than just a bit of the harbour. The place was packed, in some parts we were walking shoulder to shoulder. We had such a laugh in Whitby – I thought it was a sleepy little port but this weekend there was a goth convention there – I thought it was carnival time, or pantomime time, there were so many people in extraordinary outfits, multi-coloured hair and strange make-up – and they weren't all young either, some were about my age. It reminded me of the Kings Road in the 60' on a Saturday – everyone parading their outfits and extreme 'hairdo's – the more extreme the better. I believe they are cult-followers of an American murderer called Michael Manson, but they weren't all youngsters. One woman had a tiny baby – maybe six weeks old, dressed up in a red devil outfit – complete with horns and tail. Somebody else had dressed their dog up gothic – I had never before seen a dog wearing fishnet tights. We laughed so much. The old part of Whitby reminded me of St Ives years ago. Whitby was brilliant – atmospheric, fun, and bustling with humour. The fact that it was a brilliant hot day (even though it's nearly the end of October) added to the atmosphere.

Joanne and I went on a boat trip around the harbour and out to sea a bit. It was a smallish boat, model of Cook's Endeavour ship. It only cost £2 for half-an-hour and was really good. I took loads of photographs. And so, back on the coach to Bradford. On the coach I read today's Daily Mail, and began to feel I was in a vacuum going on forever, but seeming as if it would never actually arrive anywhere. Finally we got back to the hotel. When we arrived back at the hotel Lesley had had time to sulk-herself out and re-joined the party quite happily. We got showered and changed and went down to dinner. And that was the bit that, after such a lovely day, really spoilt things. Put a tin lid on the sunshine. Just everybody had something to moan about. And moan they did! There was a party of pigeon-fanciers in the hotel tonight – and Joanne embarrassed me by making loud and offensive remarks about Jack Duckworth. Nothing makes me so angry as rudeness – it sours the atmosphere needlessly. The pigeon-fanciers had a Disco-Party and some of our party asked permission to join it but were told no. We were moved into a smaller dining room for dinner – only the service is slow. I was hungry and got a bit irritable – but everybody seemed to be aiming to out-moan each other. I finally left them to it. I didn't wait for the coffee. I came up here leaving Joanne down in the bar and Lesley in the dining room. Moaning is something that irritates me, but rudeness really makes me angry. In Scarborough today we went to the public toilets and had to pay 20p to a toilet-warden as we went in. Joanne was really rude to him about the 20p. I was angry and ashamed. When we came out I said to the toilet attendant, "I apologise for my friend's rudeness to you." I don't know whether Joanne heard anything. She didn't say so. I've worked as a toilet cleaner, in Pleasure-land, and nobody, nobody, whether they're a toilet cleaner or the Prince of Wales, deserves to be publicly insulted. It was like the to-do with Lesley, in Southport, the other week with the fellow who sells the Big Issue. Actually, Joanne has quite a few times been publicly rude and loud and critical and insulting – it's very embarrassing. At least when Mum and I are on holiday, or out together, she is never rude to people. When a person is publicly rude and loud-mouthed the person who they show up is themselves. Well Diary, I am going to have another coffee and cigarette and get my book out and read for a while until Ann comes up with the latest tirade of insults. We are only paying £40 for this weekend, and the pigeon-fanciers do not deserve to be publicly called Jack Duckworth's. I am struggling a bit now. I am not used to being in a group of people all the time, especially one like ours where there are so many diverse characters that fireworks are going off when you least expect it, and you know when to turn the other cheek and walk away. I'm totally drained, so I think I'll put my head down now – home tomorrow –thank goodness. Goodnight Diary.

Sunday 30th Oct 2005

And so we have packed up our suitcases, taken lots of photographs of the hotel and given our last Goodbye and Thank You to our friends amongst the hotel staff. We had about four hours in the rain in York before returning to Southport. I would have gone in to look at York Minster but it cost £5 to enter. Some of our group told us that they went in the back door, and so didn't have to pay £5. Now here's a puzzle. Which is the most un-Christian? The church people who charge a fiver entrance – or the people who sneak in the back-door of the cathedral - or the people who say "I can't afford it," and go and spend their fiver in the pub across the road? Lesley was spend, spend, spend – even paying £40 for a teddy bear.

Anyway we finally got back on the coach and I made peace with Joanne. As we drove back over the Yorkshire Moors I had never seen such wonderful skies, unbelievable cloud formations and colours on the moors and the trees. I could have just sat all day drinking in the beauty of it, but of course the coach was moving, and so were the clouds. Do countries that have endless sunshine have beautiful clouds and skies like we do? And so home to Southport. Some friendships have become rather thin and stretched, others have been newly cemented – but personally I couldn't wait to get indoors to my own armchair, a cup of tea, and a ciggy (with no-one to frown at me smoking!) and to Thank God that it is all over and nothing ghastly happened.

31.10.05

Hello Diary, I didn't write up my diary last night because I was too tired by the time we arrived home from Bradford. We had left Bradford at 9.30am. I've taken loads of photographs of the lovely hotel, and trees around etc. We had three and a half hours in York – where it rained and rained just pausing for a break until it rained, again. I ended up going around York with Lesley – I sometimes feel as if Joanne and Lesley are fighting over me – that one pulls one arm and the other pulls the other arm, like one of those tug-of-war competitions. Anyway, joanne had won on Saturday, so Lesley won on Sunday – and I'm the one trying to keep the peace, as well as being the one pulled between the two of them. Anyway, to finish off yesterday's story, we arrived home about 7pm, and I was very glad to be back in my own nest, in my own armchair with a cup of tea and a packet of cigarettes and perfect peace and relaxation.

1.11.05

So, I went this morning, in the taxi to Knowsley Road, to pick up Satin. The cattery lady said that Satin wouldn't eat her food. (surprise!) So they had bought her the same tin from Marks and Spencer. She gave me a tin of M&S tuna cat food and saw that Satin had settled down back at home again. I can't afford to buy food for myself from Marks and Spencer's, never mind for the cat! As I write this she just came and sat on my knee and is now tucking into some Felix treats. She has been really performing since I brought her home so I think she is just about to make herself sick. Now she's cuddling down on my knee again – I feel like a monster because she is going to have to go to Elaine's on Saturday because Mum and I are going to Blackpool.

Anyway, I went over to Mum's today, and then to the museum. We were sorting out and classifying some old children's toys and books today – some from the time of Queen Victoria, and some more recent. I enjoyed it and the time flew by. So, here I am again, writing up the latest news and views. I phoned Elaine and asked her to wake me early tomorrow as I have an appointment with Dr.

Ronson at 8.20am. I really hope she doesn't hurt me again. I am worried about all these cervical smears – there must be some reason why they are so painful, and why the doctor keeps trying to do it. I am worried that there is some sinister medical reason behind it all. All for now Diary – I'm going to watch TV for a bit and then go to bed with Maya Angelou. G'night

3.11.05

I haven't written my diary for a few days. Nothing very exciting has happened and sometimes I just don't have the energy to do everything! I have made a decision about withdrawing from Hempton Road's support network. As soon as the doll's house has been despatched, and as soon as the Christmas meal is sorted out I will stop going to woodwork. Instead I am going to return to the fortnightly sewing group in Formby. Also I am going to withdraw from the allotment group. I spoke to Rob today, asking him if I could take a patch of the back garden and create my own allotment. He said he will speak to Kevin but cannot see any problem about it. How lovely, to be able to just potter about on my own little patch, instead of having to go all the way over to Moss Road. I will enlist my cousin Philip's help in learning how to do it all. I can spend the winter studying gardening books on how to grow veggies. I thought a good start might be the River Cottage books. I have told Mum to spread the word that for Christine's birthday I want book tokens, with doing my writing course there are lots of books I want. I was very pleased to see the Nab End books, as recommended by Elizabeth Ashworth, for only £4.99p. I am going to start it tonight, having just finished reading The Caged Bird Sings by Maya Angelou last night. What a wonderful book – it starts with childhood and completes the cycle with giving birth. I think the main impression that you get is the dignity with which the people of the Black South tackle the discrimination from the white folk. It made me think that the young, second generation, black people in London today do not maintain that dignity, or the love of learning. It is a very different world now. I need to think about this some more. Where does the attitude towards religion in both groups affect all this? I really haven't got much more to write tonight. I have been thinking about assignment two – The Diary of a Fortnight'. I thought I might work on a couple of character impressions of people in the MS group etc. And try to look at the ongoing events through their eyes – the same events from different angles – based on the Bradford holiday, and also the holiday in Blackpool. I need to do some thinking and some work on this – I will have plenty of time to think and to write about it while we are in Blackpool. I am going to fill in the paperwork for my next walking holiday in Bowness next July. Also, I am going to fill in a form applying for a Waitress job in the restaurant in BHS in Southport.

4.11.05

I can't write much tonight Diary – I am too tired. I don't know how I am going to get over the next five days with Mum – the very thought of it terrifies me – every time she and I go on holiday together the same terrifying, thoughts and feelings return and I struggle to get through the holiday. I know she is my Mum, but I have been so ill for so long – people think if they ignore my illness it won't be there, but I know different. Please God stay by my side. I just want to have some time on my own – with no one demanding, or expecting, anything from me. I keep up this veneer of wellness – the only person I can't fool is myself. I just want some time on my own. 'Nab Fed' G'night.

Blackpool, November 5th, 2005

And so, having spent the last few days gathering myself together and recovering from the shatterings of the Bradford bun-fight, I now find myself sharing a shoebox of a room with Mum in Blackpool. The hotel-owner-family are quite extraordinary. They seem to want to adopt Mum and me. Every time I go into the sitting room for a smoke, one or other of them will nobble me and start telling me their family history and all the business of the other family members. I really don't want to know! I went out on my own, along the promenade tonight – to get away from Mum for a bit and to see the illuminations which finish tomorrow night. Of course, being a Saturday night in Blackpool it was full of hen-parties and stag-parties but I was a bit surprised to see a naked man in the street. However, when I mentioned it to one of the hotel family later they said it was quite a regular thing. I'm rather glad I live in Southport. And so we struggle on

6.11.05

So, the second day of our holiday in Blackpool – and I have gone into a daze of apathy and boredom. I've just switched off and can't wait to get back to life and living again. How is it that when I'm at home there aren't enough hours in the day, but here every day is a week long? We went to a craft fair at a big hotel in Blackpool called the Norbeck Court. I am totally in Mum's control. I am the puppet, she pulls the strings, and at the same time I feel as if I have to look after her. She started talking about moving to a rest home in St Anne's today – she thinks Southport is going downhill. She only goes into Southport about twice a year. She said that if she moved to St Anne's it would help me come to terms with the idea that she won't be there forever. I still don't know what to make of that remark.

I got conned out of £2 by a bloke selling little leaflets to give money to children who need wheelchairs. I said to him, "It is a genuine charity, isn't it?" "Oyes," he said. So I handed him the money – but when I looked at my £2 leaflet of course it wasn't a genuine charity. I should have known. The welfare state might be going downhill but at least we can buy wheelchairs for children who need them. After two days in Blackpool I really don't have anything interesting to write – my brain has frozen with apathy. G'night Diary.

Tuesday, November 8, 2005

Today is Mum's birthday and she is delighted with the present I gave her. It is a hand-sewn picture of her and Dad – copied from their wedding picture in 1944. I would like to claim that it is all my own work – but it isn't. I am a sewer, and I did try to do it, but it was beyond my capabilities so I had to pay Elizabeth West to do it for me. Anyway, Mum was well pleased. The hotel people gave her a card, and put a lighted candle on her breakfast of poached eggs on toast, which made me laugh. We have been going out in the mornings, but there has been heavy rain and strong winds every day and Mum can't walk far. I have to go out – I can't stay in that shoebox all day. The sea has been coming over the sea-wall every day. I can't wait to get home. I thank God that I have survived this past fortnight – It is the time of the year that we all look forward to, and secretly dread. It is the longest fortnight of the year.

Wednesday, November 9th, 2005

Home again. Thank God. To smile, to socialise, and to silently, secretly struggle and swear. That's what it's all about – the annual Making Space winter break, followed relentlessly by our annual winter break in Blackpool to celebrate Mum's birthday. She was 88 this year, and it becomes more and more of an ordeal. We arrived home today and it is such a relief to be able to sit in my own armchair with a cuppa, a smoke (no one to glare at me when I get out the fags!). Somehow I have survived the annual ordeal. I am so tired. I want to get my assignment 2 sorted. I have just sat and re-read the last few weeks diary entries.

We got home from Blackpool today and I feel completely drained, as if I have done a long and exhausting job, when in fact all I have done is spend a few days in Blackpool with Mum, and before that the MS Weekend. I want to catch up on my writing. If I could just spend about two hours a day on it I could get a bit more organised. The time in Blackpool was mostly spent in a tiny shoe-box room with Mum, reading and watching TV. It was too wet and cold to go out much and I was a bit spooked about going out on my own in the evening – after the Saturday night when Blackpool was full of 'Stag Parties' and 'Hen Parties'. I'm so glad to be home. The time there was like sitting in a vacuum, watching the hands on a clock move – ever so slowly. The hotel owners and their family were a very strange lot – they talked so much, (especially John, and Elaine – Lyn's parents), that it became irksome and embarrassing. Every time I wanted a smoke I had to go into the dining room and listen to the family stories and histories. I think they felt sorry for me being stuck in the shoe-box with Mum.

I am so glad to be home in my little flat. I sometimes think I would like to have a partner – a bloke to share things with, but at the end of the day there is nothing like peace and quiet and just being on your own. Mum was pleased with the picture – so she should be – the price of it!

There is no phone message, or letter from BHS about the job I applied for. Another one bites the dust. Actually I'm not sure what I would do if someone did offer me a job! I got Satin home from Elaine's. She (the cat) is very sulky and miserable – she has been pushed around from pillar to post lately – I'm glad for my own sake, as well as for Satin's, that there are no more holidays booked until next July. I feel as if at least I might be able to get my bank account sorted. I went to the market to buy the pink rug that I want for the sitting room. The one I want has been there for months – but today when I went it had gone. The lady said she would have another in about five weeks. I have got new cushions and lampshades for the sitting room and Elina has given the whole flat a good clean-up. I'm packing this up for tonight. Satin is laying on my knee wanting to be stroked – and I'm going to read today's Times and then go to bed with 'Nab End'. The telly is on the blink. So that saves me any time watching that. I'll check the lotto numbers later. G'night

10.11.05

Nothing really to write about – except that I won £69 on last night's lottery. That paid for a trip to Tesco's and the week's ciggies. I am struggling with assignment 2. I have done the donkey work on it. I am going to set myself an hour, and simply sit and write it – I'll try to do it tomorrow night – the sooner I can get it all typed out, the sooner I can get back to the nitty-gritty work that I have been neglecting. That's all I've got to say tonight. I'm trying to sort out a load of paperwork – I always seem to be drowning in paperwork. G'night.

4.12.05

Well, I haven't completed my diary for many weeks. I managed to send off assignment 2 on Tuesday, four days late, but have not managed to keep up with my work. I have so many things going on, although I packed in the allotment, and woodwork, I still seem to be continually rushing around.

I didn't go to see Mum today. She is not well at the moment.

She asked me not to go today, although I offered to go over and do her lunch for her. I think she has finally realised how much I do and how tired I get. I seem to be permanently running on the spot – rushing around getting nowhere.

I have spent this morning sorting out my lifetimes paperwork. I am going to make a real effort to do some study-work daily and keep up with the work. This afternoon Elaine and I are going to the Salvation Army carol concert at the Arts Centre. That'll put us in the Christmas mood. I think Mum was quite hoping that I would go to the carol service at Queens Road. She has contributed for a light for life candle for Dad. Only we had already booked our tickets for the Salvation Army. What a pity they clash in their arrangements.

I am still weighing up whether to sign on to do voluntary work at the new PDSA bookshop, Charity Shop. I know I would enjoy it, but I seem to have so much going on at the moment. I had planned to do dozens of Christmas cards, cross-stitch, but somehow they never got done. There just aren't enough hours in the day! When I am very tired I switch on the TV. The celebrity jungle programme really does make me laugh. Also The X Factor, and Strictly Come Dancing. They call them reality TV. What puzzles me is all the (apparent) millions who spend their time, and money, telephoning all these programmes to vote for the singer/dancer/celebrity. I only once ever telephone-voted for a TV programme. It was years ago. I was watching the Eurovision Song Contest and this German singer was so bad that I had to vote for him to win. It must be the English sense of humour. The other countries hardly gave him any votes at all, but loads of British people had voted for this terrible singer.

The more I write the more I can't read my own handwriting because I write so fast. Before I sign off, I bought three money box cows in the charity shop the other day. I have named them Stripey, Daisy and Blue Bum. All for now. I am going to spend some time on my Lifetimes file now – and I'll try to spend some on my study work in the morning. Cheers.

5.12.05

I am struggling at the moment – with Mum having had a bug all last week and me looking after her. I think she has passed it on to me – only I don't have time to be ill because I have to look after Mum. I am going over there nearly every day and she is simply sitting back in her armchair giving orders to me, or to her carer called Doreen. She is being a bit Queen Victoria-ish. I nearly didn't go into the library for my work with Lindsay today. I felt so ill. I suppose I'm just stubborn. Elaine and I are going to clean Michael's flat tomorrow. A few bob extra always comes in handy. On Wednesday we are going to Birkdale Victoria Festival. I'm not sure whether it will be worth the time and journey. We shall see. Elaine and I had a problem over the Sally Army Carol Concert yesterday. I lost her, and I had the tickets. She managed to get in without her ticket whilst I was still standing outside British Home Stores waiting for her!

8.12.05

Another busy day. Gwen came first thing this morning. She showed me the annual update of the records about me, kept in Imagine offices. Once a year we have to read and sign them. It really said very little about me. They made me sound very dull and boring, which I am sure I am not. I have got the OK for my little plot of vegetable garden to go ahead. I just need for Rob to come down and work out which bit I can have. I went over to Mum's and Doreen was there. I gave her her shopping and had a bit of lunch with her. She is well again now. She really is like Queen Victoria. Although she is 88 and no longer mobile, her mind is as sharp as ever. So when she is on her own so much of the time her mind is always busy – move this, buy that, send a message to this one, post that – and then up turns Christine, and I get the lot chucked at me! She just has no idea how exhausted I get. If I go over and spend half-an-hour sitting with her it doesn't occur to her that the effort of getting to and from Stirling Court from Meals Cop Road can take an hour each way. All this sounds as if I begrudge helping her, and looking after her. I really don't. Sometimes I think of old memories. Mum and Dad weren't always kind to me. I feel a bit as if I'm playing Happy Families with Mum. But at least when she does go I won't have anything to reproach myself with. I'll be able to say I shared her old age with her and helped to make her last years more comfortable and less lonely. I got to know her as a real person instead of just waiting for her to die and then looking to see what is salvageable from her home as I know my sisters will. I know Mum has passed all her family photograph albums of her own growing up years to Yvonne. I don't know why. I wish she would talk to me about her own early life. Enough for now. G'night diary.

9.12.05

Some thoughts while I am re-reading my lifetime's file, about what is permissible, and/or appropriate: The life stories of some of my friends in Broadmoor. There is so much that I would like to tell people, stuff that would open people's minds to a world which is closed to most of the human race, and which might make people sit up and think e.g. Capital Punishment – a subject for glib, know-all, stubborn views. The old lady who had been given the death sentence, and then had it rescinded and was sent to Broadmoor instead. Every morning she woke up saying, "Are they going to hang me today? Please ask them to hang me today, I can't bear waiting anymore." Do these people who support the death penalty have any knowledge, any comprehension, of the pain that that old lady went through, every day of her life?'

Or when I view a report in the papers of race/family/social killing– I think about Ali. And when I hear about cot deaths I think about V. These are stories which might open people's minds if they could hear them and start to think. The medics only give one viewpoint. You only hear the real story when you sit and share a pot of tea with someone whose mind is broken, whose life is destroyed, and you hear their tale. Sometimes I think that I know more about the minds of murderers, rapists, arsonists, and child killers than most policemen will learn in a life of police work. The irony of it all is that I have no police record myself – but in an odd way I was privileged to share the pain of these people. I have learned not to judge people, or to be mean, or narrow-minded but to look at all sides of a tale.

At Formby, Elaine, Jen and I were sitting in the Market Cafe and I mentioned about my autobiography course. They were teasing me, saying that when my book comes out they would be first in line for signed copies. I laughed along with them, but later thought if my friends read my life-story half of them would never speak to me again. I enjoy today, look forward to tomorrow, but yesterday is a black cloud in my mind, which comes to the fore-front during long sleepless night. That is when I would like a fella – someone to hold me in his arms during the night.

A Good Day

"You're supposed to set us an example, Yvonne," I said. "YOU go on the raft."

So she did. And it sank. Dave swam for dry land. Mike was hauled earthwards. The rest just paddled about in the water laughing hysterically. I stayed on dry land. Well, I was already wet through from sitting knee-deep in water in the kayak. I'd learnt by that time. I was useless on the archery, and on shooting – missed the target by miles. My excuse was that I was only wearing one contact lens so couldn't get the sight right. It didn't matter anyway. It was a good day, despite the rain that dripped from the sky, from the trees, from our hair, from our noses. I hope the photos come out – I want one to prove that I actually did reach the top of the climbing wall and abseil down. I was terrified going up, but once I got my feet back on the mud I couldn't wait to have another go. I got lots of encouragement from the rest of the group and I think that was my favourite part of the day – with the possible exception of lunch. Rock and River is set in a magical piece of countryside and we saw a rat and a rabbit, a squirrel and some wild flowers that we couldn't name. It was a day for a laugh, we were all cold and wet all day but nothing was taken too seriously and Jim was a good leader. There were pictures on the wall of little kids performing acts of bravery but it wasn't meant to be a survival course and teamwork and helping each other was what was important. When I got home I had fish and chips, and a hot bath, and was glad I'd gone. And I'd go again. In summer.

*

Mr John Pugh MP

House of Commons,

13th Jan 2011

Dear Mr Pugh,

I am writing to you as the voice of a small and normally silent group of people in Southport – those of us who have life-long problems with mental illness.

I don't know whether you are aware that the entire 'Care in the Community' system, upon which many of us are dependent, is being dismantled in Southport. Of course, we understand that many people in all walks of life are suffering from the necessity of financial cuts at present. It seems like some 'Number Crunchers' in an office in the local area have said: Care in the Community –that's a luxury we can no longer afford' If only they knew.

The Community Mental Health Team (CMHT) is a group of professionals who have spent their entire working life supporting us. When they lose their jobs (quite soon apparently) a pool of experience and teaching will be lost. What a waste. Personally, I am now 62 years old and have been 'in the system' since the age of 15. I am one of the fortunate ones – I am now quite well – largely due to the fact that when I needed support it was there – in the shape of the CMHT staff. But when this vital service is disbanded, when there is no 'Care in the Community' more people who have 'crises' will find themselves re-admitted to the Hesketh Centre. Isn't that a more expensive and wasteful use of resources – not to mention the actual human beings affected by this penny-pinching and not-thought-through exercise. I am writing to ask you, Mr Pugh, to look into this and see if anything can be rescued – on behalf of the wonderful group of people who have spent their entire working lives supporting us, as well as the people who battle daily with their mental health problems. Thank you for your time and consideration.

Yours sincerely,

Christine Delahunty

*

HOUSE OF COMMONS
LONDON SW1A OAA,
18th January 2011

Dear Ms Delahunty,

Thank you for your letter of 13th January in which you express concerns about possible job losses in local Community Mental Health teams. I am not aware of any specific proposals for cutbacks to be made in this area of provision so I have asked the Sefton Primary Care trust (NHS Sefton) to let me know the present position. When I hear, I hall let you know their response.

Yours sincerely,

Dr John Pugh

*

MP HOUSE OF COMMONS

LONDON SW1A OAA

Christine,

Any chance you could brief me about how things are now about Care in the Community' Could you phone to make an appointment.

John Pugh

(Christine didn't have the confidence to make the appointment.)

Chapter Thirty-One

CRUISING

"Jill, is it okay for me and Phil to come down next weekend?"

"Yes of course," I replied. The request was not unusual, but the immediacy was. Since I had retired and moved to Whitstable, a place that Christine and our cousin Phil were coming to love as much as I do, they had become more regular visitors enjoying the sea, lots of lovely places to eat and drink, funky independent shops, and the charity shops, which was a love my sister and I shared.

There was always plenty to do. Canterbury is an enjoyable bus ride away, helped by us now all having bus passes and Phil would also drive us out to the many interesting places round about like Dover Castle, Sandwich and Margate. He had been a great support to Christine over the years and he and I had become close too.

On arrival the first demand was always for a cup of tea. On this occasion we had just sat down with one when the words fell out of

Christine's mouth.

"Jill, I've been diagnosed with lung cancer, and the doctor has told me I've probably only got about six to 12 months to live. I don't want any tears. I want you to book a cruise for us all." She was speaking excitedly and with a clear sense of self determination. She was already pulling holiday brochures for cruises to the Caribbean and the Canaries from her bag. I glanced across the room at Phil who was looking very solemn. I was trying to take it in. Surely not on top of everything else? Hadn't Christine had far more than her fair share of illness? It's not fair, I thought. But of course it never is fair.

I fought back the tears and got up and gave her a hug saying how sorry I was and of course I would try and sort a holiday. Then I asked her what the doctors were saying about treatment. She explained as much as she knew. She mentioned chemotherapy. I knew she was still on depot injections (slow release) and other considerable medications for her psychiatric condition and also the other conditions she had by this time been diagnosed with – the onset of Parkinsonism, and osteoporosis. I suggested that it was important to ensure that those treating her for the cancer were informed about what medication she was already on. She said she had told them. The weekend continued but we didn't speak much about the cancer. We were guided by Christine who wanted to enjoy her remaining time.

A few weeks later when I knew that Christine and Phil were coming again, I was pleased that Louise and Amelia had agreed to come for the weekend too. They arrived before Phil and Christine, which I had arranged so that I could tell them about Christine in person and we could share and dry our tears before they got here. I told them about Christine's wish for us all to go on a cruise. They both immediately agreed to come.

I had already been exploring options. I quickly decided that venturing to the Caribbean was too risky – too far should anything go wrong. A more realistic option appeared to be the Canaries. None of us had ever been on a cruise, or to the Canaries. I felt that if Christine's health, either physical, or mental should deteriorate the stops were close enough for it to be more manageable if we needed to get home. I had found a P&O Christmas cruise going from Southampton to the Canaries. All agreed happily. The hardest thing proved to be arranging travel insurance for Christine. It was very expensive but I was relieved when I finally managed to sort it as it is a requirement of going on board.

The Cruise was a great success, fortunately without incident. We even managed to get Phil into a DJ in spite of his protests of, "You're not getting me dressing up like a penguin." He received several bow ties as Christmas presents, including his favourite sparkly, rotating, flashing one, which I think Amelia was responsible for!

Fortunately Christine kept reasonably well throughout and we were all able to enjoy the holiday. Christine kept a diary.

16.12.2011

It's our first full day at sea and I'm sitting on the balcony of our cabin on the Oceana, huddled in my winter coat and hat, overwhelmed by the sheer power and beauty and glory of the sea. I could happily spend the whole holiday just sitting here watching it.

There is no way of putting into words the wonders of the sea just below where I am sitting. The colours of it are ever-changing, the constant movement, the sheer power. I have never really been at sea before so have never experienced it. The water fascinates me and draws me to it. Anne and Dad and I went on the ship out to Lundy Island once, and I've been on the occasional canal trip – even the ferry over the Mersey – they say it's because we are an Island Race – I just love it. Southport seems a world away.

I didn't really know what to expect of this trip – I was looking forward to the sunshine of the Canary Islands – it has started to rain now but that won't put me off just sitting here and looking at it. The ship is rocking now. I have to write a few words about life on the 'Oceana'. There's a collection of restaurants and bars to suit everyone at every time, and non-stop activities and events for those who need to be entertained all the time. I think at present Amelia and Louise are asleep next door, and Phil and Jill are off doing something. Tonight's dinner is I believe, semi-posh, which means I'll be wearing a dress and tights for the first time in years – I suppose they can't actually refuse to serve us and make us starve if I went down in my old corduroy trousers – but it's probably best not to chance it!

The clouds have changed and so has the sea in the last few moments. I'm afraid I'm in danger of becoming the biggest bore on the boat with my fascination with watching the sea – others are doing vital things like playing bingo or bridge, or line-dancing, or doing whatever people do in casinos. We joined the group this morning on a tour of the ship to try to find out where everything is and what is going on. We didn't go out on deck – it's too windy and actually by the end of the trail I wasn't very much wiser.

17.12.11

Sitting on the balcony of our cabin again. After a couple of very stormy days the strong winds have passed and the sea is much calmer. For the last couple of days we have all been slipping and sliding and the background noise in the bars has been punctuated by the sound of crashing crockery and glasses. Last night was quite rough and our beds seemed to be rocking from side to side with the ship. I didn't get much sleep. The sea today is not calm – we are, after all, in the Bay of Biscay in December – but we had coffee out on the deck this morning, the five of us, warmly wrapped up of course.

The colour of the sea seems to be constantly changing. Just to sit and watch the ever churning, ever changing, extraordinary beauty of the sea. Just those chances to sit and watch it – they are a gift from God. I mentally toss all the bad things overboard into the bottom of the ocean and thank God for all the good things. If I get ill in the coming months – and I probably will – then I'll re-live these wonderful few days spent with the family and just watching the sea.

As we move south in the next few days, down to the Canary Islands, the sun will almost certainly come out, which will be nice but is not essential. I think we are all rather troubled by the fact that every single passenger is white-skinned, and every single crew member, room steward, waiters, bar-workers etc are Asian men, from the Philippines, or somewhere like that I should think, South-East Asia. A shipload of white people being looked after by a large group of black people who work very, very hard and long hours. Forty years ago this might have been accepted as the norm. They run around all the time, hovering and catering to our every need. They never say no. I think it embarrasses us all.

I am now regarding the ship, the Oceana, as an aging, fading dowager – she certainly was bright and beautiful once. Everything nearly works. Everything sparkled once. From the furnishings to the way the cruise is run, to the crew themselves, 'Good morning, Madam', everything is of yesteryear, everything is of faded elegance but so long as I can sit here and watch the rocking, rolling sea. I'm not at all bothered about meeting the Commodore (Captain) tonight, or any other little frills.

It's Saturday today and we have been aboard since Thursday afternoon but still a major problem - not only for us, but most of the passengers I think, is finding our way about. The 'Oceana' is a massive ship – 15 floors I think – so we are constantly lost. Jill shepherds us around as her little flock and does all the organising – I don't know how other folk on the ship get themselves to the right places at the right times at all. Jill has been a real star. The fact of the ship being so huge makes it all the more extraordinary the way it was tossed around like a cork by the sea for about 36 hours, and is only today feeling more stable and less frightening walking around. A buffet breakfast seems like a good idea until you find yourself with a tray of breakfast and you seem to be wearing someone else's feet that just won't balance properly.

I'm having a bit of time to myself this afternoon. I do get very tired, even if I don't always admit to it. I think Jill and Phil have gone to a talk on Tenerife or some-such. I have been to a couple of the talks about the places we will be stopping at. They're quite interesting as I know nothing at all about these places – they're just the names of places where other people always seemed to spend their holidays. On Monday we dock at Madeira and are going on a boat-trip to watch whales and dolphins for a couple of hours and will then spend a couple of hours in Madeira. Magic!

18.12.11

The sea is much calmer today and the wind has dropped. This means that we can walk still (a little precariously) on deck and tomorrow we will have our first port day – in Madeira. This is a huge relief as I'm beginning to get jail fever on the ship. It's a huge liner and there really is plenty to do, although we do seem to spend large swathes of time in the bars and restaurants.

Each afternoon I spend a little time just sitting alone on the balcony writing up this diary and looking out at the sea. This bit of time is a tonic in itself. It isn't that I don't like to spend time with the others, and I'm certainly not hankering for home, this cruise is a wonderful experience and I'm very glad that we are all doing it together – it's just that it's Sunday now and we've been on the 'Oceana' since Thursday and it really is an unreal world. It's a bit like we all stepped off the edge of reality for a few days, into a very odd dream.

Tomorrow we are all, except Jill, going on a boat trip to see whales and dolphins and are then meeting up with Jill for a walk around Funchal, the capital (I think) of Madeira. Amelia is going to tell me all about the underwater sea creatures when we are on the boat. She does scuba diving so has seen the wonders of the bottom of the ocean which I have only ever seen on TV (Jacques Cousteau etc).

Phil and I went to Sunday Mass this morning. There is Mass said at 9am each morning – I would quite like to go sometimes myself, but I think the others might think I was being a bit odd, a bit eccentric. Perhaps when they are getting to the last few months of their lives they will understand. Actually I would quite like to have a chat with the Father at some point. When Amelia and I were walking together on deck this morning I told her my thing about throwing my problems overboard, which she thinks is a great idea – a real Aunty Chrissy Idea. If only life was that simple. I try to carry on smiling but I do wonder sometimes what the next year will hold. (Well, don't we all?!) and whether this will be my last Christmas. I think almost certainly it will. I'm not really afraid actually to die – my faith deals with that, and my conviction that God will not turn me away, and that the actual Dying Bit will just be a matter of switching off a light and moving from this world into eternal happiness and peace. I'm just worried about the bit in-between. When I get ill and have to get through the pain bit; and the loss of dignity bit.

I expect I'll manage. I know I'll be surrounded by kind and loving people – and that it's something that'll happen to us all. I know there won't actually be a big bloke sitting on a throne above the clouds, or Saint Peter at the gate with a notebook and pencil – I'm not daft. I think that, quite simply, my body will die but I won't – the bit that is Christine – the bit that is each of us – is the bit that won't die but will simply move into happiness – no more worries, no more illness.

It's supposed to be that when we die we each get what we deserve but I find it difficult to believe in Hell, or believe that God will turn any one of his creations away. I've met some quite wicked people in my time, some who could fairly be described as evil, but I cannot believe that God would turn them away – only that they might not move immediately into eternal happiness and peace. Here I am, trying to work it out – if I knew the answers I'd be God Himself!

21.12.11

It's nearly Christmas and today we all spent the afternoon sunbathing on the beach at Gran Canaria. What an unreal world! We went again on a coach trip, this time around the island of Gran Canaria. It was a long trip on a warm day with the Spanish travel courier droning away. I just couldn't keep awake. I christened Gran Canaria as Birmingham-on-Sea. We ended up at an amazingly beautiful little harbour area, clearly aimed at rich Europeans, but large parts of the island seemed to consist of grey, grim skyscraper flats and a general air of dreariness.

Yesterday we went to La Palma – another long coach-trip around the island. It is a volcanic island but clearly the people who are native to these islands are very proud of their home-places. Still, I like Madeira and the Madeira people best of all the places we have visited these so busy days. Each morning Jill and I have had an early alarm-call and have been up in time to see as our ship approaches the next island we are visiting. Seeing the little islands coming busily to life, and watching as the sun comes up and as we dock – the pilot ship, the other liners that are coming into port with us. It is all so fascinating and exciting. I have never travelled before, but I can see now the attraction of being a traveller – moving briefly into someone else's bubble, trying it on for size and then moving on. As I write this the 'Oceana' is leaving the dock at Gran Canaria and out to sea and to our next stop, which will be Tenerife. Gran Canaria is a very busy port and there is a lot to watch as the ship moves so silently and so quickly out to sea.

Chapter Thirty-Two

FAREWELL TO CHRISTINE

During what was to be her last year, Christine's physical health steadily deteriorated. The cancer had progressed in spite of having had an operation on her lung. Throughout her illness Christine remained brave and stoical. The worst part was when she was admitted for her first bout of chemotherapy. It wasn't until she had been attached to lots of tubes that someone realised the risk this would pose alongside her ongoing medication. The treatment was immediately terminated, and Christine was sent home. All of her regular medication was abruptly stopped. This quickly made her very ill, foaming at the mouth and in serious discomfort. The medications were restarted, and Christine decided that she would not proceed with any further treatment for her cancer beyond palliative care. She was also adamant that she would not be hospitalised having spent too many years of her life in institutions.

Weekly visits to the local hospice were added to her already comprehensive care plan. Phil also cared for her and she was able to carry on staying reasonably active and self- managing.

The autumn after the Christmas cruise, Christine wanted me to arrange a cruise around the UK, but I could see it would be too much. I found a coach holiday to Oban which Christine, Phil and I were able to enjoy, although some days she was too unwell to come out. She knew, and told me that this would be her last trip. I went and stayed with Phil in Southport for Christmas week 2012 and he collected Christine at times when she was well enough to come out with us and join us. I bought her an armchair that gave her the physical support she needed.

Even though it was the middle of winter, Christine had me out in the garden planting tulip and daffodil bulbs. Neither of us mentioned that she would never see them flower. It was a big garden and she had grown a great deal there over the years, including fruit. She loved to feed the birds, even pigeons. She fed them right up to the end.

I returned home to Whitstable on December 28, 2012. Christine died peacefully, in her own home in the chair that I bought her, on January 12, 2013. Gwen, her regular carer, was with her. We scattered her ashes in the garden she had so lovingly tended. The bulbs were still to flower.

I think about Christine most days. Now that she has died, I know that she is no longer in any kind of pain, and I am glad that she was able to live and die a normal death. There had been times when she came close to dying through suicide, and that was always a devastating thought. She didn't live a long life by today's standards, but if she had managed to kill herself in her early 20s, that would have been horrendous. In reality, most of her life was lost in institutions. Her death wasn't the horrific scenario it could have been and she had a good death, not in hospital, which was extremely important to her. Christine's death is not the part of her life that has caused me the most pain, I think the worst pain was when she was sent to Broadmoor, and that still hurts me, to think of her years locked away there. And the thought of her in solitary is an awful one. Not only was she in the worst of the worst places, where the most violently mentally ill people go, but even within that, she would end up in the worst ward for long periods of time. She is no longer in pain. I don't have to fear for her anymore.

Recollections of Christine by her niece, Louise

As a small girl when my Aunty Christine would stay, I would wake to find beautiful Sindy outfits she had hand crafted. One in particular, was a soft blue suit with red buttons and a matching hat, to help Sindy break some glass ceiling or other. I also remember her telling me about my Chinese great aunt. For some reason, this fired my imagination totally. Was I a bit Chinese then? Nope. I wasn't, she explained, as the aunt had married in. Finding me clearly unsatisfied by this, she eventually submitted, "Okay, you're two hairs Chinese." How I loved those two hairs!

Generally, I experienced Christine as a gentle woman. I remember seeing her in hospitals and not really understanding what it meant that someone who looked well was there. She could seem quiet and distant in hospital and then some time later her life would seem to drastically change. One memory in particular was of meeting her at a station, her hair in a longish ponytail and warm looking clothes. I remember thinking how pretty she looked and how together, or whatever a child's concept of together is.

There was also the struggling side to my Aunty Christine, that as a child I could construe as something of a betrayal. Once I found my mum kissing her boyfriend (I struggled for years to adjust to my parent's divorce) and ran to my aunt for comfort. She looked awkward and told my mum. I was in trouble and was told, "not to look if I didn't want to see that." This made me feel very unsafe in expressing my own emotions, but as an adult I now see Christine had so seldom had her own emotional needs met and so could not have been present for the young me in that way.

Yet there was also a deep sensitivity to her, one that travels so eloquently through her written words. As the years went by I felt an unspoken bond between us that we had often both so struggled to be in the world, both struggled with generations of dysfunction and in carrying its sad and unspoken legacies.

What I will always admire about Christine was that in spite of the many dark roads she had endured, she retained some capacity for joy. In spite of multiple betrayals she could connect in small ways with her childlike innocence. I remember her excitement at seeing a West End show, how much her face lit up as the characters circled the stage. How she unashamedly waved feverishly and delightedly, beaming like she had found paradise. How she could retreat into brilliant and inventive stories, enjoyed silly hats, delicate lace and could always see the beauty in a flower. The Threads of Hope she would later write about.

Years later I had an interview to be a nursing assistant at Broadmoor where she had been a patient. "Why aren't there any flowers in the garden?" I asked the interviewer. "Patients would use them as a prop to get over the fence," she said, without a heart. I thought of Chrissy then. I didn't get the job, but in spite of this, or perhaps because of it, I am a mental health professional now.

I liked how my aunty was not a snob in any way, in spite of a sharp and perceptive intelligence that could have led her to have been. She had a laugh that made her whole body shake and sledging with her and my dad (they retained contact after my parents divorced) was a joy to see. We would sledge on occasional visits and eat potatoes she cooked on the fire. Sometimes she had boyfriends who all seemed to have red hair? "Is the hippy still coming round?" My dad would tease her about one who wouldn't take the hint. "Not anymore," she smiled.

In my teens, Aunty Christine worked for a record company, and for my 13th birthday she had Jason Donovan sign a card with red roses on: Love Jason xx. I would look at it often and think romantic 13-year-old girl thoughts – me and Jason in x amount of years.

When I was 18 or so, Aunty Christine said I was too old to call her aunty and from now it should be Christine. I never knew what this was about, but it never felt right to me, so she always stayed

Aunt. As an older woman I saw her care for her mother with grace, until she passed. Constantly criticised by her and never knowing motherly acceptance and warmth, I marvelled at my Aunt Christine's capacity to forgive her mother for never seeing what a beautiful woman and strong survivor she was, for never telling her she was good enough, just the way she was. The truth was, she was more than good enough but carried the buried shame of a woman who lacked the skill and bravery to face and examine herself. What a heavy burden that was on a delicate soul.

Recollections of Christine by her niece, Amelia

My earliest memories of Auntie Chrissy are when we would visit her in the hospitals. I remember at the time not understanding why she was there but the vision of there being never ending narrow corridors and everything was white, white and white. It was like walking into an unknown, but scary feeling place, full of the noises of people's misery. Auntie Chrissy would be quite hunched, in a gown, like she had been eagerly waiting, and so relieved to see my mum. She would be begging her to get her out of these horrible places. She would not want us to leave. Sometimes I might have to stay in another room and not even see her myself. Looking through a window hoping Mum would come back soon, but I also wanted to see my auntie as the whole journey was to visit Auntie Chrissy. Sometimes I would see her briefly, and other times I would be kept away. I didn't then realise that as a child my life could be in danger in her company.

I remember a few years later in Southport, where she had been moved to more like a bedsit, next door to a bed and breakfast. We would stay in the bed and breakfast and take her out in the day. At the start of the day she would be okay, but at any sudden moment she could switch and need to leave immediately, then it was our mission to get Chrissy home ASAP. I remember one evening, when my mum bought us all fish and chips and me a Ribena. We sat on a bench to eat it and Mum went into a phone box to make a call. It was the first time I was alone with Chrissy. She was on mountains of medication, which made her very clumsy at times, and while Mum was in the phone box, the fish and chips fell on the floor. Chrissy's frustration and exhaustion at this time in the evening, along with the fear of making the smallest mistake, made her shout at me and I burst into tears. Then she panicked even more and my Mum came running over to see what had happened and Chrissy blamed me for the stuff falling. We got her back to her home as quickly as possible and I was hiding behind my Mum holding tightly to her hand. Then when she reached home she calmed down and wanted a kiss and a cuddle. I was terrified and didn't want to. That's the first time I was fearful of Chrissy and started to understand what was going on with her.

The mountains of medications I would see when she came to stay in Brixton in my Mum's house at this point were overwhelming. What were they all for? Why were there so many? I always wondered but never asked. I remember when Auntie Anne and Auntie Chrissy came to stay and we went to the London Eye and Trafalgar Square. This was a good day apart from the bit on the bus home when Auntie Chrissy declared to my mum that she was going to move to London and come and live with us in Brixton. She repeated this spontaneous idea all the way home. After she had gone to sleep that night I said, "Auntie Chrissy isn't really going to live with us, is she?" That was the first time I admitted my fear of her to my mum.

In the school holidays we had to visit my grandparents sometimes, yet they only came to visit me once in Brixton for the Chelsea flower show. When we would see my grandparents and my auntie, I really didn't like the way my Nan treated my Mum and my aunties or me and my sister. Her company was so cold, so careless, and as Chrissy got older, and after my Grandad died, my Nan used to order Chrissy around to do everything for her. Chrissy would be working in cleaning jobs, in cafes, and on the pier at the same time as trying to take care of my Nan. My Nan who was rude and bossy and never ever looked after her or any of our family really.

My Mum had to be a mum to Christine from the time of boarding school from Chrissy being aged 14, to the end of her life aged 64. Mum helped her when she was in need. Mum went to the tribunals. Mum did everything she could to look after her sister whilst maintaining a busy and full life of her own as a single mother bringing up two children 13 years apart. My mum supported Christine throughout 40 years of her life so it's had a massive impact on our family.

Christine was told she was never allowed to have children, and if she did they would be taken away from her. Christine had rarely been able to leave the country until she was dying of lung cancer. She smoked so much due to the stresses of her imprisoned existence.

When Christine was diagnosed, she was not scared, she was ready. She had spent most of her life trying to escape it, running in front of busses where she lost all her teeth; setting herself on fire; she had tried to escape life so many ways as well as trying to cut her wrists while staying with my mum when my sister was two and living in the house in Camberwell. Mum couldn't have done more for her.

It was always hard to see Christine in the early years as I could read the sadness and pain in her face without the real understanding that started to become clearer when I got older and understood what it was all about. My Mum's annual healing is going abroad and I was so lucky to have experienced so much of the world with my Mum. This was her escape, her time when she could get away and free herself from the mountains of responsibilities she was constantly juggling at home and weighing so heavily on her all the time.

In 2001, when I was 13, we moved to one of the remotest islands in the world, St Helena. When Christine got older, and after my Nan died, she seemed to get quite a lot better. She would still break sometimes, but she could smile and laugh and really want to try and troop through days out with me and my Mum. The excitement of going out and about was always much looked forward to as Mum would lead the pack and make sure everyone was okay and the breaking point of a day was an instant home time.

When Christine was in a supported living home in Southport, rather than the horrible hospitals she had been in and out of throughout the rest of her life, she finally had this added freedom to be allowed to make her flat a home, full not empty, colourful not white, full of pieces of Chinese furniture and oriental pieces. She was able to have a cat and that gave great comfort to her too. Most importantly it was her place and she could finally make a home however she wanted it to be. When Chrissy knew she was dying she laughed about it and wouldn't let us cry. She really wanted to celebrate by going on a cruise and for us all to enjoy it with her. My Mum, me, my sister and my great cousin Phil joined her. Being on a ship was what she had heard about me and my mum doing for three years to and from St Helena, something she could only dream of before, and see photos of, and never be allowed until it was too late to fully enjoy a travelling experience. Her favourite thing to do was sit on the balcony and watch the waves crashing by, she found it incredibly magical watching the sea, the sparkles in the sea. The stars had never shone so brightly for her. Walking around the ship with me she listened to my stories of the underwater world. I was telling her happy stories that she could graphically picture in her mind to make her feel like she could be a part of those experiences.

I also asked her lots of questions about her life, and the loves she had, and the times that were hard, and the times that were happy. I needed to learn as much as I could in the end because she was often too scared to talk about it before, too scared to reveal any of what Mum has collected as the scraps of thoughts and creative poetry she wrote over the years. She was too scared when she was younger that if she exposed any of the brutal honesty people would come for her and hurt her more than she had been hurt before.

When she had her own place, her final home and finally a real one, she had time to be creative and always got such joy out of her creative therapy. She would spend months before Christmas making, sewing, and planting gifts so they were unique and special and would be kept by the family to remember her when she's gone. She spent a lot of time planting daffodils, looking after the garden, and feeding the birds, another favourite part of her days at home with the little boy that lived upstairs. He would enjoy helping her feed the birds. And between Nanny dying and her dying she felt more comfortable talking about anything. When the Jimmy Savile thing was all over the news she told me he used to go to the hospitals and the girls were terrified of him. They would be watching television and he would march into the middle of the circle of women and change the channel to watch himself on Top of the Pops and lie down on his tummy, legs in the air. All the girls would be totally creeped out and get up and shuffle together to the corner of the room.

When we went on that cruise trip together I would take her often to the back of the ship, where you see the most waves crashing. She was fascinated by those waves and said she just wanted to take all of her worries, and all of the pain of her past, and throw those worries into the sea.

Auntie Chrissy died while I was travelling with my boyfriend in

2013, and I'm sorry I need to stop there as this is very emotional and such a hard thing to do. I am currently living on an island in Indonesia and I would really like to leave this now to go to see the sunset for my own necessary healing time. I live here to enjoy the sunrises and sunsets over the mountains, being surrounded by beautiful strangers, and taking people to the end of the pier to introduce them to luminescent plankton. They are my three most enjoyable and calming healing points of each day.

Jill

Patsy, who is referred to in many of Christine's letters, was originally a friend of mine from La Sainte Union teacher training college in Southampton, where we were both students from 1965-68. We met on our first day in college where we were both studying art as our main subject .We have always remained friends not only with each other but with a wider group of friends from that time who still now, 50 years on, all enjoy meeting up together periodically. Patsy was a close confidant and would have met Christine originally when she was well enough to come and spend a weekend with me in Southampton. After college Patsy returned to her home town of Newmarket and I was employed by Inner London Education Authority to work in a primary school in Kilburn. These were my flat sharing days initially with three other college friends. By 1969 Patsy had moved to London and for a while we shared a flat in Chalk Farm. In October 1971 Chris and I married. Patsy and Bill married the same year. We had all met in Southampton where Chris and Bill were students at the university. Chris and I then moved to Sheffield until 1974 when we returned to London. Patsy and Bill were living in Sunninghill – which is fairly close to Broadmoor, which is in Crowthorne. Patsy was brilliant at staying in touch with Christine often visiting her and writing to her. She became an important friend to Christine through those darkest of her days. The following is the recall written by Patsy:

Patsy

I met Jill at college. We were both students of the art department, training to be teachers. We spoke of our families among other topics and that is when I heard of Christine, her younger sister. When we completed our studies and began our teaching careers we continued to keep in touch. In 1969 we eventually lived in a flat in London with Andy (Lovering) who was a librarian, now retired. Christine eventually came to stay with us and all went well to begin with. One day I remember vividly was when Christine wasn't well, but resisted advice to stay home to recover, not wanting to miss a day's work. Jill and Andy had already left. I couldn't persuade her to stay in the flat. She showed steely determination to go to work. We got on the crowded tube train where it became obvious she wasn't herself. She leant against people, who objected, and then suddenly she got off and disappeared. I went on to work where I could phone Jill to alert her to what had happened. It was a very anxious time. Then Christine no longer lived with us.

Eventually Christine went to Broadmoor Hospital in Berkshire. I couldn't understand why she was there. She had never, to my knowledge, hurt anybody deliberately. Apparently she had attempted to commit suicide by sitting in the middle of a road and was considered to be a risk to herself and others. I do remember hearing that she had broken a window in the hospital with her bare hands, which was disturbing and worrying for her family.

Bill and I were married in 1971. We moved to Sunninghill, Berkshire in December 1971. I was expecting our first child in the February. That December we joined Jill and her husband Chris to visit Christine at Broadmoor to watch a Christmas Concert. I remember Chris saying in his strong Yorkshire accent, "Eh, Patsy, Why don't you get off your feet and ro-o-ll.' As I was heavily pregnant and less than 5ft tall it was an appropriate remark. It did make us laugh. Christine was overjoyed to see us all. It was a good evening.

I don't remember how old Billy was when I started to visit Christine. As I didn't drive at the time I had to wait until he could sit up in a pushchair to visit Christine using public transport. That meant catching two buses, one to Bracknell then another to Crowthorne. He absolutely loved the adventure of it all. Then a good friend, Rosemary (Gane), started to give us a lift, which meant the whole process wasn't such a long one. It all took half the time. It was good for Christine to have another visitor to chat with too. I never had cause to feel anxious visiting Christine and I didn't feel uneasy in her company. Just protective of her as I am with my own brothers and sisters. She was my good friend's younger sister, who always chatted away and wrote to me and was happy to see us. There was something innocent about her. She had a lisp when she spoke and an air of a dreamer about her. She loved books, something we shared. She was a prolific letter writer, which again I used to be. I have a large family, I am the eldest of eight children, so couldn't keep up with her correspondence as I would have liked.

Her dream was to become a librarian, like Andy our friend, and she worked so very hard to achieve that dream. She sent me a manuscript which she asked me to illustrate for her. I'm sorry to say I didn't do it. I regret that very much but once the children were born and I started teaching again life became very busy, and I wasn't confident in my artistic abilities. I found the manuscript years later and sent it back to her with apologies. She was very forgiving and happy to see it again.

Broadmoor is very intimidating. The buildings are huge, ancient and imposing with enormous walls surrounding them. The doors were large, solid and very thick wooden doors, probably made of English oak. The prison officers were polite and always present, with the inevitable keys. The whole effect was sombre and maintained the overall impression of captivity and lack of fresh air and freedom. It seemed to be entirely wrong to me that Christine was there at all. When Emily was born in 1975, I didn't see Christine quite so often for a while. Then in 1976, I learnt to drive, which helped enormously. I could fit it in with Billy's nursery school timetable. Billy remembers a room with a very large window through which the sun shine poured in, and playing with toys as Christine, Rosemary and I chatted. Emily remembers a small hand-made embroidered bag with a clock on it and 'Time to Knit' written on it which she loved. Christine gave it to her but I am not sure if she made it or not. I may still have it tucked away in the attic!

One visit I remember vividly was on the day of her birthday one November. I had made a cake but was not allowed to see her as there was a prison officers' strike. I actually pleaded with the warden to just give me time to give Christine a hug and the cake and card but there was no way it could happen. I felt very upset for Christine. It did seem so unnecessary to shut out the only opportunities the patients had for contact of the outside world. I was very relieved to hear that she received the cake safe and sound. There is one memory I have of Christine, but I cannot say when this episode happened. Christine had never visited our home in Sunninghill but knew our address as she wrote to me regularly. One day she turned up unexpectedly, which was a lovely surprise. I was able to give her a guided tour of our semi-detached, Victorian, house and the children showed her their toys, and then she had a meal with us. She left later on, and again I couldn't say where she was living at this time. We left that house in 1983 so it was before then. When she left we had a phone call from Jill who was very worried about Christine as she had apparently gone off the radar and hadn't let anyone know what her plans were. I was concerned to hear the anxiety in Jill's voice but had no news to give her. I realised then just how difficult it must have been for Jill and her parents to cope with Christine's unpredictable ways and her illness. When I heard of Christine's final illness it was with great sadness. She and her family, especially Jill and her daughters, Louise and Amelia, hadn't had an easy time of it.

Christine had such a hard life where she struggled to maintain her self-esteem and to realise her dreams despite her illness and her various stays in a variety of hospitals. She had moved to Southport to be near her parents and was a dutiful daughter to the best of her abilities. She made a life for herself and seemed to be content. It was very unfair that she was struck down with terminal illness when her life had reached an even keel. When I wrote to her about her physical illness she very quickly replied to assure me that she was positive, almost upbeat and resigned to her situation. She was looking forward to all the plans Jill and their cousin Phil were making with Louise and Amelia to go on a cruise and do all the things Christine hadn't been able to do in the past.

Christine was a brave and stoical person. She achieved so much despite her schizophrenia, her life on medication, and her forever changing circumstances. As I said to Jill, Christine appeared to have kept her Christian faith when so many of us with fewer reasons to need to pray find it hard to sustain a belief in a loving God. I read Christine's manuscript and poems with Jill's additions of family history and found it profoundly moving. Her story is one of triumph over adversity. It was riveting reading. The book has a raw honesty and is a remarkable story of an exceptional woman.

Patsy Lascelles

2015

Christine Margaret Delahunty

21.11.1948 – 12.01.2013

Farewell Christine

Thank you all for joining us today to say a fond farewell to Christine. Christine was always the bright one of the family, although perhaps also the most fragile, breaking her arm, and having her tonsils out in her earliest years when we lived in Woodford Green. She loved books and was rather shy. She was often top of the class. As a child her favourite times, like all the family, were when we lived in Bideford, in Devon. She would have been seven to twelve. It was such a friendly, relaxed place where we could all play safely outside and enjoy the beautiful countryside and the sea. Our next move to Cheltenham was more austere, steeped in class conscious appearances. When the family next moved to Caddington, near Luton, Christine and I became borders in our Cheltenham Convent School. For me this was a necessity due to 'A' Level curriculums. Christine chose to join me. It didn't work out for her and her lifelong troubles began then. She was fifteen. Christine did not always fare well in life. A trick of genes maybe- that brought her ill health from her schooldays. Unspeakable, mental health issues that plagued her life, leading her to spend many, many years in hospital. There were intermittent periods when Christine struggled to live a normal life. At one stage she started nurse training at the Radcliffe Hospital in Oxford. At another, for a while she worked for the Civil Service in London sharing a flat in Victoria. Some years later she completed the first year of a degree at Aberystwyth University. She spent some years working as a packer for a record company in Orpington. Always trying to get off benefits and earn her own living she increasingly found that the only work she could get was as a cleaner and that the low hourly rate necessitated her working more hours than her health could manage. Invariably it was crises in her health that breached her ambitions usually with yet another hospital admission. Throughout these forty years or so Christine experienced everything from the very worst to the very best of health care. Massive ECT, medication, counselling, and incarceration. Christine chose to move to Southport after Mum and Dad returned to spend their last years here in Dad's original home town. She wanted to be able to help look after them as they came to need it. While she still had some ups and downs here there is no doubt that this was a good move for her. The last decade has been her happiest, with the confidence that 'they' were finally getting the medication right. Big thanks to Sefton Health and Social Care Services. Allocating Christine her own self-contained flat in the community, with visiting carer support, enabled her to manage mainly independently. She loved the garden and took much pride and pleasure in cultivating fruits and flowers there, while also feeding the birds. She enjoyed attending several local community support activity groups- many of which have now demised due to spending cuts. These mental health support groups helped Christine to overcome the isolation so often associated with her condition, while also involving her in trips, teaching her carpentry, needlework, and less successfully to use a computer. A particular favourite was 'Imagine' with whom she went on several holidays over the years. Christine has shown the most incredible courage throughout the last year. She knew she was dying. When she told us we were instructed not to weep- and I was asked to book a cruise. This became a splendid holiday of a lifetime enjoyed together with myself, her nieces Amelia and Louise, and our cousin Phil, who has long been a tower of strength much loved by us all. They all came to Whitstable in the summer, and we followed this in September with a week touring the Highlands and Islands of Scotland. By then Christine knew this would be her last trip. Still she carried on determinedly meeting her friends, and regularly visiting our elderly aunts. She remained very caring of others even while increasingly needing care herself. I cannot list all those who deserve thanks but know they include Kathy, the palliative care nurse, Dr Jane and Dr

Meehan, Father Phillip and particularly Gwen, from Imagine. Christine opted to die in her own home being determined not to spend any more time in hospitals. The increasingly regular visits of the Community Health and Care Support teams enabled her to do this. A heartfelt thanks to you all. Christine never lost her faith – although there was often little sense of the gods being on her side. She continued attending Mass at the Holy Family Church for as long as she was able and then appreciated visits for home Communion. I hope she's right about there being a heaven, and that soon she will be at peace and happily resting there. God Bless you Christine, may love and peace go with you.